T0038675

ALSO BY DAVID CAY JOHNSTON

It's Even Worse Than You Think:
What the Trump Administration Is Doing to America

The Making of Donald Trump

Divided: The Perils of Our Growing Inequality

The Fine Print: How Big Companies Use
"Plain English" to Rob You Blind

Free Lunch: How the Wealthiest Americans Enrich Themselves
at Government Expense (and Stick You with the Bill)

Perfectly Legal: The Covert Campaign to Rig Our Tax System
to Benefit the Super Rich—and Cheat Everybody Else

Temples of Chance: How America Inc. Bought Out
Murder Inc. to Win Control of the Casino Business

The Big Cheat

How Donald Trump Fleeced America and Enriched Himself and His Family

—

DAVID CAY JOHNSTON

SIMON & SCHUSTER PAPERBACKS
New York London Toronto Sydney New Delhi

Simon & Schuster Paperbacks
An Imprint of Simon and Schuster, Inc.
1230 Avenue of the Americas
New York, NY 10020

First Simon & Schuster paperback edition November 2022

SIMON & SCHUSTER PAPERBACKS and colophon are registered trademarks of Simon & Schuster, Inc.

For information about special discounts for bulk purchases, please contact Simon & Schuster Special Sales at 1-866-506-1949 or business@simonandschuster.com.

The Simon & Schuster Speakers Bureau can bring authors to your live event. For more information or to book an event, contact the Simon & Schuster Speakers Bureau at 1-866-248-3049 or visit our website at www.simonspeakers.com.

Interior design by Kyle Kabel

Manufactured in the United States of America

1   3   5   7   9   10   8   6   4   2

Library of Congress Cataloging-in-Publication Data has been applied for.

ISBN 978-1-9821-7803-1
ISBN 978-1-9821-7804-8 (pbk)
ISBN 978-1-9821-7805-5 (ebook)

For Adam, Ben, Jack, Jackson, and Nicholas

Contents

CONTENTS

The Big Cheat

Introduction

The majority of Americans found themselves in uncertain economic circumstances in 2015, many in scary straits. Living paycheck to paycheck even with two working adults in the family had become the norm in America. By 2015 many people had been down so long, walloped by economic shocks in 2000 and 2008, they believed the future was not President Ronald Reagan's Morning in America but endless debt and potential homelessness. The rent was too high, the wages too low. It was a time of anxiety for most, even as those at the top gathered riches beyond the imagining of any generation before them.

It was a perfect time for a master con artist to lay waste to the desperate and cheat them out of what they had, all the while telling them that he was really their friend and helper. Donald Trump was a man for that time.

Trump was a master huckster. He had successfully fleeced investors, cheated workers and vendors, ripped off students of his fake university, and outmaneuvered banks that loaned him more than a billion dollars that he never paid back. He had even cheated novice roulette players at one of his casinos in what was supposed to be the most heavily regulated industry in America. And he had gotten away with it. He had never been arrested, never been charged with a crime, even though Mayor Ed Koch of New York City once said he deserved 15 days in jail for sales tax evasion.

He'd even gotten away with forgery, as his own tax lawyer and accountant testified under oath in one of his two known civil trials for income tax fraud, both of which he lost.

While Trump was known in New York society as a cheat, a liar, a manipulator, and a deadbeat, and although he had been fined $200,000 for replacing women and minorities in an attempt to placate his biggest casino customer, the worst that had happened to him was lawsuits, fines, and being shunned by some at high-society affairs like the annual Met Gala in Manhattan.

But that was not the Donald Trump most Americans knew, or thought they knew, certainly not those who lived far beyond New York City and Atlantic City.

To much of the American public Trump was a hero, a larger-than-life business genius who could turn anything to gold while thumbing his nose at the American aristocracy. He was a modern Midas with a series of trophy wives and endless riches. And he ate the same fast food they did.

Trump created this image on the NBC television network, which for years aired his shows, *The Apprentice* and *Celebrity Apprentice*. The shows made the network a fortune. They earned Trump the cash he needed to pose as a multibillionaire, and, more important, they made him famous in what he called the "real America" of small towns, farmland, and cities where no one wore bespoke suits or designer dresses. And he had that signature line—"You're fired!"—which in a perverse way gave relief to people who knew they could be fired at any time and for no good reason.

His television shows were no more real than the paint that made his name appear to be carved in gold letters. It was fool's gold all the way for anyone who believed his protean story. To anyone who understood business, his show was laughable. But his audience was largely people who had never been in a boardroom or an executive suite, didn't know what was taught in management schools, had no idea what makes businesses succeed. And so the ridiculous narratives played in prime time as believable tales of business acumen.

What people watching his show, and a majority of the rest of America, wanted was a leader who would relieve their financial distress. Trump appeared to provide them with what they yearned for: a hero who cared about them, a man who they believed would champion their desire to escape decades in the economic doldrums.

The year that Trump came down the escalator of Trump Tower to announce his campaign for the presidency, the economy was on the mend, but not fast enough to make up for the devastation caused first by the dot-com bubble bursting at the turn of the century and then by the 2008 Great Recession, which by some measures caused more harm than the Great Depression of the 1930s. Tens of millions of Americans who worked steadily, took care of their families, and tried to do their best kept being stymied by circumstances beyond their control. Their wages had stopped rising decades earlier. Ninety percent of American households had less income, adjusted for inflation, in 2015 than they had in 1973, according to tax data.

Even in households with two working adults, many people struggled to keep afloat. The vast majority of Americans had no savings, and more than a few relied on payday lenders who charged interest rates that a few decades before would have earned them prison sentences for usury. By 2015 those interest rates had been legitimized by the courts, Congress, and state legislatures. Health insurance plans didn't fully cover even routine care. Pensions were disappearing.

Many good-paying jobs, especially in manufacturing and mining, had vanished, some gone to China, Mexico, or Vietnam, others never to return, especially in coal mining, as competing fuels were cheaper and cleaner. And job security? By 2015 no one's job was secure, not even those teachers and professors who supposedly had tenure for life.

The plight of most Americans could be summed up by the acronym ALICE: asset limited, income constrained, employed. By this measure, developed by the United Way charities, a family of four in high-cost states such as Connecticut, New Jersey, or California needed more than $60,000 a year just to provide the basics of modern life. Only one in five jobs paid that much in 2015, the annual Social Security wage report showed. The median wage, including for part-time workers, was just $29,930, less than $600 per week.

And yet some Americans were rich beyond imagining. Trump had his own Boeing 757 jet; some ultra-rich couples had his-and-her private jets. Megayachts costing hundreds of millions of dollars sat at anchor on every coast. Mansions and even apartments sold for tens of millions of dollars.

It's so unfair, was Trump's message to average Americans, and it wasn't your fault.

Trump didn't waste time with 32-point plans and talk about human capital investment, labor market elasticity, and productivity charts. He spoke to people in language they understood. He told them that the elites in Washington, in that swamp along the Potomac, were rigging the system for their own benefit and were doing so at our expense. Wall Street was buying up and shuttering or selling overseas the companies that owned the mills in towns across America.

Trump blamed border-crossing Mexicans for an increase in rapes and murders even though violent crime in the U.S. was on the wane. He blamed China for stealing jobs. He blamed Muslims for everything.

And then he made the promises people wanted so badly to hear. He pledged economic growth greater than anyone else suggested possible, up to double the average of the postwar era. He promised to bring back coal mining jobs. And he vowed to defeat the elites who wanted what Trump falsely claimed were cancer-causing wind turbines to generate electricity.

The coastal elites, Trump said, those with a fancy education and a big paycheck, looked down on those who never went to college, who lived in what the elites considered flyover country. He told his audience that he alone could save them from lives of endless debt and worsening misery. No one else cared about them, he said. At every rally he told the crowds, "We love you."

Combined with this were his decades of practicing just how to appear on camera, how the angle of the camera, the lighting, the way he smiled or glowered would affect his audience, few of whom would ever grasp that they were his marks.

He told lies barefaced and bold, daring and dumb, distracting and disinforming. He lied even when telling the truth would have been better for his ego and personal enrichment. Trump, his family, and his cronies would soon train tens of millions of Americans to believe that there is no objective truth, that whatever he said was true, and anyone challenging his version of events was a liar. It was a strategy of deceit, disruption, and distraction that no high school civics text had prepared Americans to understand. And it worked, bringing to power by far the most dishonest, disturbing, and destabilizing administration America has ever seen. Trump promised to "drain the swamp" in Washington. But once in power, he stocked it with the most voracious economic predators and polluters in the country. Almost from the first day, he denounced duty, honor, reason, and rationality, all bedrock principles of self-governance on which our Constitution depends.

At the core of Trump's lying was the myth of the modern Midas, who turned everything he touched to gold just by putting his name on it. That myth had its genesis in a 1977 meeting in the New York City mayor's office, when police had to remove Trump forcibly—a story never before revealed.

*   *   *

This book examines Trump's promises against his performance. It completes a trilogy that began with my 2016 biography of Trump and continued with my 2018 assessment of his first year in office.

INTRODUCTION

The Big Cheat documents how Trump did what he has always done: promise the moon, the sky, and the stars, and then deliver rocks and sand, if that. In the closing weeks of his presidency he not only tried to overthrow our government, he left behind policy changes that showed his disregard for his promises and his contempt for the people who had put him in office, actions that barely registered in the news from Washington.

The most diligent Trump watcher could not follow everything Trump & Co. did in his four years. I know because from the day of his announcement Trump has been the focus of my work and that of the journalists at *DCReport*, an online news organization which my friend David Crook and I started to make sure the substance of what Trump did to our government would be recorded. Yet even as I researched this book I kept coming across things I had missed or forgotten or whose significance had escaped me at the time, especially actions taken on days when Trump engaged in his most outlandish or outrageous behaviors.

Through it all Donald Trump, his extended family, and his cronies, including the swamp dwellers he nourished rather than vanquished, used his presidency to get richer, to set up lucrative future opportunities, and to escape their own financial quagmires. Some gorged on tax dollars; others put their greed ahead of our national security. Some focused on small potatoes. And although Trump promised he would staff his administration with "the best people," some of them proved inept both at their assignments and in their efforts to loot the U.S. Treasury.

Topping the list of those who got richer while Trump was in the White House are his daughter Ivanka and her husband, Jared

7

Kushner. They scored 18 sweetheart mortgages totaling nearly $800 million, as we shall see in the pages ahead.

This book draws on my experience covering Trump, investigating his financial dealings, and exposing his lies dating back to 1988, when I left the *Los Angeles Times* to cover the casino industry in Atlantic City for the *Philadelphia Inquirer*. I expected that casino gambling would expand across America, which it did almost exactly as I predicted in my first book, *Temples of Chance*, much of which documented Trump's incompetence, ignorance, and dishonesty.

Parts of this story you may know, others you may learn were not as you had understood, while still other elements will be entirely new, events lost in the torrent of bad behavior that was the Trump presidency.

Public office, and in particular the American presidency, is a public trust, a position of honor. Presidential powers should be used to strengthen and improve our democracy. When that happens, freedom and opportunity benefit the American people, and America itself shines as an example to the world of what can be accomplished when the human spirit is free to flourish, aided by a government whose leaders seek to enhance the public good—not commit larceny.

Five months after Trump left office, a state grand jury in Manhattan returned an extraordinary indictment against the Trump Organization and its chief financial officer, Allen Weisselberg. The indictment detailed a calculated 15-year-long criminal tax fraud conspiracy that included all four years that Donald Trump was president. Soon after Weisselberg resigned from his Trump Organization positions.

INTRODUCTION

The indictment asserts that Weisselberg "evaded approximately $556,385 in federal taxes," plus a third of a million dollars in state and city taxes through the conspiracy with the Trump Organization. It said he and his wife received an apartment free of rent including parking, utilities, and cable television; each enjoyed a leased Mercedes-Benz; and they were reimbursed private school tuition for grandchildren among other hidden compensation.

No president or former president has ever before been a figure in a felony case, much less one covering his years in office.

The 15 felony charges, if proven at trial or by confession, would establish that the president of the United States knowingly presided over criminal activity, including criminal offenses against the United States government, that continued to the day of the indictment, July 1, 2021.

While Trump was not named in the indictment, he is the sole owner of the Trump Organization. Eric Trump testified under oath in 2011 that no business decision was made without the approval of his father, a point that others have consistently made about the tight control Donald Trump exercised over his business.

Donald Trump worked so closely with Weisselberg that their offices were on the same floor of Trump Tower while Don Jr., Eric, and Ivanka—all executive vice presidents—worked on a different floor. Numerous associates have said publicly that Weisselberg knows where every dollar came from and where it went.

Detectives brought the 73-year-old Weisselberg to court in handcuffs. Both he and the Trump Organization entered not guilty pleas on July 2, 2021. A state judge released Weisselberg on his own recognizance.

Significantly, other than the formality of not guilty pleas, no one involved denied the facts charged in the indictment, indicating that the criminal defense lawyers know that prosecutors have their clients cold with virtually no prospect of an acquittal if the case goes to trial. Were the Trump Organization convicted of felony crimes, the state of New York could have it dissolved, its assets used to recover the taxes evaded and the costs of prosecution.

In summer 2020 I said the eventual outcome of the grand jury investigation would almost certainly be a New York State racketeering and criminal enterprise charge under Article 460 of the New York State penal code. John Moscow, the Manhattan prosecutor who successfully pursued the BCCI global banking case scandal three decades ago, concurred with my opinion when we appeared together on *Brian Ross Investigate*s on Law & Crime television. Over the next year, many former prosecutors, criminal defense lawyers, and law professors appearing on national television adopted my view.

That law, upon conviction, would allow the state to seize the Trump Organization's assets as the fruit of criminal enterprise. It's also an easy charge for juries to understand, unlike tax cases, which can sometimes be defeated by confusing jurors and suggesting it's so complicated that one can innocently violate tax law. Since Trump has said he is the greatest expert in world history on taxes, and Weisselberg is a certified public accountant, those defenses likely would not carry much weight with jurors in a criminal trial.

Trump issued a statement. "The political Witch Hunt by the Radical Left Democrats, with New York now taking over the assignment, continues. It is dividing our Country like never before!"

Trump Organization lawyers also didn't try to deny the charges, an astonishing position given what that says about Trump's presidency.

Ronald P. Fischetti, a criminal defense lawyer representing the Trump Organization, belittled but did not challenge the accuracy of the charges in his statement: "This is a sad day for the Manhattan District Attorney's Office. After years of investigation and the collection of millions of documents and devoting the resources of dozens of prosecutors and outside consultants, this is all they have? In my 50 years of practice, I have never seen this office bring a case like this and, quite frankly, I am astonished."

Cases of prosecuting hidden compensation are not unusual, despite Fischetti's remarks. They are, rather, garden-variety tax fraud cases.

The indictment was the first but certainly not the last that the Manhattan grand jury will bring. A host of former prosecutors, defense lawyers, and I all said on various national television programs that the first indictment had two primary goals: to persuade Weisselberg to flip on Trump and to scare family members, employees, and anyone else who participated in criminal schemes with the Trump Organization to turn state's evidence in hope of avoiding prison.

The indictment detailed a scheme to hide $1.76 million of Weisselberg's compensation from federal, state, and city tax authorities.

While Fischetti and other Trump lawyers dismissed this as small potatoes, suggesting it is common practice, the sum is significant. An American at the median wage, about $660 a week in 2019, would have to work more than 51 years to earn that much money.

In what surely set off alarms among Trump family members and business associates, the indictment revealed that the Trump Organization kept two sets of books in some years.

Only a criminal enterprise has reason to keep more than one set of books. The whole point of accounting ledgers is to maintain a single—and honest—record of income and spending.

Throughout his presidency Trump was dogged by questions about whether he was a tax cheat. In 2018 the *New York Times* published an exhaustive inside look at how the Trump Organization, Donald Trump, and his siblings engaged along with their father, Fred, in schemes to evade income, gift, and estate taxes while at the same time jacking up the rent on rent-controlled and rent-stabilized apartments in Brooklyn and Queens. The *Times* project was based on 18 bankers' boxes of tax records supplied by Mary Trump, a cousin who says she was cheated out of most of her inheritance by Donald and his surviving siblings.

Soon after the Times exposé, Donald's older sister Maryanne Trump Barry resigned as a federal court of appeals judge in New Jersey. That stopped a judicial ethics inquiry into whether she was a tax cheat just as it started.

While federal judges have granted themselves such extraordinary favors as being able to stop an ethics investigation by resigning, former presidents do not enjoy them.

The felony charges against the Trump Organization, if proven, would establish beyond all doubt that Trump committed "high crimes and misdemeanors" while in office.

Trump sued in 2019 to prevent enforcement of a state grand

jury subpoena, which ultimately resulted in the indictments. The subpoena sought his personal and business accounting and tax records held by the Mazars USA accounting firm. The firm said it would obey whatever the courts ordered.

Twice Trump took this case all the way to the United States Supreme Court. Both times the justices unanimously rejected Trump's assertion that as president he was immune from criminal investigation. His lawyers argued that immunity applied even if he committed murder and that this immunity covered his life as a private citizen before he became president.

Trump's audacious claim of absolute immunity, a claim more commonly invoked by absolute monarchs and dictators, drew a sharp rebuke in July 2020 from John Glover Roberts Jr., the chief justice of the United States.

"In our judicial system, 'the public has a right to every man's evidence.' Since the earliest days of the Republic, 'every man' has included the President of the United States. Beginning with Jefferson and carrying on through Clinton, Presidents have uniformly testified or produced documents in criminal proceedings when called upon by federal courts," Roberts wrote, citing a 1742 British parliamentary debate to show how long this principle had been in force.

The high court sent the subpoena case back to the federal trial court for a technical review because it was the first time that a president had challenged a state court criminal subpoena. By the time the high court got around to upholding the subpoena the second time, after which Mazars immediately turned over more than a million pages of documents, Trump was a few weeks out of office.

— I —

Original Lie

D onald Trump's 2015 announcement that he was running yet again for president began with a nationally televised lie that it seemed no one caught that day. Had it been reported at the time, had it made front-page headlines and the network news broadcasts, this lie might well have turned Trump into a laughingstock. But the lie got lost amid coverage of Trump's hour-long rant pronouncing the American Dream dead and calling Mexicans rapists and murderers. He got air time to insist that, unlike any other politician in either party, he could fix what ailed America.

It was just the first of tens of thousands of documented lies he told over the next six years as candidate, president, and—to use a term he hates—former president. What I will call Lie One made Trump's campaign appear to be a popular movement Americans were aching to join. It began late on the morning of June 16. Melania Trump stepped onto a Trump Tower escalator, followed by her husband. Loudspeakers blared "Rockin' in the Free

World," Neil Young's angry 1989 protest against the presidency of George H. W. Bush, the epitome of establishment Republicanism.

"I see a woman in the night," the singer belted out as Melania descended toward the lower lobby, the networks cutting out the lyrics that followed moments later: "she hates her life and what she's done to it."

Melania's tight white dress drew eyes away from the small crowd behind her, partly visible through a low glass partition that prevents people from falling onto the escalator. Television viewers saw the crowd for just a few seconds, but close examination of the images later showed each person had plenty of room, most of them standing only two deep. Many wore white T-shirts pulled over their street clothes, with TRUMP stamped across their chest.

Down on the main floor, Ivanka Trump, in a competing tight white dress, had just finished saying that her father needed no introduction. Then she devoted five minutes to a fanciful list of virtues Trump wasn't known for, notably hard work and his desire "to make a positive contribution to society."

Affixed to the podium was a sign that said "TRUMP" in big white letters, and below, in a smaller font, his campaign slogan: "Make America Great Again!"

Soon Trump stood at the podium. He had choreographed every aspect of what television viewers could see, right down to telling journalists where to position their video cameras and lights. At many events he would tell the more docile ones which questions to ask.

Trump stood in front of a row of large, gold-fringed American flags, their crisp red and white stripes neatly angled toward the viewer's right. He positioned himself between two of the flags so that the stars framed his face in an attempt to make him look heroic.

"Wow. That is some group of people. Thousands," Trump began, trying to be folksy. He paused. He waited to make sure the live national television audience heard the burst of applause, the first of what would become forty-three rounds of clapping and hollering. He claimed the crowd was bigger than any rival had drawn. This was a lie, but it wasn't the big lie that day.

One tip-off to the lie was the applause that followed Trump's assertion, "When Mexico sends its people, they're not sending their best. They're not sending you. They're not sending you. They're sending people that have lots of problems, and they're bringing those problems with them. They're bringing drugs. They're bringing crime. They're rapists. And some, I assume, are good people."

Trump was speaking in liberal Midtown Manhattan, so the applause he got for his description of Mexicans was inexplicable. But that incongruous response to his bigotry didn't make the network news that night or the major newspapers the following day. Instead, some, such as ABC News, focused on a remark that Trump wanted them to highlight: *Sadly the American dream is dead. But if I get elected president I will bring it back, bigger, and better, and stronger than ever before.* Instead of scrutinizing the audience reaction, the *New York Times* focused on how Trump's gaudy lifestyle would play in Iowa. The paper didn't even directly quote his bigoted remarks on Mexicans, dryly noting that "he vowed to build a 'great wall' on the Mexican border to keep out rapists and other criminals, who he said were sneaking into the United States in droves."

But the next day an entertainment industry trade publication, the *Hollywood Reporter,* exposed the lie behind the crowd's 43 rounds of applause. The seemingly enraptured Trump supporters were actors and extras taking advantage of a chance to make some quick and easy money.

Extra Mile, a New York casting company that hires people to populate the background in movies and television programs, had sent out an email seeking performers to salt a June 16 event "in support of Donald Trump."

"We are looking to cast people for the event to wear t-shirts and carry signs and help cheer him in support of his announcement. We understand this is not a traditional 'background job,' but we believe acting comes in all forms and this is inclusive of that school of thought." The acting job was to last less than three hours. "The rate for this is: $50 CASH at the end of the event."

Corey Lewandowski was Trump's campaign manager in 2015. He denied paying anyone to attend the event. That, too, proved to be a lie. We know this because a campaign watchdog organization, the American Democracy Legal Fund, filed a formal complaint that August with the Federal Elections Commission. It is illegal to pay organizations and people for work on a campaign without disclosing who they are and how much they are paid. Seven months after the announcement, the Trump campaign admitted to the elections commission that it had paid Gotham Government Relations a $12,000 fee to recruit the performers, via its subcontractor Extra Mile, who feigned support for him and applauded his racist tirade. Commission staff noted that this long delay in paying and confessing could be prosecuted, but recommended leniency.

This foundational lie, Lie One, of a mass upwelling of popular support was the corrupt seed that grew into mighty crowds at rallies. There Trump found people so angry over their circumstances that they wanted to join his assault on America. These were the millions of Americans left behind economically, especially former factory workers, as new global trade rules allowed big companies to close shop at home and take advantage of cheap labor overseas.

Trump gave aid and comfort to those who feared racial minorities. He turned up the heat on long-simmering tensions between white Americans who feared that they or their descendants would become the new minority and those who embraced diversity and immigration. Those Trump attracted wanted people of color, women, and minorities to know their places as second-class citizens. In supporting Trump they found a way to express the desire of many to Make America White Again.

Among the many other lies told during the announcement of his candidacy, was one that people should embrace Trump because he was a self-made billionaire. Ivanka said in her lengthy introduction to the man who needed no introduction, "Throughout his career my father has been repeatedly called upon by local and federal government to step in and save long-stalled, grossly over-budget public projects." These were, in fact, projects he got paid for and which, in the case of Wollman ice skating rink in Central Park, he falsely told vendors he was rebuilding *pro bono* so they would not charge him for their work or only charge costs.

Trump's story that he was "really rich" held appeal even for many people who disliked, even detested him. They bought into his claim that his net worth was in the billions of dollars. During his announcement that he was running for president, Trump put a number on it: $8,737,540,000.

Days later he would claim that his net worth was much more, greater than $10 billion. That, too, was a lie, as Trump's financial disclosures after he became president would show. Assuming those disclosure statements were trustworthy, and using the threshold of $50 million for assets he said were worth that much or more, his net worth when he entered the White House was about a tenth of his highest claim. Both *Bloomberg* and *Forbes*, which run competing indexes of billionaires, put his net worth at a few billion, acknowledging that many of his properties were difficult, if not impossible, to value. Much of this wealth was the assumed value of the Trump name, a method of valuation similar to that used by luxury brands like Fairmont Hotels, Dolce & Gabbana, and Tiffany.

Claiming to possess great riches and showing signs suggestive of them, such as his personal jet, were critical to fulfilling his long-sought desire to commandeer our federal government and then squeeze every opportunity to put taxpayer money into his enterprises. And, of course, he wanted to get his family, friends, and political allies in on the profiteering as well.

Even news organizations bought into this tall tale of great wealth, routinely referring to Trump as a billionaire or multibillionaire, even though there has never been verifiable evidence that he is worth even $1 billion. Trump is certainly a rich man, but the best evidence comes from my former *New York Times* colleague Tim O'Brien. Trump let O'Brien examine his tax returns and other financial documents. O'Brien put Trump's fortune in 2015 at a few hundreds of millions of dollars. Even that assumes he doesn't have significant hidden liabilities.

The myth of the modern Midas started with the remaking of the once-grand Commodore Hotel next to Grand Central Terminal in Midtown Manhattan. The derelict hotel fell into the hands of the Trump family in the 1970s, when Fred Trump, Donald's father, arranged through his outer-borough political connections to rebuild the hotel into a high-end Hyatt.

In late 1977, Abe Beame was the lame-duck mayor of New York. Beame was also a longtime ally of Fred Trump, who had put money into his campaigns for years. Fred called Beame, saying he needed his help, and the mayor agreed to a meeting.

Beame called his advance man, Jonny Messer, into his office. Messer, six years younger than Donald Trump, had grown up down the street from the Trump home. He was among those familiar with Donald's boyhood bullying including throwing little rocks at a baby in a playpen next door to Fred and Mary Trump's home.

"Freddie's coming to see me and I may need you to get the schmuck out of the room," Beame said, referring to Donald, who was 29 years old at the time. "Freddie's bringing Donald with him and because of that, if I just need to talk to Freddie privately, I'm going to ask you to take Donald out for a walk."

When the Trumps arrived, Messer went outside to greet them and bring them to the mayor's office. "Jonny Messer, look at you all grown up in a suit and tie," Fred snarked, while his surly son said, "[Epithet deleted], what are you doing here?"

Fred explained to the mayor that he wanted to revise the Commodore Hotel deal to make it Donald's first big project. Beame threw his hands into the air, saying he doubted he could do anything about that. After all, he had only two of 22 votes on the city's Board of Estimate, which controlled city contracts, making it the center of power in New York City.

According to Messer, Donald bolted out of his chair, leaned across the desk, and jabbed the 71-year-old mayor with his index finger, shouting, "You are going to do what my father wants you to do." Fred grabbed his son and pulled him away from the mayor, who was a foot shorter.

The mayor and Fred Trump continued talking about the project until Donald jumped out of his chair a second time and again leaned across the desk and jabbed the mayor. At this point, Beame turned to his aide and said, "Jonny, take him for a walk."

Messer sized up Donald and decided he needed backup. "Push the blue button," Messer said to Beame, referring to one of three buttons under the mayor's desk. One summoned his secretary, another Messer; the blue one alerted the two cops seated just outside the mayor's office.

The cops, one tall and lean and the other short and heavy, stepped in. "Take him for a walk and lock him in a closet," Messer recalled Beame saying.

When Donald resisted, the officers put the ends of their batons under his armpits to prod him out of his chair and then muscled him into the hall and outside, Messer trailing. They forced Trump into his father's waiting limousine, then ordered the driver to give them the keys, which one of the cops tossed to Messer.

Donald got out of the car and started walking. "Where you going?" one of the cops asked. Donald touched his pockets and realized he had no money on him. "Here, take the subway," said one of the cops, tossing him a quarter, half the subway fare at the time.

Donald eventually returned to the mayor's office, where his father ordered him to apologize. "Donald mumbled something I couldn't make out," Messer recalled.

Trump was similarly threatening later to lawyer Richard Ravitch, then chairman of the New York State Development Corporation, over his demands for a Commodore Hotel tax exemption, which eventually cost the city more than $410 million. "If you don't give me a tax abatement, I'm going to have you fired," Ravitch recalled Trump saying.

Eventually, the project went ahead as Donald's, though his father's backing and influence made the financing possible. Beame issued an order in his last weeks in office: "Whatever Mr. Trump wants in this town he gets." Donald got a property tax abatement for four decades, boasting later that had he asked for 50 years he would have gotten it, such was his power to make golden deals and avoid taxes.

In this story of how the Trump saga began, we can see Donald's arrogance and his belief that rules don't apply to him. He set out to turn his run for the White House into a profit-making enterprise, to make his brand more valuable so he could get more for licensing his name. And if he had to lie and cheat along the way, none of that would be new for Donald Trump.

— 2 —

Jobs Mirage

A month after his Electoral College victory in 2016, Donald Trump called a press conference to demonstrate that he would make good on his frequent campaign promise of economic and job growth the likes of which America had never seen.

It was an event filled with good news. However, it also had a secret purpose that would not emerge for years, a purpose that proved lucrative for Trump, bad for jobs, and came with the added risk of a new kind of explosive modern horror, as we shall see.

Six weeks before the election Trump spoke at the New York Economic Club, telling the members about "a plan for American economic revival. And it's a bold and ambitious and forward-looking plan to massively increase jobs, wages, income and opportunities for the people of our country—the great people of our country." But his speech offered barely an outline, let alone a plan. It had few details. The key specifics he did promise mostly disappeared when his tax-cut bill was signed into law in 2017.

Trump's promise was something that millions of Americans desperately wanted to hear. Decades of economic woes weighed people down even as television celebrated the rise of a superrich class with mansions, personal jets, and yachts the length of a football field. Corporate loyalty to workers was gone. No one had job tenure, a fact reinforced by Trump's signature line, "You're fired." The disappearance of good-paying manufacturing jobs, coupled with rising debt and middle-of-the-night anxiety from knowing that one unexpected health crisis could mean bankruptcy had soured many people on the established order. Federal Reserve data showed that the net worth of the typical middle-income family with children headed by an adult age 35 or younger had shrunk so much that it was a smaller in 2016 than in 1986.

Trump promised economic growth of 4, 5, even 6 percent a year, figures no one else was talking about. In this century America's gross domestic product (GDP) has grown by more than 3 percent only three times, most recently in 2015 under Barack Obama, when growth was 3.1 percent. The average this century is just 2 percent per year.

Even people who couldn't explain what GDP is knew that Trump was promising to double or triple the economy's growth rate, promising boom times. They knew this would mean more money, more jobs, and more opportunity. His promises ignited hope among the dejected for a better future for themselves and their children. Millions of families, left behind as America moved on from an industrial economy to a service economy, watching as their jobs moved overseas, believed that Trump truly was their economic and social salvation.

Trump received a phone call from a Japanese executive soon after election night and invited the man for a private chat in his Trump Organization office. After the meeting, the president-elect emerged in the Trump Tower lobby all smiles, upbeat as could be.

"Ladies and gentlemen, this is Masa of SoftBank of Japan," Trump announced, indicating his companion, "and he has just agreed to invest $50 billion in the U.S." To create, Trump said, 50,000 jobs.

Trump's guest was Masayoshi Son, the richest man in Japan. Son was just 24 years old when he started SoftBank in 1981 as a software distribution company. He invested his profits wisely in emerging cell phone companies and other digital enterprises, and SoftBank soon grew into one of the world's 40 largest companies with publicly traded stock. Son's most lucrative investment was in Alibaba, a Chinese start-up loosely modeled on the e-commerce retailer Amazon. In just 14 years SoftBank's $20 million investment soared to $60 billion.

As a wealth and job creator, Son enjoyed credibility galore. Trump didn't. Trump spent money wildly for show. He overpaid for trophy assets like the Plaza Hotel at Central Park and a yacht originally built for the Saudi arms dealer Adnan Khashoggi, both of which he subsequently lost.

Trump and his siblings had inherited thousands of outer-borough apartments from their father. Donald quickly sold them so he could get instant cash to fuel the burning holes in his pockets, losing out on rental revenue that would have gushed more and more cash year after year. And he persuaded his siblings to sell those apartments to a single buyer, a strategy that meant they almost certainly got far less than what skillfully plotted sales to multiple bidders would have raised.

The inheritance and his father's cash infusions over the decades had made Trump rich, but his fortune was nothing compared to the wealth of Masayoshi Son. That day in the Trump Tower lobby, with Son at his side, Trump basked in the glow of the television lights. Then, after the cameras left, the president-elect tweeted, "Masa said he never would have done this had we [Trump] not won the election!"

That wasn't true.

SoftBank had announced its investment plans two months earlier. It had formed a partnership with Saudi Arabia to invest in high-tech start-ups. The Saudis put up $45 billion of the $100 billion in the fund that Softbank would manage, signing a contract before the U.S. presidential election. The other investors reportedly included cash-rich companies Apple, the database company Oracle, and Qualcomm, which makes semiconductors. The celebratory partnership Trump and Son formed turned out to be a lucky strategic move for SoftBank. Trump had often criticized Japan, accusing it of harming the American economy and American workers and taking advantage of incompetent American trade negotiators. But Trump adored the Saudis.

During one of his first campaign rallies Trump bragged about how much the Saudis liked his apartments. "Saudi Arabia, I get along with all of them," he told the crowd in Mobile, Alabama, in August 2015. "They buy apartments from me. They spend $40 million, $50 million. Am I supposed to dislike them? I like them very much."

That same month Trump registered new corporations to manage a hotel he planned to bear his name in Jeddah, a Red Sea city that many Muslim pilgrims pass through on their way to the holy cities of Mecca and Medina.

And it wasn't just individual Saudis putting money in Trump's pocket. In 2001, the Saudi government had bought the 45th floor of Trump World Tower in Manhattan for its diplomatic mission to the United Nations.

Just as Trump claimed credit for Masayoshi Son's planned investment, he said in February 2019 that his daughter Ivanka had created "millions of jobs." Ivanka was tasked with working on Trump's Pledge to America's Workers, a White House initiative to encourage training for young adults and professional development for workers in a variety of industries. The program did not create jobs or even training opportunities; it just encouraged them. In time it came out that the number of these opportunities was similar to numbers in previous years, not a Trumpian bonanza.

Trump soon elaborated on Ivanka's achievement, this time quoting an actual number: "Think of it: six point five million. And these are jobs that, for the most part, would not have happened" except for his becoming president.

In a November 2019 address to the Economic Club of New York Trump inflated this job claim, declaring that Ivanka had "created 14 million jobs." Six months later, on national television, he inflated the number yet again, to "over 15 million jobs."

How could Ivanka have created 15 million jobs when the economy had added only a tad more than 6 million since her father assumed office? And what did she have to do with job creation anyway? These statements went to the heart of how Trump's cons worked: he created his own reality. If he said something, that made it true, even if he contradicted himself a minute later. This making stuff up became known, thanks to his adviser Kellyanne Conway, as "alternative facts."

If any previous president had uttered such fantastical absurdities, he would have become a laughingstock. But America had become so accustomed to Trumpian nonsense, and the White House press corps so inured to Trump's "alternative facts," that he just continued lying like that every day and paid no price with his supporters. Trump had so thoroughly taken control of the Republican Party that even senators with secure seats dared not call him out.

Two years into Trump's presidency, in May 2019, ProPublica, a nonprofit investigative journalism organization known for deep dives and high-quality use of data, examined the subject of job creation. Its reporters and data specialists set out to answer the question of just how many jobs could be traced to Trump's victory.

After extensive research into corporate statements and disclosures, as well as interviews, ProPublica concluded that SoftBank's Son and other CEOs had already planned to expand hiring no matter who won in 2016. The number of additional jobs these executives created after the election numbered just 122,000 at that point. And how many of those new jobs could ProPublica connect to Trump's election victory, to companies hiring more because Trump was in the White House? ProPublica put the number at 797.

SoftBank really did follow through with the jobs it had planned when it looked like America would have its first woman president. Within three years the Japanese company had added about 48,500 jobs in America, a promise fulfilled by any reasonable measure. But there was more to this job creation than met the eye.

Softbank was famous for its hugely successful high-tech investments in an array of biotech and health companies, chipmakers, and cell phone providers. It also owned Sprint, the struggling fourth-place mobile phone company in America. Son had tried to sell Sprint through a merger with AT&T, the number 2 cell phone carrier in America after Verizon, but the Obama administration's antitrust experts had prevented that deal as anticompetitive. Son believed that with Trump in the White House he might have a shot at unloading Sprint. Trump had no real understanding of antitrust law, whose purpose is to promote competitive markets, or any law for that matter. He had spent his life denouncing regulations, especially when he got caught violating them. He claimed that regulators held back the American economy.

Son's quick action to bolster Trump's image as a job creator would pay off for both men. Among other treats, Son got approval to sell Sprint to T-Mobile, a deal worth $26 billion to Son.

Charity Doghouse

Donald Trump was the first president since William McKinley who didn't have a dog in the White House. No dogs live at his private estate in Palm Beach, Florida, which he called the Southern White House, Mar-a-Lago either. Except for a poodle his first wife, Ivana, brought along when she married Trump a half-century ago, he's never lived with a dog.

"Donald was not a dog fan," Ivana Trump wrote in her 2017 book, *Raising Trump*. "When I told him I was bringing Chappy with me to New York, he said, 'No.'"

"It's me and Chappy or no one!" Ivana insisted. Trump caved, though the Canadian poodle had to sleep on Ivana's side of the bed.

Chappy, Ivana wrote, "had an equal dislike of Donald. Whenever Donald went near my closet, Chappy would bark at him territorially."

Trump often uses dogs as negative symbols. His rhetoric is filled with short sentences that begin with the word *begging, died, fired, kicked, killed*, or *sweating*, followed by "like a dog." He also wields his dislike of dogs to describe women he dislikes or finds unattractive. At one 2016 campaign rally, for example, he suggested a barking sound came from Hillary Clinton.

Despite his antipathy to man's best friend, Trump has no aversion to siphoning money donated to rescue homeless dogs to benefit himself. He's already collected $2 million for dog charity events at Mar-a-Lago and at his golf course a few miles away in Jupiter, Florida.

The story of how Trump pocketed $2 million of charitable funds donated to rescue dogs, money that continued coming to him after he left office, is an example of how the Trump family works together to make sure that charity starts, and ends, at home. It begins with his son Eric arranging a charity golf outing to benefit children with cancer.

The Eric Trump Foundation was formed in 2007. By all appearances it was, at the start, something alien to Trump family culture: a selfless, public-spirited enterprise. Eric, who was just 23 at the time, ran it out of his apartment across from Central Park in Manhattan. The foundation had no staff. Most of the volunteer board were buddies who helped sell tickets to events, which started at $3,000. Eric devoted 200 hours a year to his foundation, which was legally classified as a public charity.

In 2007 Eric's charity held its first golf outing. The venue was his father's golf club in Westchester County, a short drive north of Manhattan. It soon became an annual event, and a typically tawdry Trump affair. After 18 holes, Hooters waitresses wreathed in cigar smoke served drinks and steaks.

Eric said that every dollar from sponsors and golfers would go to St. Jude Children's Research Hospital in Memphis. Over the years more than $16 million did.

The event was staged at virtually no cost, Eric told *Forbes* after the 10th annual golf outing. He said sponsors donated most of the food and beverages and whatnot. And then there was his father's generosity: "We get to use our assets 100% free of charge."

That wasn't true. Eric knew that, and yet he said it anyway, following his father's practice of making up facts.

Annual tax filings required of all nonprofits tell the real story. The first year, expenses were about $46,000, a reasonable sum for an event that grossed $222,000, especially a start-up. Costs were about the same for the next three years. Then Dad demanded more money, a lot more money. Eric's charity paid his father's golf club $142,000 in 2011, an exceptionally high bill for a one-day outing for about 200 golfers. Soon the fee was $322,000. That's an expense of more than $1,600 per golfer. By law the officers of charities are obligated to pay only reasonable prices and to conserve charitable assets. What Trump was charging doesn't meet that standard.

Ian Gillule, a former marketing director at Trump National Golf Club Westchester, explained what happened when Donald Trump heard what was paid for the use of his golf course in the first four years of his son's charity event. "Mr. Trump had a cow. He flipped. He was like, 'We're donating all of this stuff, and there's no paper trail? No credit?' And he went nuts. He said, 'I don't care if it's my son or not—everybody gets billed.'"

Over the five charity tournaments from 2011 to 2015 Donald Trump collected just shy of a million dollars. That was on top of the roughly $200,000 he was paid in the previous four years. But even that was not enough. Trump, so adept at lining his own pockets, came up with a way to take money from the ostensibly charitable Donald J. Trump Foundation and put it into his personal bank account.

The scheme was simple. The father's foundation made a $100,000 grant to the son's charity. In turn, Eric's charity paid that money to the Trump Organization for use of the Westchester golf club. As Dan Alexander of *Forbes* magazine smartly put it, "This maneuver would appear to have more in common with a drug cartel's money-laundering operation than a charity's best-practices textbook."

Just before the price for using the Trump golf course tripled, the board of the Eric Trump Foundation changed. His buddies were gone, replaced by 17 new members, including Trump lawyer Michael Cohen, the head of a company doing millions of dollars of business with the Trumps, and Eric's girlfriend and later wife, Lara. Any independence the Eric Trump Foundation had had was gone. It became a de facto subsidiary of the Trump Organization.

Eric's charity also stopped directing all of its support to St. Jude, but without telling supporters. It gave about $500,000 to other charities, some with no connection to childhood cancers. Three of the charities that received grants from Eric's foundation started holding events at Trump golf courses, paying Donald far more in fees than the grants they received.

It was a diabolically clever way to transform charitable donations—the fees that golfers paid—into a marketing budget for the Trump golf course. Best of all, because it was charity money that attracted the new business, it was deductible and didn't cost the Trumps a dime.

Eric insisted he had done nothing wrong in any of this, but he also announced that he was suspending operations of the foundation.

"Contrary to recent reports, at no time did the Trump Organization profit in any way from the foundation or any of its activities," Eric stated after *Forbes* published a devastating piece on the abuse of charitable funds in December 2016, just after the election. "While people can disagree on political issues, to infer malicious intent on a charity that has changed so many lives, is not only shameful but is truly disgusting. At the end of the day, the only people who lose are the children of St. Jude and other incredibly worthy causes."

Despite the denial, laws were clearly being broken. The years of excessive fees for using the golf course and the money that flowed from the father's charity to the son's charity to the Trump Organization constituted self-dealing, using charity funds to benefit the people in charge of the charity instead of applying the money to the charitable purpose donors believed they were supporting. Self-dealing can be prosecuted as a felony, although more often it is treated as a civil offense—when it is detected.

It might seem that all Donald Trump did was arrange to get his own $100,000 back from his foundation. That in itself would be illegal. But that is not what happened. The money that the Donald J. Trump Foundation washed through Eric's charity and then returned to Donald hadn't come from Donald.

The last time Donald put money into his own foundation was 2008, and it was only $35,000. The money his foundation held as a charitable trust came from vendors who were paying him tribute. Among the donors was NBC, which broadcast his so-called reality shows. The World Wrestling Federation, which had long staged its faux wrestling matches at Trump properties, and others with a financial interest in pleasing Trump were the only donors to the foundation.

Gifts from business partners and vendors to Trump's foundation are legal, though it's reasonable to view them as purely commercial transactions that provide a tax deduction, not as gifts motivated by charitable intent. Using outsider money to fund a private family foundation, other than perhaps memorial gifts when a family member dies, is pretty much unheard of in American philanthropy, which I have written about for four decades.

That $100,000 of self-dealing was not a unique event in Trump's life. Over the years he has used $12,000 of foundation funds to buy a signed Tim Tebow football helmet and jersey. Then there was the $258,000 he unlawfully diverted from his foundation to settle lawsuits that had nothing to do with his foundation. He also used funds from the foundation to buy three portraits of himself, two for $20,000 each. His former lawyer Michael Cohen testified before Congress in 2019 that a straw buyer paid $60,000 at an auction for a nine-foot portrait of Trump. After the auction, as part of his never-ending campaign of self-flattery, Trump tweeted that the portrait was valuable art: "Just found out that at a charity auction of celebrity portraits in E. Hampton, my portrait by artist William Quigley topped the list at $60K." Trump kept the painting and reimbursed the straw buyer with charity funds, Cohen told the House Oversight Committee.

Trump also used his foundation as a cookie jar to dole out money to advance his political interests, which again is illegal. He made a $25,000 donation in 2013 to support the campaign of Pam Bondi, the Florida attorney general. Bondi then shut down her office's investigation into complaints from Floridians that Trump University was a scam.

At the time Trump directed this illegal campaign donation he was planning his 2016 presidential campaign. He also knew that the lawsuit filed in 2013 by Eric Schneiderman, then New York Attorney General, alleging that Trump University was a scam could damage his chances of becoming president, especially if he was charged with criminal fraud.

Schneiderman said that for three years Trump kept "filing baseless charges and fruitless appeals and refusing to settle for even modest amounts of compensation for the victims of his phony university." And then as soon as he won the White House agreed to a "$25 million settlement agreement . . . a stunning reversal by Donald Trump and a major victory for the over 6,000 victims of his fraudulent university." They got full refunds and Trump paid a $1 million penalty, escaping criminal prosecution.

A Bondi spokeswoman defended her decision to journalists as lawful and appropriate. Team Trump tried to explain the illegal political donation as a simple name and mailing address mix-up. That story collapsed under mild scrutiny. Following news reports of the Bondi political donation, the IRS demanded that Trump pay a $2,500 penalty. He did. Bondi got the first of several Trump rewards when she was invited to speak at the 2016 Republican National Convention in Cleveland that nominated Trump. Bondi led the gathering in "Lock her up" chants directed at Hillary Clinton.

After Bondi's term ended in 2019 she became a lobbyist for Qatar. At the same time she was working for the Qataris she became a "special government employee" on the White House staff working on Trump's defense in his first impeachment trial. Normally people on the payrolls of foreign governments cannot be on the U.S. taxpayers' payroll.

The Bondi campaign gift was just one of many instances of Trump's misusing charity funds to advance his political interests. He also made grants during the 2016 presidential campaign to organizations that subsequently invited him to give speeches in Iowa and Washington. In the 2012 presidential election, which Trump later dropped out of, evangelist Billy Graham received $100,000, which he said he used for political ads. A week before the 2016 election the Graham family released a photo of the 98-year-old preacher with Trump, which many evangelicals took as an endorsement.

Misusing charitable money for personal benefit was the pattern from the start of the Donald J. Trump Foundation. In 1989, two years after the foundation launched, Trump owed a half-million dollars to the Central Park Conservancy. The money was an assessment on the Plaza Hotel, which he then owned. His foundation paid $264,631 of the obligation, by far the largest grant it ever made.

So why didn't all of these wrongful acts result in an indictment, or at least a demand by charity regulators to pay back diverted funds? The answer is that enforcement of charity abuse laws is rare. State legislatures and Congress authorize hardly any money to ferret out abusers and hold them to account.

When action does take place the perpetrators are often exceptionally wealthy men who can bring enormous pressure to bear to blunt or even stop official inquiries by bureaucrats working in underfunded offices of the IRS or a state attorney general's office.

Trump and his oldest three children eventually did get caught, but only because the patriarch ran for president, raising his profile and attracting attention to long-standing news reports about many of his questionable and sometimes obviously illegal acts. Even then the outcome didn't match the level of offense. Marc Owens, former head of the IRS tax-exempt organizations division, called Trump's dozens of abuses of foundation funds "bizarre, this laundry list of issues. . . . It's the first time I've ever seen this, and I've been doing this for 25 years in the IRS, and 40 years total."

Six weeks before Election Day 2016 Trump received a "notice of violation" from Eric Schneiderman. The Donald J. Trump Foundation wasn't even registered with the state to solicit donations, as the law required. Schneiderman made clear he was going to pursue civil fraud charges. Trump denounced it as a partisan attack because Schneiderman was a Democrat.

Then, Thanksgiving week, when Trump was now president-elect, a new IRS filing by the foundation became public. There was no announcement, just a check mark in a single box on page 6 of the foundation's Form 990 tax filing for 2015. The check mark was an admission of self-dealing and that this illegal conduct had not been corrected. Few people noticed.

Another 18 months passed before Barbara Underwood, then the New York acting attorney general, filed a civil lawsuit against Trump and his three oldest children, alleging "a shocking pattern

of illegality." Trump tweeted, "I won't settle this case!" He insisted
he had done nothing wrong and that Democrats were behind the
baseless attack.

In late 2018, after six more months had passed, Underwood got
the president to agree to shut down his foundation.

Finally, in November 2019, the case resolved. Trump agreed to
shutter his foundation. Most significant, he admitted to 19 specific
illegal acts involving abuse of charitable funds, including the Pam
Bondi campaign donation. He also agreed not to be involved in
any charity again without a host of restrictions.

Judge Saliann Scarpulla, the state court judge who heard the
case, held that "Trump breached his fiduciary duty to the Foundation and that waste occurred to the Foundation. Mr. Trump's fiduciary duty breaches included allowing his campaign to orchestrate
the Fundraiser, allowing his campaign, instead of the Foundation,
to direct distribution of the Funds, and using the Fundraiser and
distribution of the Funds to further Mr. Trump's political campaign."

Judge Scarpulla ordered Trump to pay $2 million in recom-
pense. That money, along with a nearly equal amount left in the
foundation bank account, was then divided equally among eight
charities the judge chose because they had no relationship with
Trump or his business interests. Don Jr., Eric, and Ivanka Trump
were ordered to take training on their legal obligations regarding
charitable funds, which they did.

The judge let Trump continue to do business with charities at his
golf courses just so long as he was merely selling them services, not
participating in their operations. There was to be no monitoring,

no requirement that he charge only commercially reasonable rates and submit invoices to the court. That was a curious omission given the five years of price gouging involved in the Eric Trump Foundation golf tournaments.

Meanwhile, Eric's foundation revived and morphed into the Curetivity Foundation. It was to hold golf outings to raise money for St. Jude, but that changed, too. In 2016 it took in more than $3.3 million, and its expenses for the golf outings came to just $20,000.

Many charities and businesses dropped Mar-a-Lago as a venue after Trump's failed coup d'état on January 6, 2021. But one charity didn't think associating with the ex-president would hurt its fundraising. IRS filings show that the charity has paid Trump nearly $2 million over several years for fundraising events at Mar-a-Lago and Trump's golf course in Jupiter. A party permit showed it planned to spend at least $225,000 at Mar-a-Lago in 2021.

The name of the person in charge of the charity is Lauree Simmons. Three days before the insurrection at the Capitol, she shared this on her Facebook page: "Either we TAKE back power or we will never be free again. No more asking nicely. Our founding fathers warned us. THIS IS NOT A DRILL." The message was followed by an angry orange face.

The chair of these fundraising events at Mar-a-Lago and the Trump golf course is Lara Trump, Eric's wife, which likely explains the reason the charity didn't use other venues.

The name of the charity spending so much money at Trump's properties? Big Dog Ranch Rescue.

— 4 —

Off the Books

The presidential transition team and the inaugural committee worked in a dreary federal building in Washington. Late one afternoon, just after New Year's Day, as yet another of the interminable planning meetings finished up, Stephanie Wolkoff, a close friend who was Melania Trump's choice to plan the celebrations so they would run smoothly, started thinking about how nice it would be to sleep in a comfortable hotel bed. As she walked down the hallway toward her dingy office, she realized Rick Gates, the inaugural committee's deputy chairman, was following her.

As soon as she stepped into her office Gates asked Wolkoff if her company, WIS Media Partners, would take in money directly from donors so that their gifts wouldn't appear on the books of the 58th Presidential Inaugural Committee.

For just a moment, Wolkoff was at a loss to understand the request. Then it clicked: Gates was trying to hide the identities of donors and perhaps the money itself. He had just asked her to commit a crime, especially if foreign donors were involved as it was illegal for them to contribute. Visions of life in an orange prison jumpsuit flashed in her head.

No, she said, absolutely not. One of her partners broke into the conversation at that moment, reminding Gates that he and a third Wolkoff partner had already rejected the proposal. Gates slunk away.

There is no limit on how much money a presidential inaugural committee, or any charity, can raise. So why would Gates ask Wolkoff to hide money? And why in the world would he make such a request to Wolkoff, who had tangled with him repeatedly and had complained to Trump and Ivanka about outrageously high spending plans for the inauguration? And why would Gates persist after Wolkoff's two partners had told him no? Gates had once worked for the corrupt Ukrainian president Viktor Yanukovych. Had he spent so many years ignoring federal law on representing foreign interests that he thought he could get away with flouting any law?

Six months after his request to Wolkoff, in June 2017, Gates would plead guilty to conspiracy against the United States and lying to investigators about Russian interference in the 2016 election. He would make a deal to turn state's evidence and testify against his longtime boss, Paul Manafort, who was Trump's campaign manager in summer 2016, and others.

Wolkoff later wondered what made Gates think she would go along. She told me he must have figured that, as a friend of Melania, she was simply naïve. After spending hours interviewing Wolkoff, I know that she's got boundless energy bouncing in many directions, but she's nobody's fool.

A likely explanation for why Gates made his request to Wolkoff emerged at the Candlelight Dinner and other inaugural events, where Russian oligarchs and others with close ties to the rich gang that helps Vladimir Putin rule Russia showed up as guests. This was the first indication that some of the money flowing into Trump's inaugural committee came from foreigners using American citizens as fronts. That would be precisely the kind of transaction that Gates would not want to appear on the charity's books.

Among the guests at the Candlelight Dinner for major donors was Maria Butina, the twenty-something who claimed to be a Russian activist for gun ownership. She had entangled herself with the National Rifle Association and some key Republicans and held a party for Trump campaign staffers. Butina later confessed to conspiracy to defy the law requiring agents of foreign powers to register and report their activities, a charge short of spying, and was sentenced to 19 months in prison.

Other Russians attended as well. Viktor Vekselberg heads the Renova Group, a global conglomerate in aluminum, cell phones, oil, and other businesses. It employs 134,000 workers worldwide. Vekselberg came as the plus-one of his American cousin, Andrew Intrater, who runs the Columbus Nova investment firm in New York City. Court papers show that the government has long suspected that Columbus Nova is a front for Vekselberg's Renova Group. Both Intrater and Vekselberg have denied that.

Also attending was Alexander Mashkevitch, who owns a metals and mining empire based in Kazakhstan and who six years earlier, in 2011, settled money-laundering charges with Belgian authorities with no admission of wrongdoing. Leonard Blavatnik, a

Ukrainian-born billionaire who is a dual citizen of Britain and the United States, appeared on guest lists for the Candlelight Dinner and other inaugural events. His Access Industries, with operations worldwide, is the controlling owner of Amedia, the largest producer of Russian television programming.

Sergey Kislyak, the Russian ambassador to the United States, was invited to the Global Chairman's Dinner, another inaugural committee event.

In the days surrounding the inauguration Trump's hotel in D.C. was awash in Russians, drawing the attention of FBI counterintelligence agents already anxious about the Trump family's coziness and financial dealings with Kremlin agents and Russian-speaking gangsters. For years rumors have persisted that since 1987 the Kremlin has sought to develop Trump as an asset, witting or not. The presence of these and other Russians and their associates raised questions about whether some of them had used American fronts to funnel money to the inaugural committee or Trump allies.

Trump has a powerful affinity for Russian president Vladimir Putin and repeatedly went out of his way to praise him. In Helsinki in 2018, for instance, Trump declared that he trusted Putin but not American intelligence services. He attended one meeting there with Putin accompanied only by his translator, whose notes he ripped up. He participated in another with no one accompanying him, the content of his long conversation with Putin a mystery to all but the Kremlin.

Four months after becoming president Trump held an unannounced meeting in the Oval Office with Ambassador Kislyak and Foreign Minister Sergey Lavrov, where he shared "sources and methods" intelligence, the most carefully guarded of secrets, with the Russians. We know this only because the two Russian diplomats announced the meeting via TASS, the Russian news agency controlled by the Kremlin.

Whether Russian money made its way to the inaugural committee or some other receptive pockets is an unresolved concern with national security implications. Trump's older sons have boasted about all the money the Trump Organization had been taking in for years from Russians. Trump spoke admiringly of the Saudis, who paid tens of millions of dollars for Trump apartments. Many Russians of dubious character also bought Trump apartments, as Reuters and others documented, but which Trump didn't boast about. Dmitry Rybolovlev, yet another Russian oligarch, rescued Trump from his purchase of a tasteless Palm Beach oceanfront mansion in 2008, paying $95 million, more than twice its value at a time when Trump was in default on a $40 million loan.

Weigh all of this information in the context of Trump's making Gates the pivotal official running his inaugural committee despite the fact that Trump previously alleged that Gates had stolen three-quarters of a million dollars from him. While there is no public record that Gates stole from Trump, he was a target of Special Counsel Robert Mueller's prosecutors. They found that Gates stole a quarter-million dollars from Manafort.

After the inauguration, questions arose about the money flowing out of Trump's inaugural committee, which reported raising a record $106,751,308. This amount was more than double the $53 million raised for Obama's first inauguration, in 2009, a much bigger and more lavish affair. Given Gates's request to Wolkoff, that may not even be all the money that came in.

Trump's inaugural committee reported having 208 employees, far fewer than Obama's 307. Trump listed 500 volunteers, Obama 17,500. Trump had three inaugural balls, Obama 10. Yet despite the much smaller Trump operation, his inaugural committee reported spending almost $104 million, more than double the nearly $51 million Obama spent. In both cases, charities were to get the residue.

Where did all the Trump inaugural money go?

* * *

The 58th Presidential Inaugural Committee's Form 990, a report to the Internal Revenue Service filed by all nonprofits, lists "other expenses" of $94.3 million. There is little detail in the schedules on the 990.

I have written stories based on 990s for decades, and I fill one out each year for *DCReport*, a charity. The Trump form is sloppy at best. It has irreconcilable numbers, too. Promotional gifts—the swag often handed out at high-end charity events—costing $560,000 are reported deep in the form. Yet the line for fundraising expenses on the summary front page, of which swag is just one component, shows less than $237,000.

In line 9, where inaugural ball ticket revenues should be entered along with money from selling memorabilia, the Obama inaugural committee in 2009 reported almost $2 million. Trump's line 9 is blank.

Trump's inaugural committee reported almost $4 million in ticketing expenses. It had budgeted close to $8 million. Even the lower figure is an enormous cost that should invite close examination of payments to the ticket-issuing firm. The Obama form showed less than $91,000 in expenses on the line where ticket costs should be listed. Why was Trump's ticket vendor paid so much? Did some of that nearly $4 million make its way back to the Trump family, Gates, Manafort, or anyone else connected to the Trumps? Only a subpoena can answer that question.

When guests showed up at inaugural events, the Trump ticketing system let them register using whatever address was recorded when the tickets were purchased or given away. That means Team Trump did not correctly capture their identities. The official record shows that many of the guests at the inaugural balls and other events lived at the addresses of the U.S. Senate and House of Representatives, for example, or various businesses.

Somebody seems to have falsified some ticket purchase records. For example, mathematician Katherine Johnson of *Hidden Figures* fame appeared as a $25,000 donor, her home address shown as the National Aeronautics and Space Administration headquarters. Johnson told a reporter she didn't make a donation, prompting a Trump representative to acknowledge the error. There were at least four donations attributed to people who don't exist, one of them in Singapore.

How many fake names and addresses were entered in donor records? How many were foreign agents?

Donors to inaugural events qualify for an income tax deduction because presidential inaugural committees are charities. But the value of services is supposed to be deducted. A million-dollar donor got free hotel rooms, meals, drinks, and seats at events with Trump.

The charity must deduct the value of those services on receipts pro-vided to donors. Trump receipts did not show such offsets, however.

* * *

"I've spent far more on lawyer bills than what I was paid," Wolkoff said in her family's apartment, its walls covered with x-ray images enhanced by an artist and other starkly compelling modern art.

She took on the inaugural events as a favor to Melania Trump. Wolkoff and Melania had been besties for years, two tall, elegant, and rich women in Midtown Manhattan who lunched together and shared confidences. Melania told her best friend she had no idea how to organize all the celebratory events for her husband's new role as president of the United States. She asked Stephanie to step in.

When questions arose about how the inaugural commit-tee money was spent, unnamed White House sources planted a provocative story in the *New York Times* that pointed to Wolkoff. Describing her as a mere "party planner," the *Times* reported that Wolkoff was paid $26 million. Wolkoff said she wasn't even con-tacted for comment before the first article appeared.

Wolkoff said that, without her approval, $25 million of the $26 million was passed on to two associates of television producer Mark Burnett. She said she never figured out what they did, especially since other vendors were paid handsomely for providing broadcast services. She said she thought before the tax form was even filed that the $25 million was paid first to her and then passed on so that her business, WIS Media Partners, would appear on the charity tax return as the biggest vendor. That, she said, would focus attention on her and not men with clear ties to Trump's reality television shows who are not named on the tax document. When the news broke that is exactly what happened.

Thomas J. Barrack Jr., Trump's longtime business associate and a real estate billionaire in his own right, was head of the inaugural committee. Wolkoff said that Barrack ordered that the Burnett associates be paid through her rather than directly for reasons she said Barrack never explained. "I have no idea what it was for or who ultimately got the money," she said.

Wolkoff's firm kept just under $1 million, including her $480,000 fee, which was all that she expected for her firm's services and vendors it retained as subcontractors. In the market for high-level event planners, and given the more than four months that Wolkoff put into the inaugural festivities, that is a large but reasonable fee.

The inaugural committee didn't pay to archive the inauguration website, www.58pic2017.org, or keep it alive. Go to it now and you will be transferred to the website of a payday lender, which advises on page after page that it makes loans almost instantly and charges the "maximum" rate each state allows, in some cases an annual rate of more than 500 percent.

In February 2018, more than a year after the inauguration, Barrack issued a statement as head of the Trump inaugural committee praising the group he nominally led. The inauguration "was executed in elegance and seamless excellence without incident or interruption, befitting the legacy and tradition that has preceded us," he announced.

The FBI arrested Barrack in July 2021. A seven-count indictment alleged that he engaged in illegal influence peddling on behalf of the United Arab Emirates, a close ally of Saudi Arabia, as well as conspiracy, obstruction of justice, and lying to the FBI. Also charged were a Barrack business associate and Rashid Sultan Rashid Al Malik Alshahhi, who authorities believe fled to the U.A.E.

Jacquelin M. Kasulis, the acting United States Attorney in Brooklyn, said Barrack and his associates "engaged in a conspiracy to illegally advance and promote the interests of the United Arab Emirates in this country, in flagrant violation of their obligation" to disclose their influence peddling.

The indictment described foreign influence that succeeded, including when Trump spoke language sought by the U.A.E. Barrack emails glowingly described this success, prosecutors said.

After Barrack spent nearly a week behind bars, a judge freed him on a record bail of $250 million. He pleaded not guilty.

5

Collecting Tribute

Watching an Inauguration Day video of Donald Trump's first presidential motorcade, Zach Everson noticed something that most Americans missed even if they were watching when The Beast, as the presidential limousine is called, came to a stop and the First Family got out for a brief stroll on the asphalt.

Along much of the two-mile route to the White House from the Capitol, where Trump had just been sworn in, crowds were sparse. Supporters were often outnumbered by police officers, soldiers, and other security personnel. There were plenty of protesters, however, displaying signs and sometimes shouting epithets. This was in contrast to the joyous crowds of well-wishers who packed the sidewalks on both sides during Barack Obama's motorcade to the White House eight years earlier. The paucity of Trump supporters infuriated the adoration-seeking 45th president of the United States. He made that clear later in the day with the statement he ordered Sean Spicer, his first White House press secretary, to read. The statement declared it was beyond dispute that Trump's was the largest inaugural audience ever, despite many photographs and other evidence showing that it wasn't even close to the largest.

What struck Everson, a seasoned freelance writer, was where The Beast stopped. It was one of the few places along the route where the applauding crowd was thick, filling the sidewalks, as if someone unseen had urged people to gather there.

The spot where the Trumps took their stroll was in front of the second tallest building in Washington, the Old Post Office, erected in the late 1880s under the supervision of Senator Leland Stanford of California, a robber baron who made his money in a way that has never gone out of fashion: by cheating taxpayers.

Under a contract with the federal government, Trump had recently transformed the long-neglected Old Post Office into the swanky Trump International Hotel Washington, D.C. It had opened just four months earlier.

"It was definitely an advertisement," Everson thought to himself as he studied the video. "Pennsylvania Avenue is a long street, and there are plenty of places to get out for a walk. The fact that it was such a beautifully framed shot, to have the Trump logo included in the shot, it was free marketing. So why would this be different from anything else Trump does?"

Everson realized that the free advertisement wasn't for Joe and Joan Sixpack or even their prosperous cousins, given the five-star room rates, but for a very select audience. The pitch was aimed directly at corporate executives, dictators, foreign diplomats, lawyers, lobbyists, and anyone else who would need attention from the new administration.

This was a subtle announcement to opportunists that it would be smart to show their respect by paying tribute to Donald Trump before asking for favors. The easiest and most obvious way to do this was to spend money at his newest hotel, located just five blocks from his new home. Smart people would figure out that his Doral, Bedminster, and Westchester golf courses and Mar-a-Lago, as well as his Scottish and Irish golf courses, would also do nicely as collection plates for the tribute. Without saying so, Trump was declaring that his newly acquired powers were, if not for sale, then available for rent to those who pleased him.

Everson knew from experience that Trump could learn the identities and affiliations of anyone who came to his new hotel, what they spent, and who they came with or to see. That's because on assignment from Condé Nast's *Traveler* magazine, Everson had just enjoyed a weekend there.

"When I arrived at Trump's D.C. hotel the first time I was greeted by name," Everson recalled. "It was clear they knew who I was. Within minutes two of the managers were at the bar where I was ordering a meal, providing me with a glass of Veuve Clicquot and giving me their business cards. Later, I asked the hotel general manager, Mickael Damelincourt, how they knew who I was, and he said, 'The attaché department researches all of our guests.'"

Everson spent $2,600 of the magazine's money on his room, drinks, meals, and a massage in the Ivanka Trump–branded salon. He gave it a balanced but on the whole quite positive review. He also noticed that many of the other guests wore MAGA hats, Trump lapel buttons, or other accessories or talked openly about being Trump fans. In this Everson saw an opportunity.

Realizing that the hotel would become the best place to observe legalized corruption, Everson started a newsletter named for the hotel address, 1100Pennsylvania.com, charging readers $5 a month. He relentlessly chronicled all the goings-on he could uncover at the hotel, showing that over the next four years the Trump International Hotel Washington, D.C. was ground zero for observing those eager to participate in Trump's pay-for-play schemes.

Everson might not have been so savvy about goings-on at Trump's Washington hotel but for an earlier experience he had reporting about luxury. One evening in Rome he was eating at La Pergola, the prime restaurant in Hilton's Waldorf hotel, when he noticed something extraordinary on the menu.

"They have this really high-end menu with 150 types of water, with some bottles of water at a thousand dollars each. I asked the server who buys thousand-dollar water, and he said, 'The Russians do.'"

"For whatever reason, these rich Russians didn't care for staying in the hotel, but they soon learned that the restaurant gave preferential seating to hotel guests. All of a sudden, the Russians started booking rooms without staying in them, so this Hilton property was making bank on empty rooms."

Everson realized that those seeking favors from Trump would stuff his pockets with money that was, to them, like tap water. Indeed, soon people, organizations, and governments that could drop unlimited sums on Trump did so. The government of Saudi Arabia, among others, rented out entire floors at Trump's Washington hotel. The Saudis rely on the U.S. military to maintain their iron grip on that nation's people. The Al Sabah family, who own the oil-rich country of Kuwait that was freed from Iraqi control by American troops during the undeclared Gulf War, moved their annual freedom celebration from the Four Seasons Hotel to Trump's place, knowing that the president would notice if they didn't.

"I can prove that officials of thirty-two countries visited Trump's hotel," Everson said, "but the actual number is certainly higher, and that's without counting a Taiwanese party that made a show of going to five Trump properties."

That money was pouring into Trump's hotel was clear after a document was inadvertently, though briefly, put online that showed it was a huge moneymaker. Trump's Washington bar and restaurant alone were raking in $68,000 a night. That could work out to $25 million per year, an extraordinary sum even for a five-star hotel. It was not at all what Trump had anticipated in documents he filed as part of his lease of the government building. Those papers showed that he expected the hotel to lose money at the start. But he wasn't president when his people filed those papers.

Everson was in the hotel lobby one day in January 2019 when there was a commotion at the entrance. A large group had arrived in what Everson and his companions believed to be African attire. His host, Ilya Marritz of WNYC, the public radio station in Manhattan, who was there to make a podcast, went over to investigate. Everson eventually learned that the man with the entourage was running for vice president of Nigeria, an opposition candidate in a field with dozens of others.

"The Trump hotel was his swing state," Everson explained. For decades Nigeria had counted the United States as a major customer for its oil, making Nigerians intensely aware of the importance of relations with Washington.

"It was surprising he was even allowed to be in the United States," Everson added. The Nigerian had been involved in a political scandal in which a congressman from Louisiana was caught keeping gold bars in his refrigerator. "But by checking into the Trump Hotel, video cameras in tow, it would tell people back in Nigeria that he was close to Trump, and that could be enough to make him stand out." A second candidate for the same office showed up at the hotel some days later, copying the strategy of creating the appearance of rapport with Trump.

Everson also observed John Legere, the president of T-Mobile USA, arriving at the hotel when he was seeking Trump administration approval to acquire cell phone competitor Sprint. "Legere made a beeline for Corey Lewandowski," Everson noted, referring to the one-time Trump campaign chairman and ongoing adviser.

Legere later got Trump administration approval for the merger of T-Mobile and Sprint. Legere's employers at T-Mobile paid Sprint owner Masayoshi Son's SoftBank $26 billion, as previously mentioned.

Paying tribute to Trump was especially critical for novice Republican candidates seeking his endorsement. Consider Michael G. Adams of Paducah, who wanted to become Kentucky's secretary of state, a job that would give him vast authority over how elections there are run. He ran in a field of eight for an office to which few voters give much thought.

Adams enjoyed solid Republican connections. He had been a lawyer for Mike Pence, Trump's vice president; had served on the staff of Senator Mitch McConnell of Kentucky; had once worked for President George W. Bush; and had been general counsel for the Republican Governors Association. He had the backing of Pence; McConnell; McConnell's wife, Elaine Chao, the transportation secretary; and Rand Paul, the Bluegrass State's junior senator. Adams's campaign issue was requiring voters to prove their identity at the polls, something Trump also supported.

Given all those Republican Party bona fides and support, Adams should have been a shoo-in for a Trump endorsement. And yet Adams felt paying tribute to Trump was crucial, so he spent at Trump's Washington hotel what at the time was more than a tenth of the donations made to his Kentucky campaign. The tribute paid, donations flowed quickly. Adams won his November 2019 election.

Everson also pointed to Kevin McCarthy, the California Republican and House minority leader, a job that requires constant traveling across the country raising money for Republican incumbents and challengers to vulnerable House Democrats. "McCarthy spent $743.93 on one stay at Trump's Chicago hotel and then dropped $200,000 on the D.C. hotel," Everson told me. And McCarthy made sure that reporters knew this, guaranteeing that Trump would get the word.

It wasn't just the Washington hotel, however, where favor seekers turned out to pay tribute. Lobbyists and their regulators posted photographs from their time at Trump's golf course in Bedminster, New Jersey, for example. Everson said, "The language in the captions they provided on social media insinuated that they had played with the president in a 'game of golf to never forget.'"

The same was true when the trade association for payday lenders, who loan money at interest rates that just a few decades ago would have qualified them for long prison terms, moved their convention to Trump's Doral golf resort in Miami.

Trump himself showed up at his D.C. hotel from time to time, once shaking Everson's hand and engaging in chitchat. His hotel steakhouse was the only Washington eatery Trump visited during his presidency. And except for a round of golf in Japan with Prime Minister Shinzo Abe, Trump played exclusively at his own courses, teeing off about twice a week, even though as a candidate he had vowed to never visit the links while in office.

How did Trump get to run a hotel in a building owned by the federal government he was elected to lead? Such mixing of elected office and profits has been illegal since 1808, and the story of how Trump got around the law is next.

6

Don't Ask, Don't Know

W hen Trump contracted with the U.S. government in 2012 to convert the Old Post Office into a hotel, he agreed to a condition dating back to the early days of our republic. An 1808 law, updated and still in effect, made it a "high misdemeanor" for members of Congress to participate in federal leases.

This anticorruption measure was consistent with the actions of our Constitution's Framers, who just three decades earlier had devised what was then a radical idea: that the people would govern themselves through popularly elected officials rather than bow to a monarch or other dictator. The Framers worried a lot about corruption, both venality by individuals and the vulnerability of corruptible institutions like the Office of the President.

To guard against profiteering by elected federal officials and their appointees, the Framers put the word *emoluments* into our Constitution in two places. A hoary word, it refers to *compensation, profit, economic gain,* or *advantage.* Old as it is, that word is today boilerplate in national security clearance agreements signed by millions of federal workers and contractors. Those agreements require, among other things, preclearance by the government of any publications based on classified work. Those who failed to do this have had their royalties seized by the government.

Trump faced a different kind of emoluments issue. It involved national security and the need to keep the nuclear launch codes near the commander in chief close at all times.

The problem was where to stage the so-called nuclear football. Access is highly restricted at his Manhattan home, Trump Tower; his northern New Jersey golf course, where he often stayed on weekends; and his Florida home, Mar-a-Lago.

At Trump Tower, a trailer on the street wasn't a viable option since if power went out it would be a 55-floor climb to his triplex. So when Trump was president-elect, the Defense Department started looking for space to rent in Trump Tower. That, however, raised an issue since paying to use any space Trump owned would constitute an emolument, unless Trump wanted to provide the space gratis. That's not Trump's style.

The Pentagon eventually found an owner of a Trump Tower apartment willing to rent to the military. That ended the emoluments problem, but at a high price. The apartment cost $130,000 per month, far above comparable rentals in midtown Manhattan, for a space that was needed for only a handful of nights during the four years of his presidency. The owner collected more than $6.2 million.

The Pentagon refused requests by Congress and journalists for information about what rent, if any, Trump was paid for a space to stage the nuclear football near him when he stayed at his Bedminster golf resort or Mar-a-Lago.

That left the emoluments issue in which Trump leased the repurposed Old Post Office building in Washington, which had become one of his hotels.

Our Constitution contains two emoluments clauses, both relevant to Trump's lucrative government lease. The Domestic Emoluments Clause, sometimes called the Presidential Emoluments Clause, limits the president's income to that which Congress determines before he assumes office. The clause bars the president from receiving any other compensation from the federal government or any of the fifty states. Since counties and cities are creations of the states, they too are covered by Article II, Section 1 of our Constitution, which addresses the role of the president.

The Foreign Emoluments Clause is in Article I, Section 9. It provides that "no Person holding any Office of Profit or Trust [in the U.S. government], shall, without the Consent of the Congress, accept of any present, Emolument, Office, or Title, of any kind whatever, from any King, Prince, or foreign State."

The 1808 law states that "no member of Congress shall, directly or indirectly, himself or any other person whatsoever in trust for or for his use or benefit or on his account undertake, execute, hold or enjoy in the whole or in part" any lease with the government.

This law invoked language similar to the "other high Crimes and Misdemeanors" language in our Constitution's Impeachment Clause. The 1808 law imposed a fine upon conviction of $3,000, a fortune at that time.

The anticorruption language in federal leases was strengthened and expanded over the past four decades. In 1999, when Kimpton Hotels converted the former General Post Office building, a historic landmark, into the Monaco Hotel, the language in the lease became the template for future leases. It stated that the lease prohibition applied to "any elected official" of the federal government. That expanded the ban to the president and vice president, though not to federal judges.

Trump's Old Post Office lease states in Section 37.19, "No member or delegate to Congress, or elected official of the Government of the United States . . . shall be admitted to any share or part of this Lease."

His lease also provides an exception. This grew out of the 1983 federal lease of the historic Willard Hotel site to the Marriott lodging chain. The prohibition in Trump's lease would not apply if he merely held stock in a publicly traded corporation such as Marriott. The Trump Organization is a private corporation, however, so this waiver doesn't apply.

This lease language makes it crystal clear that Trump had to exit the Old Post Office building lease once he assumed office. Indeed, the 1808 law, updated and still in effect, provided that "every such contract or agreement shall moreover be absolutely void and of no effect." That is, the lease is supposed to be self-cancelling if any government employee is a participant.

Given this clear language, how did Trump get to keep his lease and operate his Washington hotel? After all, Trump was both a federal employee and an elected official. Under the terms of his lease, he could, and I would argue should, have been thrown out on Inauguration Day.

Arguably, from the moment he became president, Trump was continuously committing an impeachable offense by violating the emoluments clauses. The attorneys general of Maryland and the District of Columbia thought so; they filed lawsuits making this point and were gaining traction until the issue came before the U.S. Supreme Court. Five days after Trump left office, the High Court dismissed the cases. It held that since he was no longer president there was no reason to resolve the issue, another example of Trump's running out the clock in litigation. This was a trick the notorious Roy Cohn taught him to do a half-century earlier. Cohn had been the lawyer for Senator Joseph McCarthy's committee that fabricated claims of communists infiltrating our government, notably the Army. Cohn later became the premier fixer in New York City for everyone from mobsters John Gotti and Anthony "Fat Tony" Salerno to Rupert Murdoch and Yankees owner George Steinbrenner. In this case, however, Trump had not intended Joe Biden to be the one to stop the clock.

The Foreign Emoluments Clause references kings and foreign states. Since corporations are creatures of government, many constitutional scholars believe that this clause covers foreign corporations. For instance, allowing officials of the German cell phone firm T-Mobile to stay at Trump's hotel and so put money in the president's pocket would seem to violate the Foreign Emoluments Clause. After all, what is the difference between the de facto ruler of Saudi Arabia and his entourage renting out entire floors of Trump's hotel and a company owned or authorized by the Saudi, or German, government doing the same? In terms of corrupting influence, does it matter from which Saudi interest the president's profits came? The courts have never resolved this issue, however.

Alexander Hamilton wrote in *Federalist 73* that the Domestic Emoluments Clause was necessary for "the independence intended for [the president] by the Constitution," so that neither Congress nor the states could "weaken his fortitude by operating on his necessities, nor corrupt his integrity by appealing to his avarice." If ever we had a president prone to let his avarice rule his decision making it was Trump, who for decades boasted of his unbridled lust for money and the power it brings. Hamilton's reasoning about preventing Congress or the states from corrupting the president by "appealing to his avarice" would also apply to the Foreign Emoluments Clause.

There was a way for Congress to let Trump rent rooms without raising questions about constitutional violations. While Article I, Section 9 bars emoluments, it has an escape clause: "without the Consent of the Congress." Republican majorities controlled the House and the Senate when Trump became president. They could have voted to let him receive gifts and other emoluments from his Washington hotel as wells as his other hotels, golf resorts, and restaurants. But the Republican leadership didn't choose to do this.

The leasing agency, the U.S. General Services Administration, let Trump keep his D.C. hotel, even issuing a letter blessing the arrangements, despite the clear language in Section 37.19 of the Old Post Office lease.

The inspector general for the GSA scrutinized all of these issues in a richly detailed report completed in 2019. Investigators interviewed two dozen lawyers, managers, and Kevin Terry, the contracting officer on the Trump lease. It's an informative story of how bureaucracies bend to power and find creative ways to avoid doing their duty when it might upset their ultimate boss. The lawyers in this case took a trip into an *Alice in Wonderland* realm of legal nonsense.

Among those the IG interviewed were lawyers Lennard Loewentritt, the GSA deputy general counsel, and his colleagues Barry Segal, Timothy Tozer, and Paula DeMuth. The former top lawyer at GSA, Kris Durmer, refused to be interviewed.

One of the first discoveries the IG made was that three years earlier, in December 2016, the top lawyers at the GSA had "decided not to consider whether the President's business interest in the [Old Post Office] lease might result in his receipt of emoluments under the Constitution's Emoluments Clauses." The lawyers "all agreed early on that there was a possible violation of the Constitution's Emoluments Clauses. Nonetheless, the attorneys decided to ignore the emoluments issues. They told us that the agency generally does not deal with constitutional issues. . . . Consequently, the Constitution's emoluments issues were not in GSA's purview."

The GSA lawyers said that they were "only responsible for rendering an opinion on an explicit provision of the [Old Post Office] lease, such as Section 37.19. Emoluments raised larger issues regarding the President's business interests. One attorney told us that they decided not to 'spin their wheels' on something that was not before them and, if necessary, they could address the issue another day."

The GSA attorneys "also told [the IG] that they made this decision without conducting any research of the two Emoluments Clauses or checking" with the Justice Department's Office of Legal Counsel. That was a crucial act of willful blindness because those

Justice Department opinions are binding on all government agencies. If lawyers know about them, they have to comply with their conclusions. But by not requesting them, the GSA lawyers could feign ignorance.

One of the GSA attorneys acknowledged that he had read one of these opinions that allowed President Ronald Reagan to collect the pension he had earned for his eight years of service as California's governor while he was in the White House. That GSA lawyer, unnamed by the inspector general, came up with a clever excuse for not acting with regards to Trump's lease as his duty and oath of office required. He said that he read the binding opinion only "as a matter of personal interest."

Kevin Terry, the contracting officer supervising the lease, was just as uninterested in looking into whether Trump should be thrown out of the lease. "Terry told us that he immediately formed an opinion, based on his 'plain reading' of Section 37.19, that there was no breach."

Only after Trump became president did his lawyers contact the GSA. They "notified Terry that the President had transferred his interest in the Old Post Office to a revocable trust and relinquished his management . . . for the period of his presidency; however, he still retained his financial interest in the property."

On January 31, just 11 days after Trump became president, Don Jr. and Eric, along with their lawyers, met with the GSA. Contracting officer Terry said he "strongly encouraged the President's divesture" and "pushed hard for divestiture" in his meeting with the Trump sons. Terry "wanted to get the [lease] out of controversy so he encouraged divestiture to try and prevent any issues related to emoluments, even though emoluments issues were not GSA's responsibility to consider. However, Terry stated he did not have a solid position to force a complete divestiture since there was not a breach of the lease."

Days later, Terry asked the GSA lawyers whether the agency should terminate the Trump lease. He sought their advice because Trump's lawyers insisted that Section 37.19 was irrelevant since Trump was "admitted to" the lease before he assumed office. The GSA lawyers sent two responses to Terry, both blacked out in the inspector general's report.

Then, in late March, Terry certified that Trump was in full compliance with the lease. Terry said press reports and analysis by legal experts outside the government had drawn simplistic "black and white" conclusions. "It has been less widely reported," he wrote, "that other legal professionals and former government contracting officials have reviewed the language and come to different conclusions."

Terry didn't mention the willful blindness of GSA lawyers and his own instant conclusion favoring Trump without any review of the facts.

The inspector general didn't buy any of this.

"The notion that GSA can disregard selected parts of the Constitution fundamentally ignores Article VI of the Constitution [which] establishes the whole Constitution as 'the supreme Law of the Land' and, therefore, it governs every agency," the IG concluded. "As an executive agency of the United States, both GSA and its employees have an obligation to ensure that agency actions comply with the law, whether the lease incorporates the Constitution or not."

The IG also noted that to understand their duty the GSA officials only needed to read two other sections of Trump's lease: "Section 6.2 of the lease prohibits [Trump's] use of the premises 'for any purpose or in any way' that violates the applicable laws (including the Constitution)." The IG rejected the idea that GSA could ignore any activity or law "because they are not stated verbatim in the lease."

More important, Section 37.2, which immediately follows the section barring elected officials from participating in the lease, "provides expressly that 'federal laws of the United States'" govern the lease terms.

"The Constitution certainly is the law of the United States and, consequently, applies to the lease, even if those terms are not mentioned expressly in the lease," the IG stated. Thus Terry's, the GSA lawyers', and others' "assertions that the Constitution's emoluments provisions fall outside the four corners of the lease" were wrong. Those assertions made "an artificial distinction that simply cannot be reconciled with the very provisions of the lease that incorporate the laws of the United States. Like any other federal agency, it is not only appropriate that GSA address potential violations of the Constitution that arise with its activities, GSA cannot ignore them. GSA did not fulfill that obligation."

The IG report summed up its findings in plain but harsh language: "We conclude that GSA's decision to ignore the Emoluments Clauses was improper."

The Old Post Office lease was far from the only conflict of interest that would enrich Trump while in office, as we shall see next.

— 7 —

Conflicts of Interest

Having a president whose businesses shoveled millions of dollars in cash into his personal accounts was a prospect America had never experienced before.

All presidents since World War II who had assets had put them into blind trusts, which were then invested in Treasury bonds or broad mutual funds to avoid even the appearance of a conflict between their duties and their bank accounts. For instance, before Jimmy Carter assumed office in 1977 his team acknowledged that "the existing law is extremely strong in prohibiting outside earned income. Governor Carter heavily approves of that law and its policy." Carter then put his profitable peanut warehouse into a blind trust (and when he left office discovered that he and Rosalynn were more than $1 million in debt).

Trump dismissed any conflict of interest. He insisted again and again that he had every right to run his businesses and our federal government at the same time, telling Fox News, "You know, under the law, I have the right to do it. I just don't want to do it. I don't want to do deals, because I want to focus on this." Presumably, "this" refers to the presidency.

Speaking to the *New York Times* he said, "In theory, I could run my business perfectly and then run the country perfectly." And he told a news conference, "I could actually run my business and run government at the same time. I don't like the way that looks, but I would be able to do that if I wanted to."

Still, he placed the Trump Organization into what he said was a blind trust. It was a very unusual trust. Trump appointed his grown sons as trustees so they could run his more than 500 corporations, partnerships, trusts, and other entities. He said that Don Jr. and Eric were free to tell him whatever they wanted or, though he didn't mention this, whatever he demanded to know. That would include telling Dad who was spending money at Trump hotels and resorts as well as who, among those seeking government favors, was not spending at Trump properties. Trump said he was also free to reach in and take cash from his businesses whenever he wanted. Although he promised that as president he would not initiate any new foreign business deals, past deals that remained in effect brought him millions of dollars each year from Turkey, Dubai, the Philippines, Indonesia, and elsewhere. Had Trump been an appointed official he would never have passed a security clearance because of his foreign dealings. This was the Donald J. Trump Eyes-Wide-Open-Blind-Trust.

Having a president who relied on his businesses rather than tax-payers for his income presented many risks, even if all the income had come from within the United States. It went to the very heart of the emoluments clauses in our Constitution.

When Trump proposed in October 2019 to host the G-7 meeting of world leaders at his Doral golf resort near the Miami Airport he was surprised that he drew criticism. "You people with this phony Emoluments Clause," he scoffed, mocking Article 1, Section 9, Clause 8 of the Constitution he had sworn to uphold. Eventually he relented, and the summit was held at Camp David, the government-owned presidential retreat in the Maryland hills.

The attempted profiteering at the Doral showed that controlling his businesses, even at one remove, created financial opportunities for him but, more significant, opportunities to extract money from those seeking favors or even just good relations with the Trump administration.

One obvious risk was that Trump could use intelligence secrets to coerce foreign government officials and business figures into spending money at the overseas enterprises bearing his name. Were Trump to avail himself of such an opportunity, he would not even need to get directly involved; he could deputize his favorite daughter and her husband, whom he had hired as White House advisers. Trump did send son-in-law Jared Kushner on numerous missions involving U.S. national security interests, especially in the Middle East. A foreign adversary could gain leverage by arranging to squeeze Trump's cash flow. Just as worrisome, and arguably more compromising, was how foreign interests could benefit by opening cash spigots, especially if they could shower Trump with money while avoiding attention. Don Jr. and Eric, being in charge of the blind trust, could also change the terms of existing deals to Trump's benefit.

But the promise not to undertake new foreign deals was a big problem for Trump and his family. It posed an especially tricky problem given how Trump had always conducted business. The business model that made him rich and famous wasn't based on long-term business partnerships or integrity and trust. For at least four years Trump would have to get along with his existing business partners. He would have to make them happy enough to keep sending him the cash he relied on to keep his house of cards from collapsing. Maintaining such long-term business relationships required Trump to restrain his grasping instincts. And it exposed him to a whole new kind of risk from partners smarter and more devious than he. He could no longer stiff or cheat his business partners and move on to the next victim, which had always been his modus operandi.

In spite of all this, Trump managed to pull off some very lucrative deals, small by his standards but huge for most Americans.

The first serious questions about Trump's "no new foreign deals" pledge began less than two weeks after he was sworn in. His son Eric showed up in the Dominican Republic at a resort that originally was to bear the Trump name.

Cap Cana was a massive resort project covering more land than the island of Manhattan. The centerpiece was to be the Trump Farallon Estates on the cliffs above the waves. The local developers carved 68 expansive lots out of jungle for luxury homes. Temporary wooden platforms were built so prospective buyers could climb up and see what a magnificent unobstructed view they would have of the turquoise Caribbean waters beneath the cliffs.

After Trump announced the project in 2007, promoting it on videos and in person, buyers snapped up 95 percent of the lots. Then the Great Recession hit, and construction ground to a halt.

A promised Eden Roc Hotel was eventually built, but no sign bearing the Trump name was ever erected. Dozens of investors complained that they had been abandoned. Some told journalists they had lost their life savings. These complaints were not unlike those I documented in the past involving failed Trump projects in Manhattan, Arizona, Florida, and Baja California, where Trump got paid and investors lost their shirts.

Trump was furious with the developers, Ricardo and Fernando Hazoury, leaders of a wealthy and politically connected Dominican family. Although court records show he had been paid $12 million, he claimed he had been cheated out of $14 million more from land sales. A Trump Organization lawsuit accused the Dominicans of "textbook fraud." After an audit gave Trump a look at the project books, he demanded $5.8 million. The suit was settled in 2013 for an unknown amount of cash and two of the lots. But the Farallons were not developed, and in time some of the property reverted to its natural state as jungle.

Given this history it was surprising when Eric Trump showed up at Cap Cana in 2017, less than two weeks after his father moved into the White House. All smiles, he posed with the brothers Hazoury for a photo. The Hazourys issued a press release characterizing their relationship with Eric as "incredibly strong." It appeared as though the Cap Cana deal with Trump was back on track.

Alan Garten, the Trump Organization general counsel, insisted the promise of no new foreign deals stood. Eric was there only to explore potential involvement in a revival and expansion of a dormant project. Garten pointed to the 2007 deal to show that the

Cap Cana project wasn't new. He also noted that the dormant plan to license the Trump name for the Dominican resort was listed on the financial disclosure Trump filed in 2015, shortly after he announced his campaign. However, the project was not in Trump's 2016 financial disclosure.

Global Witness, a nonprofit that exposes global corruption, especially as it relates to land use, sent an undercover investigator to Cap Cana in 2018, after Eric's visit. Posing as the agent for a wealthy investor, the investigator met with a sales representative who was captured on video. "And then here," the sales agent says, pointing to a map, "we're [going to] have a new development with the Trump Organization of apartments and [a] commercial area."

Despite the evidence in the video, the Trump Organization denounced the Global Witness report as a lie. It could well be that the sales agent, trying to make a sale, improperly invoked the Trump Organization name. But Global Witness reported that it spoke with a second sales agent who also discussed the Trump Organization. Only when its undercover investigator pressed for more information in a subsequent conversation did the second sales agent suddenly become circumspect, referring questions to the Trump Organization.

The Dominican Republic had long limited buildings near the water to four stories, but for Cap Cana the Hazourys suddenly got approval for a 22-story hotel, tax breaks, and other goodies. Critics in that country, including a columnist for the newspaper *Hoy*, questioned whether the Dominican government had bestowed these favors in an effort to ingratiate itself with the Trump administration.

*　　*　　*

Then there's India, where the Trump Organization had its biggest deals. Five Trump-branded projects worth $11 million annually in fees to Donald were underway in India when he became president. As with Trump-branded projects in the former Soviet satellites Azerbaijan and Georgia, in Panama, and at the Trump SoHo tower in Manhattan, the principals in the India projects involved people under criminal investigation. Most were accused of tax evasion, hiding money, filing false building plans, forging documents to steal land, and, in one case, setting a building on fire to force residents leave, which they did by leaping out windows to escape the flames. Continuing to do business with such people posed potential violations of a host of U.S. laws, including the Foreign Corrupt Practices Act, which Trump often denounced for inhibiting his investments abroad, and laws requiring business partners to report suspected money laundering. Trump's investments in India raised serious questions about whether his actions advanced his interests rather than national security.

During a 2014 trip to India, where he made his first deal to put his name on a building, Trump praised the newly installed prime minister, the Hindu nationalist Narendra Modi. The two men shared a hatred of Muslims and antagonism toward Pakistan, a majority-Muslim country. As president in 2019, Trump shared the stage with Modi at a Houston rally attended by 50,000 Indian expatriates living in America. This occurred after Modi's far-right political party had called for expelling India's 200 million Muslims, calling them "infiltrators."

In June 2017 Modi personally invited Ivanka Trump, now a White House aide, to India for a meeting of entrepreneurs. Soon after her November visit officials suddenly approved the planned Trump Tower in Gurgaon, a New Delhi suburb. Indian newspapers took note of this because the process for building permits in India is usually agonizingly slow, often lasting years. "Shortly after her visit, clearances for the Gurgaon Trump Towers went through in 'no time,' based on directives from" leaders of Modi's ruling BJP political party, investigative reporter Anjali Kamat soon revealed in *The New Republic*.

Just three months later, in February 2018, Don Jr. made his 10th known trip to India, where he announced he would give a policy speech on Indo-Pacific relations, which his father had been promoting as a way to counter China's influence. That mixing of U.S. government and Trump family business prompted complaints in both countries. Don Jr. then changed course, telling the audience, "I'm here as a businessman" and "I'm not representing anyone."

But he was. As P. V. Sunil, a managing director of a construction firm, said, "Though he claims that it's not an official speech, we take it as an official statement. . . . He speaks to his father more than anyone here."

On another trip to India, Don Jr. and two developers met with Prithviraj Chavan, then the chief minister in Maharashtra state. Don Jr. asked the minister to override the rejection of permits for a Trump Tower Mumbai. Chavan took offense. He told journalist Anjali Kamat that the "special concession" being sought would be "blatantly illegal."

*   *   *

And then there's the 2019 sale of the Beverly Hills mansion where Donald Trump had his brief fling with the porn actress Stormy Daniels.

The house, built in 1927, features five bedrooms and six baths on a large, oddly shaped lot where curving Canon Drive crosses both busy Sunset Boulevard and the far end of Rodeo Drive, known for its luxury shopping district about six blocks away. The Beverly Hills Hotel is just across Sunset Boulevard. The house was not in a prime location.

Trump bought the 5,400-square-foot mansion for $7 million in 2007 but insisted to the Los Angeles County assessor that it was worth less than that. As late as 2016 he was paying a property specialist lawyer to argue for a $6 million valuation.

Then in 2019 Trump sold the property for $13.5 million, nearly double what he had paid for it and more than double what he insisted was its market value.

The price seems high based on unrelated research by the real estate website Property Shark. It analyzed Los Angeles County home sales in 2008 and 2017, so a year after Trump bought and two years before he sold. It found that price growth was modest in Beverly Hills during that time: "There was only a 20 percent median increase from 2008 to 2017, which indicates that prices didn't increase as drastically as you would expect in this lavish city. The median sale price for these Beverly Hills homes was $2.2 million in 2008 and $2.5 million in 2017."

Trump had owned the house next door, too, suggesting a loophole. He had sold that mansion in 2009, ten years earlier, at an $850,000 loss. Who was the buyer of the properties? Records show it was a firm called Hillcrest Asia Limited. That the buyer sought to shield its identity would, in previous administrations, have raised questions aplenty. Hillcrest Asia turned out to be a front for Hary Tanoesoedibjo, an Indonesian media and real estate baron. A foreigner was paying the American president what at the very least was a very good price for American property.

Tanoesoedibjo wasn't moving to Beverly Hills. In addition to running a media company that reaches into every aspect of Indonesian life, he is a politician. He heads Perindo, the United Indonesia Party. The billionaire says he expects to become president of Indonesia in a few years. He calls himself the "Donald Trump of Indonesia."

He was also a source of money for Trump before and potentially long after the mansions deal. In 2015 he and Trump had made a deal to build two Trump-branded luxury resorts. Both were licensing deals in which Trump got paid for slapping his name on the projects but wasn't the developer. Trump's financial disclosure forms show that Tanoesoedibjo paid the Trump Organization between $2 million and $10 million up front for the use of Trump's name. Both men had every reason to expect years of cash going to Trump. Tanoesoedibjo valued the developments at $1.7 billion, suggesting future payments would be greater than the upfront money because such licensing deals are usually scaled to revenues.

The larger project was called the Trump International Resort & Golf Club Lido, part of Lido City, an 11-square-mile development with a theme park, its own hospital, and residences. The site is about 40 miles from Jakarta, the Indonesian capital. The other project is the Trump International Resort, Golf Club & Residences Bali, on a site overlooking an ancient temple on a rocky outcropping in the sea that is popular with tourists.

In 2019, the year the mansion was sold, Don Jr. flew to Jakarta to promote the Lido and Bali projects with Tanoesoedibjo. The men held a press conference and talked to investors. Tanoesoedibjo insisted there was no link between his business dealings with Trump and politics in Indonesia, the world's fourth most populous nation, right behind the United States. "The business with the Trump Organization has nothing to do with my political career," he said. Don Jr. took the same position, saying that Tanoesoedibjo "wouldn't make decisions on a country based on a real estate deal." He called any suggestion of linkage of business to his father's personal wealth "nonsense." But Tanoesoedibjo had reason to want to keep Donald Trump happy for his own business and political ambitions.

Perhaps not incidentally, Tanoesoedibjo's MNC Group is in serious debt to the Chinese government. The Metallurgical Corporation of China, a state-owned construction company, provided MNC with $500 million to build a theme park. China sees the financing as part of its Belt and Road Initiative, which aims to expand Chinese economic influence across Asia and into Europe. High-speed rail lines, new or improved seaports, roads and construction projects from Southeast Asia all the way to Turkey are designed to create Chinese hegemony in that part of the world. President Xi Jinping regards the Belt and Road Initiative as one of his highest priorities.

The theme park would be in Lido City alongside the Trump resort. That means if things were to go badly, the project Trump was counting on for income could get drawn into a dispute between Tanoesoedibjo and the Chinese government. This would be all the more problematic because the family of one of Trump's cabinet members was deeply involved with Chinese government banking, as you will read in another chapter.

That the Indonesian projects mattered a lot to Trump, and he didn't want the American public to pay attention to them, is suggested by what he did just days after losing the 2020 election to Joe Biden. Trump met with the Indonesian coordinating minister for maritime affairs and investment, Luhut Binsar Pandjaitan. Also attending the White House meeting were son-in-law Jared Kushner, Vice President Mike Pence, and Robert O'Brien, the national security adviser.

What made the meeting noteworthy is that the White House didn't announce it. As with Trump's May 2017 meetings with Russia's foreign minister and ambassador to the United States, we know of the meeting only because Jakarta issued a statement that mentioned it.

There is one obvious explanation for the meeting and why Trump kept it secret. The minister was in the U.S. to seek $15 billion for infrastructure improvements in Indonesia. When the unannounced meeting was held, Tanoesoedibjo had yet to build either project that was to bear the Trump name. But if some of that $15 billion could be steered to the projects, that might change, and Trump might reap a payday.

— 8 —

Tax Scam

Three months after launching his presidential campaign, Trump held a tenuous lead in the polls. He sought a way to avoid falling out of contention, as had happened to Newt Gingrich four years earlier and his friend Rudy Giuliani four years before that.

Trump needed a way to cement his support. With his attacks on Mexicans and Muslims he'd given a strong shout-out to people who feared anyone they didn't consider white. Now he needed something that would work for a larger audience, that would appeal to the people who'd seen the mills close and their jobs go to China. But he also wanted to appeal to the big moneymakers, some of whom had profited from sending those jobs offshore.

His solution: tax cuts for everyone. Combine that with insisting that he was so skilled in the ways of money that he could cut taxes without adding to the federal budget deficit and the accumulating national debt. He bet that he had a winner.

That bet was too good to be true, and yet to many of those who had suffered years of economic stagnation it was too tempting to reject. And to the very wealthy it was a promise that at least their taxes wouldn't go up.

The tax con was similar to those Trump had run many times on banks that gave him loans without checking who else he had borrowed from; on investors who bought his bonds and stock in casinos that he said were licenses to print money; on unpaid vendors who continued delivering goods on the promise he would pay them later; and on the gullible who maxed out their credit cards paying tuition for his fake Trump University. This time what Trump wanted wasn't other people's money, at least not up front, but votes that would put him in the White House, with its vast opportunities to rake in cash.

The design and timing of this scam were perfect. Its key promise was made to the vast majority of Americans who, after inflation was taken into account, were averaging about 10 percent less income in 2015 than in 2000. They were long on debt, short on savings, and had endured decades struggling to make ends meet in a nation with constant reminders of the riches of people like Trump, who said his wealth was proof he knew what the country needed. Trump's pitch confirmed the insight of Adam Smith, the philosopher and economist who in 1755 observed that human beings possess a "disposition to admire, and almost to worship, the rich and the powerful" and too often regard them with "the respect and admiration which are due only to wisdom and virtue."

Stepping before television cameras in the Trump Tower lobby in September 2015, Trump said, "We are going to be discussing something so important to our country, for our country, and for getting us all working again, and working well again. It's a tax

reform that I think will make America strong and great again."
He promised to "provide major tax relief for middle income and
for most other Americans. There will be a major tax reduction. It
will simplify the tax code. It will grow the American economy at
a level that it hasn't seen for decades. And all of this does not add
to our debt or our deficit."

The key line, intended to dominate the television news reports,
was this: "If you're single and earn less than $25,000 or married
and jointly earn less than $50,000 you will not pay any income
tax, nothing."

That year 90 million of the 150 million income tax returns that
Americans filed reported income of $50,000 or less. The typical
taxpayer near that ceiling paid about $3,800 in federal income tax,
with singletons paying more and married couples with children
less. It would be great not to have to pay anything at all.

Only tax policy wonks would likely know that the income tax
savings Trump offered to those making $50,000 equaled the drop
in their income since 2000.

Trump also asserted that 93 million people wanted jobs but
couldn't get hired because business taxes were too high. That was
both illogical and a fantastic exaggeration. By the broadest measure, only about 15 million people wanted work but were either
jobless or able to find only part-time employment. But as Trump
knew, hardly anyone paid attention to details, and numbers like
93 million were too big to be meaningful.

Trump smartly followed up this big scary number with what
he said would be a solution to create more jobs: "Business of any
size from a Fortune 500 company to a mom-and-pop shop, to a

freelancer living from gig to gig will pay no more than 15 percent of their business income in taxes. Big reduction." That was an understatement. The corporate tax rate then was 35 percent. For individuals like Trump, who owned their businesses directly, the rate topped out at almost 40 percent.

Then Trump added an element that is necessary for every successful scam: he had to show that he was not in it for himself, but because he was a good guy trying to help the little guy. Without providing specifics, he said his tax plan "reduces or eliminates most other deductions and loopholes available to special interests and to the very rich. In other words, it's going to cost me a fortune, which is actually true."

It wasn't true, not even close.

Trump sacrificing himself for others became a campaign theme. After the Republican National Committee nominated him for president in July 2016 he declared, "I have joined the political arena so the powerful can no longer beat up on people who cannot defend themselves. Nobody knows the system better than me, which is why I alone can fix it."

His rhetoric helped deflect attention from the absurdity of his tax plan. There is no way to make large universal tax cuts without running up large budget shortfalls unless you make large cuts in federal spending, which in turn eliminate jobs supported by that spending. Yet, again and again Trump told his supporters, "This [tax cut] does not add to our debt or our deficit."

Trump knew from experience that instead of treating his plan as a joke, journalists and the policy wonks in Washington would start analyzing the details, running computer simulations, and producing mind-numbingly complex reports. Would Trump's promises add $10 trillion to the federal debt, or would it be $11 trillion? As if those numbers held any meaning for the vast majority of Americans.

Two of the nation's most prominent antitax organizations, the Club for Growth and the Tax Foundation, dismissed the Trump plan as not credible because it would require massive borrowing. When asked about one of these critiques on ABC's *This Week*, Trump dismissively replied, "What do they know?"

Lily Batchelder, a New York University law professor known for smart insights into tax policy, was among the wonks who tried to warn people that Trump was selling pie in the sky. She explained that half of Trump's income tax cuts would go to people in the top 1 percent. That's households making more than $50,000 per *month*, not per year. Some in that rarified group make millions of dollars *every day*. Under Trump's plan the superrich stood to save much more in taxes each year than most people would earn in a lifetime of work.

What Trump intuitively understood, and I learned from many years of interviewing people about income and taxes, was that to someone making $50,000 a year, someone making $500,000 is no different from someone making $5 million. As one blue-collar worker with three kids told me some years back when I asked about that difference, "They're all rich, doesn't make any difference. They're just rich."

Batchelder offered revealing examples of how Trump's plan would in fact raise some people's taxes. A single parent with two kids, for instance, who made $75,000 a year would see her taxes go up because the Trump plan would take away the three personal exemptions the family was entitled to use to reduce their taxes.

The Tax Policy Center's Howard Gleckman neatly summed up the Trump tax plan scam: "Don't be fooled by those who call the Trump plan reform. While it may include some random elements of reform, it would firmly retain the basic structure of today's code. At heart it is merely a giant tax cut designed to benefit mostly businesses and high-income households."

Trump countered this criticism with a clever image to sell his scam. Instead of paying someone to fill out a tax return, he said, people would send the IRS a postcard saying "I win."

The prospect of making $50,000 a year before owing any income tax resonated because Trump offered what a majority of Americans desperately needed: economic salvation on terms they could understand. He refused to engage his critics because he knew he'd lose. The critics were trying to win with facts, reason, and rational argument. Trump reached people in their hearts and stomachs, reminding them often that he was going to sacrifice some of his own riches for them.

*   *   *

A few days after Trump announced his tax plan he was a guest on ABC's *This Week*. Host George Stephanopoulos pressed him on how much he would personally save in taxes. Stephanopoulos started off by suggesting Trump made about $250 million in 2014.

"Six hundred and five million," Trump said instantly.

That was a figure that could not be verified because Trump held tight to his tax returns, but it was about as believable as his statement that if he were president he would do for $2,000 projects on which the government currently spent $2 million.

Stephanopoulos accepted the $605 million income figure, which implied tax savings to Trump of up to $150 million under the plan Trump had outlined. "You're not going to be paying more taxes . . . you're going to get a tax cut," Stephanopoulos said.

Trump first employed a standard con man trick, shifting the subject. But Stephanopoulos wouldn't let him off the hook, reeling him back to his own situation. "I don't know," Trump replied, "because I have very big deductions. Frankly, some of them are ridiculous. You're entitled to deductions. So, I don't know that I am . . . I think probably I'll end up paying more under this, to be honest."

After that interview Trump ramped up his tax promises to supporters, telling them he would sacrifice by paying more income tax so that they would pay nothing. He told a rally in Scranton, Pennsylvania, that his plan would "massively cut taxes for the middle class, the forgotten people, the forgotten men and women of this country, who built our country." And he insisted again and again that his plan would raise taxes on people like himself.

After Trump won the White House it was time to put his promise into law.

What would become the Tax Cuts and Jobs Act of 2017 was beginning to take shape in 2016 when Trump went before the Economic Club of New York to sell the legislation. There he said, "A married couple earning $75,000 per year with two children and $10,000 in childcare expenses will receive a 30% reduction in their tax bill from what they're paying right now."

Then he softened up the audience of business economists with a line that made them erupt in appreciation: "By contrast, someone earning $5 million—like the people in this room—will receive virtually no change in their tax bill at all."

The business economists had to know better. They had to know that last point was a lie. Yet not one of them had the courage to call him on it. That was another piece of con artistry that Trump understood. Few people take brave stances, especially if that means challenging someone prominent like the prospective president of the United States.

He emphasized that his tax legislation would "benefit working and middle-class families. We've got to take care of our middle-class families." In particular, he asserted, "A married couple earning $50,000 per year with two children and $8,000 in childcare expenses will save 35% from their current tax bill. That's a tremendous savings."

The economists applauded.

What apparently no one in that audience remembered was Trump's original promise, that a married couple would pay nothing on their first $50,000. In this speech, however, he was admitting that a married couple with two children would still be paying federal income tax.

I calculate that a married couple making exactly $50,000 that year would pay $2,282 in federal income tax. Assuming the 35 percent reduction Trump mentioned, they would pay $1,483, or about 3 percent of their income. That's a savings of $799.

That's not what Trump promised in his September 2015 announcement. Had the economists been skeptical instead of laughing and applauding they might have sat in silence or even booed. Their response showed instead how successfully Trump had run this scam.

Major tax bills usually are preceded by extensive public hearings where experts testify about the expected and possible effects that may flow from an overhaul of our federal tax code. Changing American tax law is like playing Jenga. Move any one piece, and the dynamic of the whole pile may shift in ways no one foresaw. To avoid costly blunders Congress had always insisted on detailed studies. The 1986 Tax Reform Act signed by President Reagan, for example, was preceded by so much careful analysis from so many perspectives that just the summary of the research ran to 500 pages. The result was a reform that time has shown made some significant improvements in tax law.

In contrast, Trump's tax cut legislation moved through Congress more quickly and with less effort than any major tax bill in more than a century. Congress did not hold even one public hearing on the bill. Not one Democrat voted for it, either. But since Republicans held the majority in the House and the Senate, they didn't need any Democratic votes. And by not holding hearings they denied Democrats a forum to alert voters to who would actually benefit from the legislation and to point out that the legislation was nothing like what candidate Trump had promised. The Republican leadership aided and abetted Trump's scam.

The Tax Cuts and Jobs Act of 2017 was just as Gleckman had described it. In 2016 a married couple were entitled to earn $20,800 before owing any income tax. Trump's law raised that modestly to $24,000, less than half the $50,000 he had promised would be tax free. His law also took away middle-class tax benefits, especially personal exemptions that made a big difference for large families.

Under Trump, the tax rate for people in the lowest bracket remained 10 percent, then rose to 12 percent; but the next bracket jumped from 15 to 22. Trump's tax law did the opposite for the rich: the old top tax rate of 39.6 percent was reduced to 37. That's a savings of $26,000 per $1 million of income. For the 200 people who make $100 million a year in salary and bonuses, the Trump tax cuts were huge.

Trump's plan was twice as generous to the richest Americans as President George W. Bush's 2001 tax cuts. Bush gave the richest one in 1,000 households 12.5 percent of the tax cut's savings; Trump gave them 24 percent.

And what about that married couple making $50,000 who Trump promised would no longer pay income taxes? Americans who made $40,000 to $50,000 in 2017 paid on average around $4,500 in all federal taxes, not just the income tax, according to the Tax Policy Center's computer model. For people at this income level, the combined burden of Social Security and Medicare taxes was bigger than the income tax. In 2018 the Trump tax law lowered their total federal tax burden to $4,130.

That's a savings of $370, just a dollar per day.

Compare that to a household making about $3 million: their tax savings came to $47,000. That's $129 per day against the $1 per day for the married couple with two kids making $50,000. If the cut was proportional the rich household would save $60 per day because their income is 60 times greater but instead they save 129 times more. The Trump tax cut was, this comparison shows, heavily weighted in favor of the richest families.

The net effect of Trump's tax law was insignificant relief for those on the lower half of the income ladder and a big tax cut for the richest Americans. Trump's ironclad promise of ending the income tax for 60 percent of Americans filing tax returns never materialized.

Worse, Trump's tax law was actually a stealth attack on the middle class and the working poor. That dollar-a-day tax savings was financed by Uncle Sam's borrowing. A tax cut financed with borrowed money is not a tax cut at all. Team Trump had taken his preposterous promise and applied a clever accounting trick to create the appearance of a tax cut.

Looking at how the tax cuts affect the amount of extra after-tax money people will have to spend over their lifetimes is revealing. Professor Laurence Kotlikoff of Boston University, who studies the flow of income over lifetimes and across generations, used his computer model to estimate the increased spending individuals can expect over their lifetime.

"The richest 1 percent received a $278,540 lifetime tax cut," Kotlikoff wrote; this is the same as saying how much lifetime spending will increase. He described that sum as "miles higher than the $21,704 going, on average, to those in the middle." For the poor, it's only $4,975.

Borrowing to make up for the reduced revenue simply shifted the tax burden into the future, where the true cost will be greater. Every dollar people didn't pay was added to the federal debt. It also required more government borrowing to pay interest on the debt. Over time the interest will compound until it overwhelms the tax savings. And who benefits from the interest that has to be paid on that debt? Mostly insurance companies, banks, and foreign governments such as China.

By 2019 the official congressional estimate put the required borrowing at $2.3 trillion. That was for just 10 years. That means that more and more federal resources would have to be diverted to paying interest. As the federal debt grows, so do demands that government reduce spending, especially on programs that benefit the middle class, like Social Security, Medicare, medical research, and pollution regulations.

But in the short run Trump had pulled off a perfect scam. The rich were happy, and many in the middle class wrongly believed he had come through for them. Millions of people saw him as a problem-solving hero who should be given more power.

Trump and congressional Republicans successfully shifted the income tax burden onto less-wealthy Americans by using a simple strategy: lie, never acknowledge critics, and deny critics the forum of congressional hearings. It was the kind of authoritarian approach to governing suited to an unaccountable and dictatorial regime beholden not to the people as a whole but to oligarchs. Trump made many comments hinting at his belief that he should be president forever and act as a dictator, always framed as a joke, or so he said. But in 2019 the pretense ended when he said, citing Article II of our Constitution, "I have the right to do whatever I want as president."

Before the Trump tax bill came up for the final House and Senate votes many changes were made, some of them handwritten in the margins by congressional staff, some seemingly dictated by corporate lobbyists. Lawmakers didn't know about some of these changes when they voted on them—not that it would have mattered. The changes added more tax benefits for the rich and the corporations they control, benefits that were never mentioned during the campaign. Among these freshly sprouted provisions were tax favors for real estate and restaurant developers like the Trump-Kushner family.

*   *   *

The Tax Cuts and Jobs Act that Congress passed in December 2017, which Trump signed into law three days later, was his only significant legislative accomplishment as president. He had built public support for the bill by emphasizing that ordinary people and not the rich would be the big winners. And that it would personally cost him money.

"I don't benefit. I don't benefit," Trump told a September 2017 rally, one of several where he repeated variations of this lie. "In fact, very, very strongly, as you see, I think there's very little benefit for people of wealth."

Trump, however, stood to benefit to the tune of $146,000 in lower taxes on every $1 million of profit from his more than 500 businesses. Had the law been in effect in 2005, the year of Trump's tax return that I obtained and published at *DCReport*, his and Melania's nominal savings would have been $16 million. Trump's income on his 2005 federal tax return was almost $3 million a week, yet he paid regular income tax at a lower rate than the poorest taxpayers, who averaged a tad more than $300 a week.

Thanks to the 2017 tax cut, Trump's son-in-law and daughter, unpaid White House aides Jared and Ivanka, also stood to save a fortune in taxes. Like Trump and other White House officials, they had to disclose their income in broad categories. Disclosure forms showed their income during the Trump presidency was at least $172 million and could have been more than $640 million. Assuming all of their income was from pass-through or flow-through businesses, at the high end they would have saved at least $93 million in federal income taxes. At the lower end their savings would have been $20 million over four years.

Flow-through businesses are not taxed directly on their profits the way companies like General Motors and General Electric are. Instead, the profits and losses from these enterprises are attributed to the business owners as income. Trump receives nearly all of his income from his more than 500 businesses, all of which appear to be pass-throughs.

Partly by using paper losses for the presumed loss of value in buildings, Trump paid zero income taxes in 15 years in this century and just $750 in each of two other years. That was the conclusion of the *New York Times* in September 2020, after it obtained two massive troves of Trump accounting and tax records.

But Trump's real estate holdings have mostly been fully written down for tax purposes. He depends increasingly on income from licensing his name on products and buildings, which, as of the 2017 tax cut, will be taxed at 25 percent.

The 2017 tax law will also affect Trump's alternative minimum tax (AMT). He paid $31 million in this "stealth tax" in 2005. As a real estate owner, however, he only loaned the money to the government for a few years. That's because under a 1992 law he personally lobbied for, real estate developers subject to this alternative tax system get a special deal that is denied the millions of other Americans who must pay it. Real estate investors can get their stealth tax back in future years, when they aren't subject to the alternative tax system, a system they typically flow into and out of depending on their financial circumstances each year.

From an economic perspective, what Trump really did in 2005 was loan that $31 million of AMT to Uncle Sam at zero interest, knowing he would eventually get it back. He continued paying this tax through 2008. Then in 2010 he got a tax refund of almost $73 million, according to confidential tax documents obtained by the *New York Times*, which would almost certainly include the AMT he paid in 2005.

It was an IRS challenge to that refund, made after it sent the money back to him, that formed the basis of Trump's repeated claims during his candidacy and presidency that he was under audit and that only a fool would release their tax returns while under audit. That was nonsense. Once Trump and his wife signed their returns, disclosure would have changed nothing with regard to his tax status, not the refund or anything else.

Trump's 2017 tax law allowed some people who own businesses that they operate to exclude 20 percent of their "qualified business income" on their tax returns. The Trump-Kushners appear to make too much money to qualify, but without access to their tax returns there is no way to know if they found a work-around to take advantage of this new tax break.

The 2017 tax law also put a limit on how much real estate owners like the Trump-Kushner family could use their paper losses for depreciation of their buildings to offset income from work and unrelated investments. For married couples the limit was $500,000. But they didn't lose these write-offs; they can use them in future years. Delays just made them less valuable. Those delays ended in 2020 when Trump signed the 880-page Coronavirus Aid, Relief, and Economic Security (CARES) Act. Language deep in that bill revoked the $500,000 limit, allowing people like the Trumps and Kushners to take any delayed tax losses and thus lower their taxes.

This change could be especially lucrative for Jared and Ivanka. They disclosed salary and investment income of $1.7 million in 2015 but would not have paid any income taxes because their paper losses from real estate totaled $8.3 million, as shown in documents obtained by Jesse Drucker and Emily Flitter of the *New York Times*. In future years they could use the excess losses they reported in 2015 plus any additional losses to offset qualifying portions of their other income.

The CARES Act also allowed business owners to immediately write off up to $1 million a year for new equipment, which could be anything from a metal press to a fleet of luxury cars for family employees. Only one in 185 small businesses even has gross revenue of $1 million, IRS data show.

Trump's claims during the 2016 campaign and early in his presidency that he would not benefit from new tax laws proved to be as false as so much else that he said.

9

Polishing Apple

More troubling than the increased federal borrowing required to finance Trump's tax cuts was how the new tax law ran counter to his repeated promises that he would force American companies to bring back jobs they had moved offshore. His tax law doesn't do that. Indeed, it does something much worse: it encourages companies to invest and hire abroad.

If this is news to you, that's because the Trump White House did a masterful job of spinning what was in his Tax Cuts and Jobs Act of 2017. They sold it as a victory for the American worker. They created the impression that the corporate tax cuts would prompt massive new investment, faster job growth, and much better pay. Nothing was further from the truth.

First, a quick review. Trump's tax cut law took away many benefits and increased the tax bracket that raises the most money, other than from the very rich, from 15 percent to 22. Only rich people got a significant tax rate cut. The top rate, paid by the 1-percenters, was lowered to 37 percent from 39.6.

Stark as those numbers are, they're nothing compared to what Trump did for corporations, especially multinationals. First, there was a two-fifths across-the-board reduction in the corporate tax rate: from 35 to 21 percent of annual profits.

Trump's tax law also let companies immediately write off every dollar they spent on new capital equipment, like machinery, corporate jets, trucks, and robots. Usually, companies must write off these investments over three to 15 years.

Immediate total write-offs, known as "expensing" in tax jargon, are a powerful incentive to buy new equipment. With one caveat. Companies invest in new plants and equipment only when they foresee demand for their products. If people don't have money to buy appliances, bicycles, cars, furniture, and lawn mowers, there's no point in building a new production line, now or later. Trump and his team addressed this by saying incomes would rise $4,000 a year on average, even $6,000, figures high enough to establish that demand would grow if those increases materialized.

The biggest tax break of all, though, was a special one-time forgiveness of a significant portion of corporate taxes that multinational corporations owed since as long ago as 1987 but had not paid because they moved their profits offshore.

That wasn't all. Trump didn't require these companies to pony up right now in return for the discounts. Instead, his tax law gave them eight years to pay their deeply discounted taxes. In economic terms, Trump's administration loaned these companies, at zero interest, the amount of the taxes they still owed. This repayment was backloaded. In each of the first five years, the companies paid only 8 percent of the discounted tax bill. They will pay 15 percent in the sixth year, followed by payments of 20 percent and finally 25 percent. Imagine if Trump had offered you that deal: eight years to pay off just your current-year income taxes, interest-free.

The biggest beneficiary of this combined tax-discount-and-interest-free-loan program was Apple, which designs its iPhones, wristwatches, and the like in California but hires overseas firms to manufacture the electronics. Much of the work is done in China to take advantage of super-low wages, meaningless labor laws, and weak pollution controls.

Apple had stashed more than a quarter of a trillion dollars of profits offshore without paying any tax. The income tax it owed but had yet to pay was $88 billion. That deferred tax bill is greater than the total revenue of all but the 35 largest companies in America.

The Trump tax law forgave $50 billion of Apple's obligation, roughly the same amount paid each year in total income taxes by American households with pretax income of less than $800 a week.

Trump then loaned Apple the remaining $38 billion. Apple is extraordinarily profitable. It earns more than a 35 percent annual return on its equity. That means investing the loan proceeds should make the company close to $70 billion over eight years. Its final payment isn't due until September 2026.

The awful reality is that, thanks to Trump, Apple will pay no tax when the benefits of that zero-interest loan are taken into account. Instead, it turned a profit off his tax law. Combine the $50 billion tax discount with the nearly $70 billion of investment earnings on the interest-free loan that Trump gave Apple, and the company was ahead by $120 billion. Deduct its original $88 billion tax bill, and Trump gave the company back all of the taxes plus an extra

36 cents on each dollar. Would you like that deal? Well, Trump didn't give it to you, only to the big multinationals he claimed were unfairly treating you.

That gigantic $120 billion tax favor to Apple equals all the income taxes paid by the poorest 71 million American income tax filers for more than two years. And it benefited not the people who rushed to support Trump in the belief that he would save them from economic hard times, but instead one of the most profitable enterprises in history, the third largest company in America by revenue after Walmart and Amazon. Every multinational with untaxed profits stashed overseas got the same deal, though few earn such high returns as Apple.

A large majority of Fortune 500 companies have created more than 7,800 subsidiaries to hold their untaxed profits in tax havens like Bermuda and the Caymans, what British journalist Nick Shaxson calls "Treasure Islands."

These offshore subsidiaries own corporate patents, logos, and manufacturing techniques and other intellectual property. This property includes everything from the Nike swoosh and the formula for Viagra to the secret behind those nooks and crannies in Thomas' Original English Muffins. Paying offshore subsidiaries to use such property converts profits earned in the United States into tax-deductible expenses.

Here's how simple this is in principle. Take a dollar bill out of your left pocket and move it to your right pocket. Now imagine Congress gave you a tax deduction for moving your money from one pocket to the other. That's what multinational corporations do. But while your transfer is meaningless, Congress lets multinational companies take a dollar of profit earned in America and move it to an offshore subsidiary. Voilà! Those taxable profits become tax-deductible expenses even though they never left the pockets of the parent company.

This is exactly the kind of abuse of ordinary Americans by elites that Trump promised to stop. Instead, he cheated his followers by making it worse. And from remarks he's made alluding to these transfers out of the country to avoid paying tax, it's possible he may have done it himself.

Once they got their untaxed profits offshore, multinational corporations like the Trump Organization had a choice to make: they could hold the money in bank accounts, money market funds, Treasury bonds, and other liquid financial instruments, or they could invest in offshore facilities, such as factories or golf resorts.

The 2017 tax cut gave multinationals a 56 percent reduction in their tax obligation if they chose to hold the money as cash. Companies that invested their untaxed profits in offshore factories, however, got an even better deal from Trump. His law forgave 77 percent of the taxes they owed.

The signal Trump sent to corporate executives and owners of multinational businesses was loud and clear: if you invested your untaxed profits creating jobs overseas, then Trump and the Republican majority in Congress would give you a better deal than if you simply held the money in the corporate equivalent of a savings account.

These extraordinary tax favors could have been accompanied by requirements that the offshore capital be reinvested in America to create jobs, expand research and development, or pay higher wages to workers, all of which would have stimulated economic growth. Trump didn't do that. His law imposed no restrictions on how the money would be used. Indeed, companies did not even have to repatriate the money. Many chose to leave the money overseas, knowing they could bring it back to America whenever they wish.

Not requiring the companies to invest at home ignored an opportunity to create American jobs. Increased domestic capital investment is fundamental to creating jobs. Each new high-tech job requires a capital investment of about $1 million. Industrial jobs require less, but still the necessary investment can be in the hundreds of thousands of dollars per new job.

Trump and his allies had insisted that his tax law would spur levels of capital investment not seen in decades, with a boom in jobs, especially factory jobs.

That didn't happen.

There was a brief surge in early 2018, when Trump's tax law took effect. However, that surge likely had little to do with the tax cut. Trump announced that he would be imposing tariffs on imported aluminum, steel, and some other industrial materials and products later in 2018. Many companies responded by speeding up orders and buying extra to avoid the tariffs. Starting in the second quarter of 2018 such investment began falling. By the end of 2019 the growth rate was zero.

Repeatedly Trump asserted that his tax law was the reason for various capital investments announced by major corporations. For example, he touted plans by ExxonMobil to invest $25 billion over a decade in the Gulf Coast region. That turned out to be the same level of investment Exxon had been making and had disclosed in statements to shareholders long before the Trump tax cut became law in December 2017.

So what did the multinational companies do with the money they saved on their taxes? They spent the bulk of it buying back stock in their own companies. That doesn't create any jobs. It does, however, increase the value of stock options, which are the principal way that corporate directors and executives get paid. If a company buys back 10 percent of its shares, then the value of the remaining shares should rise by about the same amount. It's a way to make the already rich richer without doing anything to expand the economy, create new jobs, or invest in the research and development on which future profits depend.

Anyone with a degree in economics from a good college, which Trump claims to have, should know this. So much for his boast to be one of the world's leading experts on finance and the single greatest expert in the history of the world on taxes.

Just 17 days before taking office, Trump claimed he had browbeaten Ford Motor Company into halting construction of a $1.6 billion factory in Mexico, persuading it instead to build in Michigan. That version of events was deceitful. Ford went ahead with the expansion of its factory in Mexico. But it decided for two major reasons that its factory for making the new generation of electric vehicles should be built close to its headquarters in Dearborn, Michigan. Ford management calculated that building electric vehicles, or EVs, would require significantly higher skills than the Mexican workforce could provide. And it wanted to keep a very close watch on this risky bet that buyers of fossil fuel–powered pickup trucks would switch to electric motors.

That's a big deal for Ford since its F-series pickups have been the most popular vehicle sold in America for 44 years, with sales of about $42 billion per year. That's greater than the revenue of all but the 80 biggest American companies. So Ford did build a new factory in Michigan for its F-series electric pickups, introduced in May 2021.

This story matters because it shows that Trump believed he had the political power to make Ford move jobs back to the United States. So why didn't he apply that power in the tax law?

Under the Trump tax law that car factory Ford built in Mexico will never pay American income taxes, provided its profit on the value of the plant is less than 10 percent. If the plant costs $1 billion and earns a profit just under $100 million, no tax would be owed to the U.S. government.

What if it made a profit above that high threshold? The company could eliminate the tax just by investing some of the profits into expanding production at that factory, converting taxable profits into tax-deductible expenses. That's a good idea when it happens at home. But rewarding companies for doing this overseas makes no sense as American tax policy. Trump cheated the people who supported him with their votes.

Trump's tax law also shifted the burden of supporting our federal government from companies and onto workers. In 2018, the first year the new law was in effect, the share of federal revenues paid by corporations fell by a third, to 6 percent from 9 percent.

That year individuals paid more than eight times as much income tax as corporations did. In Obama's last three years, the ratio was much lower, about 5 to 1. From the end of World War II through the 1960s, the period when the middle class saw its greatest income growth, that ratio was less than 2 to 1.

These ratios matter because ownership of corporations is highly concentrated. Among the richest 10th of American households, virtually everyone owns stocks. More than two-thirds of the poorest households don't own a single share of stock or any mutual funds. Consequently a corporate tax rate cut benefits the wealthiest Americans, including the swamp dwellers, rather than the middle-class Americans whom Trump said he would champion.

Thanks to Trump's tax law, in 2021, for the first time, individual income taxes will generate more than half of total federal revenues. Add on payroll taxes—Social Security, Medicare, and unemployment insurance—and individuals provide 86 percent of federal revenues.

10

The Koch Papers

The very rich are different from you and me. They pay a small fortune to armies of professionals who help them avoid paying their taxes, and they make huge donations to support politicians who promise to do the same. In 2016, wealthy voters appeared to have found their champion in Donald Trump, a man who boasted in the first presidential candidate debate that he had paid no taxes: "That makes me smart."

Libertarian brothers Charles and David Koch (David died in 2019), whose privately held Koch Industries are into everything from Angel Soft toilet paper to oil pipelines, didn't find Donald all that smart. They didn't contribute to his campaign despite the substantial money they spend on politics. The Koch Network employs 1,600 political operatives and organizers in 38 states, people who move so stealthily that their influence goes largely undetected. Many in the Tea Party, which arose after Obama's 2008 election, thought they were participating in a purely grassroots movement. Most didn't realize that the Koch Brothers were picking up the bill for events, advertising, and promotion and quietly guiding Tea Party ideology.

Charles and David, two of four immensely wealthy Koch brothers, have long been very generous to candidates who promised to remove regulations and lower taxes. In 2012 they, and the 300 wealthy donors to their political action committee, spent $400 million influencing elections by funding political campaigns, making grants, and endowing 300 professorships. The grants and professorships shape the issues in political debates where specific ideas are marketed the same way as Madison Avenue creates desire for particular brands of shampoo and beer. At their PAC fundraiser in January 2016, the brothers pledged to double their influence budget in that election to $889 million, roughly what each party's presidential campaign spent.

Yet despite Trump's low-tax agenda, Charles and David Koch snubbed him. Trump acted like he didn't care, claiming he was so rich, he didn't need their support. He was the one who had turned down their invitation, he said, taunting them: it would be "much better for them to meet with the puppets of politics."

Tim Busch, a California real estate attorney who once joined the brothers in making a $3 million gift to a Catholic college, explained why Trump was not a fit for the Kochs. The brothers believed Trump didn't stand for anything, and supporting him was inconsistent with their libertarian principles. If they compromised their values to support Trump, Busch said, they'd never be able to hold a politician to account again.

Another Koch brother, William Ingraham Koch, wasn't inhibited by principles once he discovered that special agents from the

IRS's criminal division were investigating him for a suspected billion-dollar tax fraud. Bill Koch happens to live in Palm Beach, two mansions down from Trump, and he belongs to the exclusive Mar-a-Lago club. Certainly, if you're a rich guy under audit from the IRS, Trump has a lifetime of experience to offer you.

In 2016, in contrast to his brothers, Bill Koch threw his money behind Trump. Perhaps if he supported Trump, the new president would get the IRS to drop its investigation of his shell game to hide the profits from his highly lucrative fossil fuel product known as "petcoke."

Petcoke is nasty stuff, a fuel made from the residue from refining oil. It's carbon-dense and burns very hot. Inhaling it can cause damage to your heart and lungs. India banned it, but there's a thriving market for it elsewhere in Asia. Higher grade petcoke is used to anodize aluminum and in other industrial applications. Bill pretty much had the exclusive right to sell petcoke manufactured in Southern California to Asian markets. His company enjoys revenues of more than $2 billion annually, much of it from Southern California petcoke sold with built-in profits of as much as $90 per ton.

You are reading about these tax issues because I received nearly a thousand pages of internal Bill Koch business documents in 2019, what I call the Koch Papers. They provide an extraordinary look into the inner workings of a privately held company and its tax-avoidance practices.

If the taxes were fairly assessed on those profits, Koch would owe our federal government about $35 million each year on every $100 million of profit from his firm, called Oxbow. Yet for years, Oxbow paid little or no tax on that profit. If the IRS criminal investigators uncovered the complex arrangement that Koch's team constructed to hide his earnings, paying back taxes plus penalties and interest could mean a $1 billion tax bill. Bill Koch also faced the prospect of prison, which could amount to a life sentence for a man born in 1940. He sure could use a good friend in the White House.

In a 2019 statement to me, Oxbow said IRS auditors found nothing amiss when they examined Koch's and his company's 2011 and 2012 tax returns.

Like his richer brothers, Bill is known for being studious, even scholarly. He separated his finances from his brothers in 1983, the year he turned 43, when he sold his shares in Koch Industries. According to *Bloomberg* magazine, Bill did so well on his own that in 2018 his net worth was around $4 billion. He has a well-earned reputation as a serious businessman who intensely analyzes deals and watches his money closely, particularly his tax exposure.

The ingenious sleight of hand that supported Koch's tax scheme likely would have impressed Trump had Koch described it to him. Koch managed to scatter the various functions of his fossil fuel enterprise across three countries and not pay taxes in any of those places, the Koch Papers show. Bill Koch established three offices for this enterprise. Let's call the one in California Oxbow America, the one in Geneva Oxbow Switzerland, and the one in Nassau Oxbow Bahamas.

Although petcoke is too dirty to burn in California, more than 300 Koch employees manufacture it there, shipping it to Asia out of the Port of Long Beach. It would make sense to manage the business there too, but the finances of this operation are allegedly run out of Oxbow Bahamas, which operates from a 1,200-square-foot storefront in a Nassau shopping center. The three to five people who work at Oxbow Bahamas must run a lean operation considering how this handful of employees, some of whom work part time, apparently are all that is needed to manage the complex affairs of a multinational corporation that takes in about $40 million each week.

Since petcoke isn't made in the Bahamas, it's not taxed there. Oxbow Switzerland, a holding company that owns Oxbow Bahamas and shelters the company's profits, is not taxed in Switzerland. Oxbow Switzerland got the Swiss government to issue a formal ruling that Oxbow Bahamas wasn't subject to Swiss tax either because it didn't do business or make any money in Switzerland. And the United States doesn't tax Oxbow America because its profits are supposedly the property of a company headquartered in the Bahamas. And all this is thanks to clever use of an S Corporation, such a marvel of tax dodging that Americans have created almost 4 million of them.

Congress designed S Corporations to give tax benefits to the corporation's owners. The S corp. pays no corporate taxes on the enterprise's profits, which flow through to the owners. That means Oxbow America losses flow through to Bill Koch's personal tax returns, where he can use those losses to offset profits from selling other assets, such as stocks, real estate, and objets d'art. Even if Koch and the other 26 individual owners had only $1 of equity in Oxbow America, they would still share in write-offs.

Koch could even use these losses to reduce or eliminate taxes on the record $22 million paid for a portion of his vast wine collection in an auction that Sotheby's conducted in 2016. There is no way to know whether he took advantage of these opportunities since personal tax returns aren't among the Koch Papers. But he would be a fool not to, and Bill Koch is certainly no fool.

Even more promising for Koch's future taxes, the S corp. allows him to bank some of those losses. Losses greater than gains in one year can be used to offset taxable profits in subsequent years, a tax advantage working people don't have but one Trump has also used.

Sure enough, once again this structure enabled financial magic. Oxbow America reported profits of $229 million in 2009. By 2015 Oxbow America was losing money, while profits were being allocated instead to Oxbow Bahamas, which was raking in cash taxfree. This is precisely the kind of tax dodge that I started exposing in the previous century. Congress needs to investigate and then craft new laws to levy the billions of dollars in profits that disappear into tax havens like the Bahamas every year.

While Oxbow's complex arrangement for avoiding taxes was a wonder to behold, Koch knew the whole thing was shaky. The scheme had to be carried off with precision if the company was to have a shot at slipping profits past the IRS tax-free. Koch could see how this structure might collapse with even a cursory investigation by the IRS.

His apprehension was justified. The execution of the tax dodge was very sloppy.

If the IRS examined travel and expense account records, they could quickly establish fraud. The whole claim to tax-free profits rests on the assumption that the Bahamas was the main center of business activity and that Oxbow Bahamas is a Swiss company doing business in Nassau. But Oxbow Bahamas doesn't appear to be a real company.

Oxbow America sent a very junior executive to run the Bahamas operation; it covered his $115,000 salary until at least 2013, suggesting the actual parent company is in Florida, not the Bahamas. One key Oxbow Bahamas executive spent, at most, 15 days a year there, mostly playing golf. Another worked from New York. And another person employed by Oxbow Bahamas spent about a third of his time in Florida.

Oxbow Bahamas didn't even pay for its storefront. Oxbow America covered the rent and picked up many other costs to create tax-deductible expenses for Oxbow America. Still, Oxbow Bahamas claimed the income from the petcoke operations, even though not a single pound of the product was produced on that island. The U.S. tax code states that a product made in America but whose ownership and finances are in another country is still taxable by the IRS. Taking tax-free profits in the Bahamas while simultaneously recording tax losses in the United States generated additional tax benefits. It permitted its U.S. owners to use phantom U.S. losses to offset other U.S. taxable income.

The pressure on Koch and Oxbow increased in 2016, when the IRS started sniffing around. Auditors examining Oxbow America and related firms repeatedly requested essential accounting, analytical, and contractual records, as well as Koch's personal tax returns. Koch's executives stalled, complaining to the IRS that finding the documents was too burdensome and that diligent searches had failed to locate them.

Meanwhile, the company, aware of its perilous position, hired an outside accounting firm, Grant Thornton, and other consultants to evaluate how to keep this Oxbow gambit operating as designed and undetected by authorities. The news from the consultants was not good. Grant Thornton indicated the company would likely be audited by the IRS.

Another consultant wrote that one of the Oxbow's tax lawyers "does NOT believe that Oxbow is acting correctly with regard to the tax implications/exposures concerning . . . His philosophy seems to be 'we can beat them in court.'"

All of that screams "Sham!," and emails and other documents show Koch and his business associates knew they needed to hire someone to shore up this scheme in a way that would raise no questions at the IRS. "I am very worried that it is not being done properly," Koch wrote in an email, adding in capital letters, "HIRE SOMEONE WHO UNDERSTANDS THESE TAX ISSUES."

Oxbow hired Charles Middleton, a specialist in international tax transactions, to serve as the company's chief tax executive, hoping he would find a way to help them protect the company from the IRS. But shortly after he was hired, Middleton grew suspicious about Oxbow's insistence that documents the IRS auditors kept asking for were too hard to find. One day he sat down at a company computer, logged into a database, and quickly located every one of the requested documents.

Middleton said he promptly notified Koch and other top executives that the company should furnish the documents to the IRS and amend the 2010 tax return, which he considered fraudulent. The executive reaction was swift. Middleton was removed from representing Oxbow on the audit. He says this could only have happened with Koch's explicit approval.

Surely the IRS auditors noticed that the company's top tax executive ceased to be involved. Still, they closed the audit without seeing many of the documents they sought. That reflects IRS practices, ordered by Congress in 1998, requiring that audits be done quickly, not thoroughly. The IRS is even required to tell medium-size and large companies in advance what its auditors will be looking for. They may not look beyond those bounds unless they find clear and convincing evidence of fraud. Some auditors derisively call this "audit lite."

As soon as the IRS closed the audit in 2015, Oxbow America fired Middleton. That turned out to be a big mistake. It transformed Middleton from a perplexed employee into a whistleblower.

After his firing, Middleton found two lawyers who have long experience representing tax whistleblowers. One is Bill Cohan of Rancho Santa Fe in Southern California, who has been a reliable source of mine for decades. The other is John Colvin in Seattle, who often works with Cohan. After they sent me the Koch Papers, *DCReport* used the information for a five-part series in 2019 about Bill Koch, tax avoidance, the inexplicable conduct of our federal tax police, and what happened after Trump became president. No other news organization followed up.

Cohan suggested the withholding of documents alone justified the IRS reopening the audits. And he noted that, given Koch's hands-on management of his enterprises, his track record of serious analysis of business deals, and the order that Middleton stay away from the IRS auditors, more than enough grounds existed for a whistleblower complaint. "Bill Koch is intensely involved in his businesses, so there is no way that Middleton was muzzled and then fired without direct approval by Bill Koch," said Cohan, who characterized the behavior as a cover-up.

Armed with its more expansive set of the Koch Papers, the IRS in 2016 started digging into Koch's taxes, which we know from phone calls IRS agents placed and an email to Cohan. That's when Koch decided he needed to cement his ties with the man who would soon become president. With his wife, Bridget, he opened their Cape Cod vacation home to a high-end Trump fundraising reception. Guests had to donate or raise from others $100,000 to be in the top tier at this "Trump for President" event. Simply attending cost $2,700.

Many among the rich supported Trump and his position on taxes, which is another way the rich are different from you and me, a difference enshrined in law. Under the American tax system, Congress trusts businesses and their owners to file honest tax returns and accepts them as such, subject to audit. Absent an audit, or if auditors don't detect tax cheating, dishonest business owners get away with not paying what the law requires.

Wealthy business owners often play what tax professionals call "audit roulette." They spin the wheel on the chance that they can get away with hiding income here and there or not reporting expenses accurately.

Many among the wealthy take their chances because the risk of an audit is small and shrinking. The IRS now has less than half the resources, compared to the size of the economy and the number of tax returns, that it had in 2000. IRS executives have told Congress that the service lacks the expertise, time, and staff to unravel many tax dodges. This is especially true at the international scale. The disclosure undoubtedly emboldened many individuals, business owners, and executives already inclined to take their chances with audit roulette.

In the 2020 budget year, the IRS referred just 1,336 cases to the Justice Department for prosecution, half of which Justice declined to pursue. Many of the few cases that are prosecuted are not straight tax dodges but instead involve drugs, bribing politicians, and failing to turn over taxes withheld from paychecks. Congress has so reduced the IRS staff that it has difficulty just processing paper returns and issuing refunds, some of them still unpaid years later.

The very few pure tax cheats who do get caught can hire exceptionally skilled lawyers who specialize in persuading the IRS and the Justice Department to drop criminal investigations in return for a civil settlement. Deals like that make for better measures of performance in the annual statistical analysis the IRS, like all government agencies, does to show its effectiveness. In contrast a single criminal trial can tie up many tax lawyers and IRS agents for years. It also means that the errant taxpayer sometimes pays only dimes on the dollar of tax evaded.

Workers, on the other hand, cannot play audit roulette because Congress doesn't trust workers. It requires that workers pay their taxes before they get their paychecks. Employers also must report to the IRS what they paid workers.

That Koch Cape Cod fundraiser was a welcoming home for anyone interested in playing audit roulette. The party took place in what had been for decades the summer home of socialite Rachel "Bunny" Mellon, an heiress to the Listerine mouthwash fortune and the widow of art collector Paul Mellon, whose father,

Andrew, was treasury secretary for 12 years under three Republican presidents.

The size of the estate keeps paparazzi away, but among those attending were former U.S. senator Scott Brown, conservative radio show host Howie Carr, and former Massachusetts state treasurer Joe Malone.

The mansion is prominent in the Koch Papers because Bill Koch committed another outrageous tax dodge in acquiring it.

The Sotheby's brochure for the auction of Bunny Mellon's home described it as "one of the most significant parcels on the entire East Coast," a 7,000-square-foot house with extensive and exquisitely maintained gardens, more than a thousand feet of waterfront, a beach house, and tennis courts. Koch paid more than $63 million for it, three times its appraised value. Then he did something homeowners normally cannot do: he deducted the $42 million he overpaid as a tax loss. And he didn't even sell the house.

Sell your home at a loss, and Congress says "Tough luck." Whether you paid too much or the market collapsed, it's a personal loss. You get no tax deduction. The loss is 100 percent yours and yours alone.

Koch got around this by acquiring the home through Indian Point LLC, an S Corporation he owned, rather than in his own name. Then he closed Indian Point, claiming the overpayment on the house was a loss to that company, which he then could use as a tax deduction.

Middleton told the IRS that the losses taken on the Cape Cod vacation home were tax fraud. Koch's spokesman responded, "It is not Mr. Koch's personal residence. It was an investment property." The statement, a classic nondenial denial, didn't address the issue of whether the tax deduction was legitimate. Congress could find out the truth by asking for Koch's tax returns, which it has the right to do. Each year numerous tax returns are reviewed by staff of the Joint Committee on Taxation in Congress, several of whose professional employees are housed at the IRS to make access to tax records efficient. Some staffers gave the strong impression that the lawmakers they work for are of no mind to investigate any Koch brother. That's as understandable as it is lamentable, given the tremendous political power of all three living brothers, who easily could finance a challenger in an attempt to defeat any politician who throws a spotlight on them.

Congressional staff were also intrigued by what happened to the IRS criminal investigation into Koch, expressing hope to me that Congress would hold hearings.

In late 2016, when Obama was still president, IRS Special Agent Michael Galdys, whose office is in Palm Beach, Florida, arranged to fly out to California to meet with Middleton's lawyers, Cohan and Colvin. Then Inauguration Day came, and Trump moved into the White House and surrounded himself with people tied to the Kochs.

Cohan and Colvin both say that after Trump became president, the IRS and the Justice Department suddenly stopped acknowledging their calls, emails, and letters. Special Agent Galdys sent a short email to Cohan on June 13, 2017, making it clear he was no longer pursuing the case, but not why. Cohan believes Trump signaled that the IRS should lay off Bill Koch. Michael Cohen, Trump's longtime lawyer and fixer, told me pretty much the same thing.

In a written statement, Koch's company said he "has not approached President Trump to discuss any significant Company business issues, tax-related or otherwise." That statement too is a nondenial denial since it doesn't cover comments to anyone except those made directly to Trump.

Koch maintains he did nothing wrong. Through his spokesman, he noted that the IRS audited his personal and business taxes for 2011 and 2012, closing the audits with no changes. He has never been charged criminally. Indeed, in April 2021, the IRS issued a letter indicating it never collected a dollar of additional tax from him. However, in spring 2021, with a new administration in the White House, the IRS sent another letter to Cohan that suggested that the whistleblower case was not closed, but had merely been temporarily inactive.

Law enforcement should not look the other way because of someone's political connections. At least, that's the textbook model of government; it certainly doesn't hold true when someone like Trump, with his contempt for taxes and law enforcement, holds the most powerful position in the country. Going after a perceived Friend of Donald could be career suicide.

The simple truth is that the only Koch brother who supported Trump's candidacy was under criminal tax investigation until his friend and neighbor moved into the White House. The fact that the IRS revealed four years later that it never collected a dollar even though a former Koch employee presented clear evidence that Koch was hiding documents from IRS auditors and other misconduct means that Bill Koch is getting richer every day. Your taxes are in part taking on the burden that by law belongs to others, especially the owners of successful businesses who set up sham overseas structures like Oxbow Switzerland and Oxbow Bahamas.

11

Wall Scam

C hants of "Build That Wall" became staples of Donald Trump's 2016 campaign. Sometimes he said he would use his supposed skills as a master builder to quickly erect a wall mightier than the Great Wall of China, built over about two thousand years.

"We will build a great wall along the southern border—and Mexico will pay for the wall, hundred percent. They don't know it yet. But they're gonna pay for the wall," he told audiences. "On Day One we will begin working on an impenetrable, physical, tall, powerful, beautiful Southern border wall. We will use the best technology, including above and below ground sensors" to "keep out criminal cartels."

Just how Trump would force a sovereign foreign nation to pay for a wall to benefit the United States was something he never explained. That's because there is no way to do that short of going to war and plundering Mexican wealth. But there were people in his own family and circle of advisers who came to realize that there was a lucrative opportunity in promoting a wall. All they needed was the right pitch, gullible donors, and endorsement from the Trump family.

Brian Kolfage, a veteran who lost three limbs in the Iraq war, conceived the plan to raise charitable funds for the wall project. Kolfage called his effort We Build the Wall.

It began at the end of 2018 as a GoFundMe campaign on the internet. Kolfage said he started the campaign out of frustration that Congress didn't fund the wall, not even when Republicans controlled the House and Senate during the first two years of Trump's presidency. Congressional inaction reflected the recommendations of construction, geography, and security experts who concluded that it was impossible to build a wall along large portions of the 1,954-mile border between the U.S. and Mexico. And they insisted that any barrier could be overcome in a variety of ways.

To build a wall along the border, even if possible, would cost $21.6 billion, the Department of Homeland Security estimated just days after Trump took office. That's $11 million per mile.

That this estimate was absurdly low became evident after the Army Corp of Engineers let contracts for 135 miles of fence—not wall, but fence. The cost? $22.2 million per mile. That implies that just a fence along the entire border would cost $43 billion, while to erect the kind of wall Trump promised would cost so much that it would be like stacking greenbacks high enough to kiss the clouds.

But reality has never been an obstacle to the Trump family and its enablers.

In July 2019, Donald Trump Jr. and his girlfriend, Kimberly Guilfoyle, flew to El Paso and then, with Kolfage, crossed the state line to a fundraising event in Sunland Park, New Mexico.

Among those attending were two former Trump campaign managers: Steve Bannon, who became chair of the We Build the Wall advisory board, and Corey Lewandowski, Trump's first campaign manager.

Also attending was David Bossie, the president of Citizens United, which favors "dark money" in political campaigns given by donors who conceal their identities. His appearance was intriguing since just two months earlier the Trump 2020 campaign distanced itself from Bossie after allegations that he used his group to enrich himself by scamming elderly Republican voters.

Other Wall charity advisory board members included Kris Kobach, the Kansas secretary of state best known for pursuing the "birther" conspiracy and trying to purge voter rolls to ensure Republican wins at the ballot box; Erik Prince, the operator of mercenary armies and brother of Education Secretary Betsy DeVos; Tom Tancredo, a former Congressman from Colorado; and David Clarke, the cowboy hat-wearing sheriff of Milwaukee County in Wisconsin until he resigned in 2017 to join Trump's America First Action, a super PAC.

These people were eager to associate with Kolfage because of his success gathering donations to build the wall with Mexico. The effort had made Kolfage a frequent guest on Fox News and Fox Business, also known as Trump TV, where he defended Trump and said critics suffered from "Trump Derangement Syndrome."

Kobach told the *New York Times* in January 2019 that President Trump gave his "blessing" to the fundraising effort, after which more donations poured in.

To assure donors that the nonprofit wall project was legitimate, Kolfage promised that he would "not take a penny in salary or compensation" and that "100% of the funds raised will be used in the execution of our mission and purpose."

In 2018, long before the Sunland Park fundraiser, Kolfage wrote on the Wall website that "I'm credible and a real person" and he included a section titled "How do you know this is not a scam?" That would have set off alarm bells for many people and suggested a background investigation, but not to the Trumps, Bannon, Kobach, and others.

Don Jr. delivered strange remarks at the live-streamed charity event at Sunland Park. Instead of talking about invading hordes from south of the border as his father did or how much generosity it would take to do what Congress would not, he took an unusual direction that suggested he didn't understand business or charity.

"Brian, thank you so much for all your sacrifices, doing this, and showing really what capitalism is all about," Don Jr. said. "This is what private enterprise is at its finest."

Guilfoyle, the national chair of the Trump Victory Finance Committee, said, "it's really impressive at [sic] what you've been able to accomplish."

A month earlier, Kolfage had boasted that the short section of the wall his group had paid for was effective. "We plugged the hole of the worst smuggling route on the entire border!" Kolfage declared. "We cut them off." But days later, people crossed over from Mexico into Sunland Park.

That any wall would be ineffective was apparent even to doubters after various Mexicans, perhaps having some political fun, showed how easily border crossers defeated sections of the wall Trump did build. Using electric saws purchased for under a hundred dollars at Home Depot, they quickly sliced through the steel barrier while others quickly scaled the government-built wall using ropes and make-shift ladders, all of this captured by television cameras on the U.S. side.

The notion that any private group, even one endorsed by the Trump family and promoted on Fox News, could build a multibillion dollar project nearly 2,000 miles long didn't deter Kolfage, Bannon, and the others. Nor did the investigation, begun more than a month before the Sunland Park fundraising event, by Amy Topol, director of Consumer Services at the Florida Department of Agriculture, which regulates charities in the Sunshine state, where Kolfage is based. Topol acted on complaints suggesting that Kolfage's promise to keep his hands off the money and use it all for the wall was belied by, among other things, a fancy boat he had bought.

In 2020, a federal grand jury in Manhattan indicted Bannon, Kolfage, and two confederates on wire fraud and money laundering charges. The money laundering charge stemmed from what prosecutors said was a scheme to hide the money they had diverted from the wall charity once the four men realized they were under federal investigation.

The Southern District of New York prosecutors alleged that Bannon had created an organization to divert more than one million dollars to his benefit while Kolfage took $350,000. The other two men indicted, Andrew Badolato and Timothy Shea, were alleged to have created a shell company that Shea controlled and used fake invoices from sham vendors to steal additional funds.

It was, in the end, just another scam facilitated by Trump and his family. We Build the Wall never had any capacity to build a wall other than the shoddy short section of fencing that Kolfage and his confederates managed to erect. The wall Trump promised to build, raiding Pentagon funds intended for military base housing, schools, and childcare, didn't produce much, either. On Trump's watch, government contractors completed only 69 miles of fencing, not the 450 miles of wall that Trump claimed, the Government Accountability Office reported in June 2021.

Just before leaving office Trump pardoned Bannon, accused of stealing more than a million dollars, but not Kolfage and the two other men. Kolfage asked the judge in his case for permission to use some of the donated money to pay his criminal defense lawyers. His request was pending at this writing.

— 12 —

Opportunity Knocks

When the first American coronavirus infection was confirmed in late January 2020, Trump had already known for two months that an especially nasty pathogen was killing people in Wuhan, China. The authoritarian Chinese government had put that city of 11 million on strict lockdown; people were not allowed to leave their home even to visit the market. Government agents delivered meals door to door.

This was Trump's opportunity to show greatness, to demonstrate leadership, to fulfill his promise of acting always on behalf of America's Forgotten Men and Women by defeating an invisible killer through swift, decisive action. Of course, he blew it.

Instead, Trump's initial response was to insist in late February that America had only 15 cases, "and the 15 within a couple of days is going to be down to close to zero, that's a pretty good job we've done. . . . We're going very substantially down, not up."

You might think that Trump would be alert to the risks of a pandemic since his paternal grandfather, Friedrich Trump, had died in 1918 from the misnamed Spanish pandemic. That virus killed at least 50 million people, including about 675,000 Americans.

Despite this, during a White House briefing on March 10 Trump said of the coronavirus, "This was unexpected." Six days later he said, "This came up—it came up so suddenly . . . we were all surprised." And a week after that, at a Fox News Town Hall, he said of Covid, "Nobody ever expected a thing like this."

Actually, a pandemic that could kill millions of Americans had been long predicted. In 2005, after a newly discovered severe acute respiratory syndrome, better known as SARS, killed just eight Americans, President George W. Bush recognized that the nation and the world had dodged a biological bullet. "Our country has been given fair warning of this danger to our homeland," he acknowledged. In 2009, after the swine flu killed 12,000 Americans, President Obama initiated a series of steps to make sure the government was prepared for future diseases before they grew into pandemics. In 2017 the Pentagon warned that America was woefully short on supplies of masks, gloves, ventilators, and other equipment for an inevitable pandemic. Just before Trump assumed office, the outgoing Obama administration ran a tabletop exercise for the newcomers about how to deal with a pandemic.

Despite all this, shortly after Trump became president he shut down the White House national security team that Obama had assembled to track and deal with pernicious viruses before a pandemic erupted. Trump also shut down Obama's $200-million-a-year program to train American and foreign scientists in how to detect and slow the spread of such viruses. This followed his pattern of endeavoring to expunge everything Obama had done.

After these policy mistakes by Trump, he still had an opportunity to fulfill his inaugural promise that his every action would champion the interests of the Forgotten Americans. He decided to provide the people economic relief, starting with the $2.2 trillion Coronavirus Aid, Relief, and Economic Security (CARES) Act.

A third of that money was designated for the Payroll Protection Program (PPP). Its purpose was to mitigate the economic harm to both workers and their employers during the pandemic by replacing workers' paychecks. What followed, however, showed just where Trump's thoughts and actions were focused.

To see this, let's consider a $3.7 million PPP loan our government made in spring 2020 to the owners of a high-rise tower in Honolulu. It wasn't really a loan, certainly not in the conventional sense in which you get cash now and pay it back over time with interest. It was more like the kind of borrowing that made Trump infamous—money you borrow but never pay back in full and perhaps not at all.

The Hawaii loan was made with the understanding up front that it was "forgivable." In other words, it was not so much a loan as a government grant. As such it was pure corporate welfare. And it came with fewer strings than are attached to a typical welfare recipient's relief checks.

Our government made more than 7 million such PPP loans. The idea was to loan companies money to cover their payroll so they didn't lose trained staff and demands for individual welfare would be lessened. The Hawaii loan is important because, like the coronavirus, it was novel, a federal welfare benefit that indirectly helped a sitting president of the United States. And it was not the only such loan.

The Hawaii PPP loan was given to Irongate Azrep Bw LLC. That oddly named real estate investment group, based in California, owns the Trump International Hotel & Tower Waikiki. Despite the name, it isn't actually on famous Waikiki Beach. The tower is a block back from the sand and waves and on the other side of busy Kalia Road. Trump and Irongate Azrep lured buyers to its more than 400 premium-priced condo units by telling them Trump was the developer. But the 38-story building wasn't built by Trump. He was not an owner, and he had no employees at the property. He never operated it, though he often said he did. Those lies and others prompted 11 unhappy buyers to sue. As late as March 2016 candidate Trump continued lying about his role. "I employ many people in Hawaii at my great hotel in Honolulu. I'll be there very soon. Vote for me, Hawaii!" he tweeted.

Trump's actual connection to the hotel was to collect about $2 million every year for putting his name on the building. The money is paid to Trump Marks Waikiki LLC, one of many firms Trump created to license his name.

The loan our government made to the Hawaii high-rise was part of a select group of loans that helped few workers but sure did help their owners, including those that owed money to Trump. But for that loan the high-rise tower might have been unable to pay Trump his annual naming fee.

Nearly $771 billion of PPP loans were extended in two rounds.

In the first round only one in 60 of these loans was for $2 million or more, but they accounted for a quarter of the money loaned out. The second round was not quite so egregiously oriented to larger businesses. Only one in 300 loans was that size, accounting for 15 percent of the money loaned out.

Much of that money went to businesses with little apparent need for a taxpayer handout. Only 2 percent of American businesses have more than 100 employees, but the Trump Administration defined small business as up to 500 employees. Many borrowers were actually big corporations that qualified because they were allowed to count each of their business locations as if it were a separate small business with fewer than 500 workers. Three hundred of these businesses received loans above the maximum allowed by applying through subsidiaries in this way.

The maximum PPP loan was $10 million, except for restaurants, hotels, and related hospitality businesses, which successfully lobbied Trump to let each location with a separate tax identification number qualify for up to $10 million. That was a huge benefit to chains with many restaurants, hotels, and other hospitality businesses. And those are, of course, businesses in the same industry as Trump's.

Meanwhile, the lightly capitalized mom-and-pop small businesses that desperately needed such loans fared poorly in the PPP process. Minority-owned businesses had an especially tough time during the pandemic.

Terence Dickson owns Terra Café, a Baltimore soul food restaurant that also has an arts and events space. Dickson was among the many minority business owners who said they were told they didn't qualify for PPP loans. Only after NBC News asked about his loan did Bank of America issue one to Dickson.

Only one in five of America's 2.6 million minority-owned businesses has any employees other than the owner. Those one-person firms generally didn't qualify for PPP loans. Also, loan approval rates in majority-white zip codes were typically twice that for minority zip codes.

The loan forgiveness mechanism that Trump's team created can take 15 hours to complete, the Government Accountability Office calculated. That's no big deal for large firms with specialists on staff to handle government paperwork. Besides, once they learn the process, they can replicate it for each loan they apply for. But qualifying for forgiveness is a difficult hurdle for mom-and-pop operations whose owners already put in long hours and are unlikely to be expert at navigating bureaucratic rules.

For the better part of a year the Trump administration tried to keep secret who got PPP loans. Treasury Secretary Steven Mnuchin told Congress, "The names and amounts of specific PPP loans, we believe that that's proprietary information." Eleven news organizations sued for the PPP and Economic Disaster loan data. The Trump administration refused until a court order forced the disclosures just seven weeks before Trump's term ended.

One reason the Trump administration was so determined to keep the identities of loan recipients secret emerged from the files. More than two dozen loans totaling more than $3.6 million were made to companies owned by or connected to the Trump-Kushner family.

The biggest of these loans, close to $2.2 million, went to

Triomphe Restaurant Corp. in the Trump International Hotel & Tower at Columbus Circle across from Central Park in Manhattan. The purpose of the PPP loans was to save jobs, but no jobs were saved at Triomphe because it permanently closed.

A company called LB City Inc., with the same address as the Kushners' Bungalow Hotel in Long Branch, New Jersey, received a loan for a little more than a half-million dollars. Loans totaling up to $1 million were made to Observer Holdings, which publishes the *New York Observer*, a gossipy weekly newspaper known at one time for columns by Candace Bushnell that inspired the television series *Sex and the City*. Jared Kushner owned the company from 2006 until he joined the White House and transferred it to a Kushner family trust. His brother-in-law Joseph Meyer then became publisher of the online *Observer.com*.

Princeton Forrestal LLC, which Securities and Exchange Commission filings show was 40 percent owned by Kushner family members in 2018, received between $1 million and $2 million in PPP loans. So did Joseph Kushner Hebrew Academy in Livingston, New Jersey, which the family supports and which is named for Jared's grandfather.

Esplanade Livingston LLC, another Kushner-connected company, borrowed as much as $1 million. Another $350,000 was loaned to Hollwich Kushner Architecture, which is run by Jared's first cousin Marc Kushner.

Two businesses that are tenants of Trump Tower in Manhattan received more than $100,000. Four Kushner tenants at 666 Fifth Avenue received a total of more than $200,000.

Sonny Perdue, Trump's agriculture secretary, also appeared

to benefit. He is the founder of Perdue Inc., a Georgia trucking company that received as much as $350,000 in forgivable loans. His 2017 ethics filing revealed that he had received almost $600,000 of passive income from his investment in the trucking company. Perdue signed an agreement promising to resign from the business, but when he returned to private life he stood to benefit from the loan to the trucking firm.

While these are not huge sums by the standards of such large businesses or the wealth of the Trump-Kushner family, some do seem to violate Article II, Section 1, Clause 7 of the Constitution, the Emoluments Clause. As I discussed earlier, that clause stipulates that beyond his government salary, the president cannot receive money from the federal government or any of the 50 state governments. Even if these loans had saved many, many jobs—which they did not—they subverted the stated purpose of the PPP as a program to aid small businesses and they violated the Emoluments Clause of the U.S. Constitution.

Apart from these benefits to the Trump-Kushner family, the PPP situation illustrates three important problems of the Trump presidency. And the Hawaii loan, along with some others, underscores the threats to American constitutional government when a president owns and operates businesses instead of putting his assets into a blind trust controlled by an independent trustee.

The first problem involves how Trump, his family, and courtiers benefited from pandemic relief spending, exactly the kind of institutional corruption that vexed the Framers when they wrote our Constitution more than two centuries ago.

Second, the PPP was heavily weighted to favor businesses that needed the least help. Because there was no provision limiting bank fees or paying larger fees for small loans, many banks had little interest in lending to the smallest and most lightly capitalized businesses. Many mom-and-pop operations couldn't get the attention of loan officers at whatever bank they had done business with for years, and when they did, couldn't qualify without devoting lots of time to fulfilling cumbersome PPP loan application rules. Some banks opened their PPP loan window and then closed it within hours or a few days, saying they had taken all the applications they could.

The rules also required applying traditional underwriting standards on capacity to repay the loans, which made qualifying difficult or impossible for many small firms. Applying those standards strictly makes no sense for loans that are intended to become grants unless there is a hidden and sinister purpose, which was to help the rich and not the small business owners.

Third, the design of the loan program made it a taxpayer-funded marketing plan that strengthened ties between the big banks and their most lucrative customers. When small banks and credit unions, which tend to count smaller family businesses as customers, asked for government help, the administration granted them just one day of assistance.

Erik Sherman, a *DCReport* financial reporter, explains, "For the big banks, that first big round of money, eventually followed by more when the bungling turned public, became a great marketing tool. It helped those financial institutions cement relationships with their most important customers. . . . The dough, filtered through the discretion of big banks, went to those least in need.

Among them was a lucrative professional basketball franchise, an exclusive homeowner's association and hundreds of public companies."

As designed by the Wall Streeters the Trump administration brought to Washington—among them, Treasury Secretary Mnuchin and economic adviser Gary Cohn, a former head of Goldman Sachs—the PPP loan program wasn't so much a balm to mom-and-pop firms as a boon to the banks that administered the loans. The cost to process a $50,000 loan to a small business was the same as for a $5 million loan to a big business posing as a small business. The signal to banks was to loan as much of their assigned share of money as possible to big companies, then to medium-size companies, then to small businesses the banks regarded as having a big future or that were owned by people the banks needed to please, such as the relatives of politicians.

Making loans and grants to businesses, especially to keep experienced staff around, would be crucial to reviving many firms once the pandemic was over. But making loans to a sitting president's business had never happened in America. George Washington was so ethically punctilious that when he wanted a piece of government land, he bid for it just like everybody else. His bid turned out to be the winner.

Given all of the Republican rhetoric about cutting not only welfare but benefits people pay for with their taxes, such as Social Security and Medicare, the idea of giving taxpayer money to a president, even indirectly, as with the Hawaii high-rise bearing his name, was inherently problematic. Now throw in that Trump claimed to be a multibillionaire, a man so rich he didn't have to sully his campaign with donations from outsiders, and the idea of welfare for the president becomes not just ethically dubious but absurd.

As the final details of the first pandemic relief bill were being negotiated with Congress, a reporter asked Trump, "Will you commit publicly that none of that taxpayer money will go towards your own personal properties?"

In response, for nearly two minutes Trump wandered down an irrelevant verbal path, moving into a hedgerow of half-finished lines, twice saying "I have no idea" without making clear what he was referring to, before moving on to complain that no one thanked him for donating his presidential salary.

A day earlier a reporter had asked Trump about "reports that the coronavirus is really hurting your businesses, especially your hotels—"

"My businesses?" Trump said.

"Yeah."

"Sure," Trump replied.

"So, is that true and can you speak to the financials—." Trump cut the reporter off.

"Well, I wouldn't say you're thriving when you decide to close down your hotels and your businesses. No, I would say—but, you know, I'm very under-levered and everything, so that's good. But is it hurting my—yeah. It's hurting me and it's hurting Hilton and it's hurting all of the great hotel chains all over the world. It's hurting everybody. I mean, there are very few businesses that are doing well. Now, there are some that are. Like, as an example, the Walmarts of the world, because everybody's lined up to get things and stock up their house, and this and that. But sure, it hurts my business. But—"

The reporter then asked, "Did you or anyone in your administration talk to anyone at the Trump Organization about the potential effects of the coronavirus?"

"No, I didn't speak to anybody," Trump replied. Then, without missing a beat, he contradicted himself. "I speak to my sons, but—I talk about the coronavirus, but not as it pertains to my business."

"Will you no longer go to Mar-a-Lago or Bedminster?"

"Well, I have nothing planned at Mar-a-Lago. But, right now, I think Mar-a-Lago, I guess—I haven't even asked, but I imagine that's closed down, just like a lot of other businesses in Florida.

Washington Post reporter Seung Min Kim then asked, "Do you expect your family company to seek government assistance if it's eligible?"

Trump answered, "I don't know. I mean, I just don't know what the government assistance would be for what I have. I have hotels. Everybody knew I had hotels when I got elected. They knew I was a successful person when I got elected. So it's one of those things. I guess I get paid $450,000 a year; I give it up. I put it back into the nation. I usually—I have to—by the way, you have to designate where you want it, so I oftentimes give it to opioid research and things."

"I meant to the company specifically, not you," Kim clarified, trying to drag Trump back to her simple question, which could have been answered yes or no.

"But, as far as the hotels and everything, I mean, I have to do what everyone else is doing," Trump said. "I would probably decide to close things up. I think it's a good thing nation—you don't want people getting together. And hotels and clubs and everything, you get together. We want to beat this deal. So I have many of them—hotels, clubs, things like that—where people get together. I would think it would be a good practice to close them up."

While his comments show skill at evading the question about seeking welfare for his businesses, his remarks make clear that Trump was thinking about his own businesses and whether he could get his own administration to grant him welfare. He spoke as a provision was being proposed for the CARES Act by Chuck Schumer, the Senate minority leader, that would block the president, vice president, representatives, senators, and heads of federal agencies from pandemic relief loans.

"Those of us who write the law shouldn't benefit from the law," Schumer said of his provision. It had a loophole, though. It applied only to businesses that the president and other named officials control. It didn't apply to the Kushners or to businesses that paid Trump to use his name.

In the end just 1 percent of PPP borrowers pocketed a quarter of the money. The top 5 percent received more than half of the forgivable loans. That means the Trump administration's design of the PPP loans and other pandemic relief generated federal welfare totaling at least $522 billion for big companies. The PPP in particular, *Fortune* magazine concluded, was "poorly designed and irresponsibly run."

There was also rampant fraud in the loan programs. The

Economic Injury Disaster Loan Program limited money to firms which had existed in 2019, yet the Small Business Administration made more than 6,000 loans to businesses that were created in 2020. Many of these firms exist only on paper. These fake borrowers bought Lamborghinis and Cadillac Escalades and blew money gambling in Las Vegas. Many of the borrowers remain unknown because the money was wired overseas.

The Trump administration had been warned about weak loan controls at the SBA, where fraud and loans to unqualified borrowers has been a long-standing problem. Exactly one week after Trump signed the CARES Act on March 27, 2020, SBA Inspector General Hannibal Ware issued an eight-page report on past experience with economic stimulus loans. It suggested five actions to ensure that money was distributed promptly, but not so quickly that fake businesses could collect the dough and make it disappear overseas. Ware detailed a strategy to "mitigate the risk of financial loss." Team Trump essentially ignored that wise counsel. As a result, holes in the program were never filled.

An SBA pandemic relief program to make immediate grants of up to $10,000 to small businesses operated for only 10 weeks before closing in July. "In the span of 71 days," Inspector General Ware reported, the SBA approved pandemic relief loans totaling more money than "previously approved in its entire history for all other declared disasters combined." Ware announced just days after the program ended that his staff had discovered "potentially rampant fraud." Grants were made to people using stolen identities; some loans went into investment accounts instead of being applied to payroll, as the law required. Some pandemic relief loans were funded twice, some were made to firms that didn't even have names or addresses, and other loans went to companies that used fake names and addresses.

By the time Trump left the White House, more than a half-million Americans were dead from the coronavirus. That's as many deaths as Americans killed in combat in World War I, World War II, and the undeclared wars in Korea, Vietnam, Kuwait, Iraq, and Afghanistan—combined. The pandemic was an opportunity for Trump to demonstrate the greatness he always claimed, to show leadership that would save lives. Instead, being who he is, he belittled the scientific advice he didn't understand and oversaw a massive program to enrich the already rich.

Dangerous Favors

In an earlier chapter we met Masayoshi Son, founder of Soft-Bank. In this chapter I want to tell the story of what happened after Son and his partners acquired a financial firm notorious for enriching its managers at the expense of investors and for its less well-known generosity to the Trump-Kushner family.

In 2017 SoftBank purchased Fortress Investment Group, a combination hedge fund and private equity and alternative financing firm that was launched in 1998.

In 2007 Fortress became the first firm of its kind to issue publicly traded stock instead of allowing in only investors it invited. Before the first share was sold to the public, the Wall Streeters who founded Fortress had extracted nearly $1.7 billion from the firm for themselves. In a move audacious even by the standards of Wall Street, ahead of the initial public offering the managers took out a loan to pay themselves a quarter-billion-dollar dividend. Part of the IPO proceeds were used to retire that loan, which came to roughly 40 percent of the $631 million that the IPO raised.

David Swensen, the very successful manager of Yale University's $31 billion endowment, wrote that the Fortress stock offering was unusual for two reasons, both of which spelled likely trouble for investors. One was that the prospectus, the required document that is supposed to inform would-be buyers of shares how their money would be used, revealed no clear investment strategy. The other, intended as a dark financial joke, was that the prospectus was missing a disclosure section titled "Greed."

Swenson's concerns proved accurate.

After nearly doubling to $35 a share on the first day of trading, the stock price slid downward, hitting just $1 in January 2009. In 2017, as Trump became president and Son and his partners bought Fortress, the stock was trading above $5 per share. By another measure, called "book value," Fortress shares were at that time worth only about $4. SoftBank paid more than $8 per share, twice book value for a deal that created no jobs.

Fortress had once been an important source of money for Trump, a loan that follows him to this day. In 2005, together with some other lenders, Fortress extended a $130 million loan so Trump could build Trump International Hotel & Tower downtown on the Chicago River. A few years later Trump couldn't, or didn't, fully repay the loan. Fortress could have foreclosed. It could have demanded an ownership stake in the 98-story building. Instead Fortress generously forgave all but $48 million of the debt.

Money that is borrowed and not paid back is income under both federal and New York State law, which applied to Trump as a Manhattan resident. Therefore Trump was required to report the amount forgiven as income and pay taxes on it. Whether he did is unknown. However, when Letitia James was sworn in as New York State attorney general in 2019, she launched a broad investigation into Trump's finances, including whether he reported the forgiven amount as income on his state tax return. Subpoenas for documents and notices for sworn testimony were issued. Both the Trump Organization and Fortress resisted James's efforts, as did Eric Trump, who tried to avoid giving a deposition. They were not, as the saying goes, cooperating fully with the investigation. That litigation has widened considerably since then, and as this book went to press is ongoing. Ominously for the Trump family, AG James loaned two of her prosecutors on the case to the Manhattan District Attorney who has empaneled a grand jury that is taking testimony from key Trump associates as this book goes to press.

In 2018, a year after Son had appeared in the Trump Tower lobby with the president-elect, SoftBank's Fortress division extended a $57 million loan to the Kushner Companies, which had been run by Jared until he resigned to become a White House aide. Jared didn't sell his shares in the family business when he joined the White House staff. He simply put them into a trust.

The loan from Fortress was intended to shore up a troubled and scandal-ridden Kushner project in Jersey City, just across the Hudson River from Manhattan. Strategically located next to a commuter train line into the city, One Journal Square, if it ever gets built, is to be a 12-story office building on top of which will rise twin 52-story apartment towers with about 10 acres of retail space and more than 1,700 apartments. The original plans were for a much larger project that the Kushners were unable to finance. The Kushners needed that Fortress loan because, among other things, the city government refused the family's request for a package of subsidies, and the deadline to qualify for a state tax break had passed.

Earlier the Kushners had played on their White House connections to raise money in China for One Journal Square. In May 2017 Jared's sister Nicole Kushner Meyer hosted an investment seminar at the Ritz-Carlton Hotel in Beijing. To draw an audience of rich Chinese to the Saturday night seminar the family bought an ad that promised, "Invest $500,000 and immigrate to the United States."

The reference was to EB-5 visas, which allow wealthy foreigners to buy entry into the United States by investing $500,000 or more in a profit-making business and then showing that within two years at least 10 jobs were created. The visa holder gets a green card, which grants permanent residence and the right to work in the United States. The visas are meant to attract entrepreneurs and promote the formation of new businesses.

At the event Kushner Meyer dangled her White House connection to prospective investors, pointing out, "In 2008, my brother Jared Kushner joined the family company as CEO, and recently moved to Washington to join the administration." She didn't name Donald Trump, but she did display his photo.

She said that connection mattered because only 10,000 EB-5 visas are granted each year. Anyone listening to the pitch could reasonably believe that if they handed over $500,000 to Kushner Meyer, she had the pull to secure one of the visas. Kushner Meyer was not the first to use a green card and residency as a lure to raise capital for construction projects, but she did stand out in her brazenness in promoting the family connection to the president.

After the visa story got out, the Kushners told business publications that they expected to raise about 15 percent of the nearly $1 billion cost of the One Journal Square project through the visa program.

The $57 million Fortress loan for One Journal Square was not the first Fortress loan to the Kushner family. Christine Taylor, a spokesperson for the family, said, "Kushner Companies and Fortress Investments have been long-time partners in various real estate transactions over the years. We have had many successes together and value their faith in our business."

SoftBank maintained that even though it owned Fortress it had no influence over its operations, a story that spokeswoman Taylor stuck to, telling *Barron's* that the Kushner Companies had never done business with SoftBank.

Trump walked away from almost $1 billion of debt in 1990 in a privately negotiated equivalent of a bankruptcy, overseen not by a federal bankruptcy judge, as would have been standard practice, but by New Jersey casino regulators. In 2008 Trump persuaded Fortress Investment Group to forgive most of a loan for $130 million, at a high rate of interest, and to waive a $49 million "exit fee" attached to the loan. Fortress was later acquired by none other than Softbank, the giant Japanese firm run by Masayoshi Son whose promise of 50,000 American jobs would buoy Trump's stature in 2016.

After making these loans to both sides of the Trump-Kushner family, Son's people sought a favor from the Trump administration. In buying Fortress, SoftBank had acquired a business called New Fortress Energy, which proclaimed a desire "to provide capital, expertise and vision to address" energy needs "while making positive and meaningful impacts on communities and the environment." The firm also asserted "the belief that access to affordable, reliable, cleaner energy is not a privilege, but a human right."

The favor SoftBank sought involved transporting natural gas from the rich and recently developed fracking areas of northern Pennsylvania to Delaware River ports near Philadelphia, where the fossil fuel would be transferred to ships headed overseas. But instead of building a pipeline, as is standard practice, the Soft-Bank division wanted to send the natural gas on rail cars 255 miles through small cities and Philadelphia to the river port. It was a monumentally dangerous idea.

Most natural gas flows through pipelines buried deep in the ground, and for good reason. Pipelines are exceptionally efficient. The natural gas pipelines used to transmit huge volumes over long distances are constructed with steel pipes several feet wide. The gas flows under tremendous pressure, as much as 1,500 feet per square inch, which means the pipelines must have thick and strong steel walls, and each of the thousands of welds connecting the pipe sections must be just as strong. The natural gas must be dried before going into the pipelines lest moisture allow the formation of corrosive salts that over decades can slowly eat away at the steel walls, weakening them as they thin until the metal tears, creating a spark and explosion.

To move natural gas by rail, it is first chilled until it becomes liquified natural gas (LNG). You can get an idea of just how much energy LNG packs from the fact that when restored to its natural gaseous state its volume expands by 600 times. The SoftBank unit that calls inexpensive energy a human right wanted to send not one railcar at a time but as many as 100 LNG cars barreling along at up to 50 miles per hour through cities like Reading, a Pennsylvania town of 88,000, and across Philadelphia, the sixth most populous city in America.

Critics call these "bomb trains." They have a point. In 2013 a parked train with much less dangerous oil got loose and rolled downhill into the Quebec city of Lac-Mégantic, burning 47 people to ash and destroying the town center. Just 22 LNG rail cars would pack as much energy as the bomb that flattened downtown Hiroshima in 1945 killing about 80,000 people, a third of that city's population.

In 2014 Karl Alexy, chief safety officer at the Federal Railroad Administration, warned that cars even sturdier than what Soft-Bank proposed would likely puncture in a crash at just 30 miles per hour. "When you begin to look at cars that are derailing at speeds of 30, 40 miles per hour it's very difficult, it's a big ask, to expect that a tank car gets hit" and doesn't leak, he said. Alexy added that LNG does not have the foul-smelling mercaptan that warns homeowners of a natural gas leak, so its vapors could spread undetected for miles until something as simple as starting a car engine created a massive conflagration.

Trump responded to Masayoshi Son's request with Executive Order 13868, authorizing new rules to "permit LNG to be transported in approved rail tank cars" and directing Transportation Secretary Elaine Chao to "finalize such rulemaking no later than 13 months after the date of this order."

Earthjustice, a nonprofit that litigates policies it considers damaging to the environment, called the proposed rules unlawful and in direct opposition to the intent of the Hazardous Materials Transportation Act of 1975. That law was enacted to "protect against the risks to life, property, and the environment that are inherent in the transportation of hazardous material in intrastate, interstate, and foreign commerce." The Act also requires the transportation secretary to "prescribe regulations for the safe transportation, including security, of hazardous material."

"There seems to be no compelling need" for the Transportation Department's Pipeline and Hazardous Materials Safety Administration "to be moving so quickly on the issuance of a nationwide rule for LNG transport by 100-cars-plus unit trains of rail tank cars, in the absence of reasonably supporting agency research," Earthjustice attorneys wrote.

The District of Columbia and 14 states sued Secretary Chao over the new rule, which they describe as unlawful. That litigation is ongoing at this writing.

The loans and loan forgiveness deals between SoftBank's Fortress group and the Trump-Kushner families are among the issues that the Manhattan district attorney is investigating.

— 14 —

Expensive Juice

T rump and his team tried to enrich many industries, especially fossil fuel companies, usually in ways that inflated profits at the expense of the American people. But there is one industry that showcases all of these plans, an industry that touches every one of us: electricity.

On his first business day as president, Trump sent a clear signal to Wall Street about how his policies would affect hundreds of billions of dollars in annual spending by consumers, business, and industry for electricity. No major news organization covered Trump's action and what it meant, only *DCReport*.

Candidate Trump had told voters that Wall Street and other elites had made Washington a swamp and he would drain it. But he gave Wall Street electricity investors a green light to gouge customers by manipulating the so-called electricity markets.

Trump first forced the ouster of Norman C. Bay as chairman of the Federal Energy Regulatory Commission (FERC), a tiny but immensely powerful federal agency. Bay had been the U.S. attorney in New Mexico. At FERC he had been its chief of enforcement. When he was named to the commission he favored strong enforcement of the rules against market manipulations. The industry challenged Bay in federal courts and lost.

Trump initially replaced Bay with Cheryl LaFleur, a former electricity company chief executive. LaFleur had a solid track record as a sightless sheriff, blind to blatant price manipulations by Wall Street firms, especially in New England. A few months later Trump replaced her with lawyer Neil Chatterjee, who had been the energy policy aide of Senator Mitch McConnell. FERC quickly developed a love for what Trump liked to call "beautiful coal," a policy that helped endear McConnell to his Bluegrass State voters.

These were the first of many decisions involving electricity in which Trump and his team favored Wall Street and coal companies and other fossil fuel interests over the people. Raising electricity prices while increasing pollution became consistent Trump administration policies that almost never made the news.

Paying more for juice hurts families. It also damages the profits of factories that are big users of electricity as well as convenience stores that must refrigerate foods. Buyers of hotels and office buildings take the local cost of electricity into account in making offers for real estate. Charging factories more for power makes American manufactured goods less competitive in global markets, contradicting Trump's promise to increase exports of manufactured goods.

Electricity defines modern life. Only because we have mastered electrons and built millions of miles of copper wires to carry them wherever we choose do we enjoy automobiles and elevators, jetliners and air conditioning, cell phones and computers.

Electricity is so wired into our lives and minds that we don't give it a thought until the neighborhood goes dark or, as happened in Texas in the winter of 2021, the new electricity markets produce $16,000 bills for a household for a single month.

Each year America generates about 4 trillion kilowatt hours of electricity. With that kind of volume the slightest change in prices has a huge impact on whose wallets thin and whose fatten. Raise the price by a penny per kilowatt hour, and customers must fork over $40 billion more each year. Given the relatively small number of investors compared to the massive number of customers, you can see why price gouging makes Wall Street predators salivate.

A corrupt Texas energy trading company called Enron changed the energy markets a couple of decades ago. Enron argued that the business of generating power could and should be broken off from delivering energy and turned into a separate competitive industry. The company persuaded lawmakers in half the states to break up the traditional electric utilities. Power plants were sold to JP Morgan Chase, Goldman Sachs, and many other Wall Street firms, some of whom paid such low prices that they soon flipped the plants for two to five times what they had paid.

The shrunken distribution utilities, left with only their power poles, wires, and meters, would henceforth buy electricity in auctions run under Enron's rules by independent agencies called "systems operators." In theory, energy producers would compete to sell electricity to utilities. If each power plant had a separate owner, this plan would be effective. But Wall Street firms typically own fleets of power plants of various types that often run for just a few hours a day or only on hot summer days or cold winter nights. The Wall Street firms were thus able to strategically bid their fleets to manipulate the selling price of electricity. They were, after all, experts at trading.

But even better, energy producers, instead of building new power plants, could close power plants or withdraw them from the auctions at which energy was sold. In New England an investment group called Energy Capital Partners, a group of former Goldman Sachs traders, paid $650 million in 2013 to acquire a fleet of power plants. Just five weeks later they announced that they would shut down the biggest plant they had bought, called Brayton Point in Massachusetts.

In the Enron-designed electricity markets, that shutdown caused New England families, businesses, and industries to pay an extra $2.6 billion for electricity in just the first year. When this matter came before Trump's FERC chief, Cheryl LaFleur, she insisted there was nothing she could do, a position that a federal judge declared dubious but acknowledged was within her discretion.

Trump would later add to the FERC Robert Powelson, who had been a utility regulator in Pennsylvania. Powelson had the kind of contempt for critics that Trump admired. When protesters picketed the homes of FERC commissioners, accusing them of favoritism toward pipeline companies, Powelson declared, "The jihad has begun."

Neil Chatterjee, the McConnell energy adviser who succeeded LaFleur as FERC chair, set out to take the commission back to the pre-Enron days, when there were no rules to prevent manipulating energy markets. Investigations of price manipulation fell by half. Total yearly penalties fell about 85 percent to just $14 million, a pittance to an industry that takes in more than $1 billion a day.

Senator Maria Cantwell of Washington and four other Democrats wrote to Chatterjee about electricity auctions that they said violated the rules against price manipulations: "Several recent actions seem to indicate that the commission may not be fully committed to finding, stopping, and punishing manipulative acts that can stifle competition and result in unjust and unreasonable prices." Chatterjee ignored them.

Then there was the proposal to charge significantly more for electricity from solar and wind. Expectations were that the falling cost of solar- and wind-generated electricity would reduce wholesale energy prices by at least a fourth. That would be a disaster for coal-mining barons such as Joseph Craft and Robert E. Murray. Craft had donated $1 million to Trump's inauguration, Murray $300,000. To rescue them and other coal companies, Trump's commissioners came up with a plan to double the price of solar and wind energy by manipulating rules to favor coal.

The rule, at least initially, was to apply only to PJM Interconnection, the system operator in America's largest wholesale electricity market. It serves 13 states, from New Jersey and Pennsylvania south to the District of Columbia and Virginia and as far west as parts of Illinois. This is the part of America where coal from mines owned by Murray and Craft tended to be used. Under this new rule the total price of electricity in the PJM service area would rise by as much as $24 billion over 10 years. That's $379 for each of the 65 million people PJM served.

This was one of many Trump assaults on Obama-era efforts to shift away from coal because of the environmental damage it causes and to foster solar and wind power. Trump made crazy claims that wind turbines were wiping out bird populations and that the sound from the turbines causes cancer as he continually talked up his love of coal, by far the dirtiest fossil fuel.

At about the same time as the PJM plan was under consideration a new entrant sought FERC approval to participate in the wholesale electricity auctions. Goldman Sachs Renewable Power Marketing LLC shared the same address and telephone number, as well as some employees, as the better known Goldman Sachs Group, the biggest, richest, and most influential Wall Street investment bank. Goldman insisted there was no connection between its power marketing firm and the investment firm.

The Goldman Sachs Renewable Power Marketing company had three corporate directors: Andrew Galloway of ICG Management Ltd., Andrew Johnson of Circumference FS, and John Lewis of HighWater Ltd. The trio were also directors of 60 other companies, all of them affiliated with the better-known Goldman Sachs Group. They all listed their addresses as the Cayman Islands, a notorious Caribbean tax haven. That fit the pattern set by Energy Capital Partners, which relied on offshore investment strategies to escape taxes when it bought its fleet of New England power plants and then closed its biggest plant.

Back when the Obama administration was watching for price gouging, JP Morgan Chase had tried a similar ploy to establish that its energy arm was not affiliated with the bank. It failed. JPMorgan paid $410 million in 2013 to settle charges of manipulating electric power markets, which it neither denied nor admitted.

The risks of allowing Wall Street firms to work every side of the street in electricity were explored by investigators working for the Senate Permanent Subcommittee on Investigations. Senator Carl Levin of Michigan chaired that subcommittee for years and issued reports with bipartisan support. The Detroit Democrat said that mixing these electricity financing and trading interests could bring down the national economy. He cited the 2008 mortgage debacle that brought on the Great Recession. Pointing to the catastrophic California wildfires caused by faulty electric wires, Levin warned that the cost of damages for deaths, property destruction, and environmental damage could destroy Wall Street firms with far-reaching consequences.

The Trump Administration persisted in trying to raise the price of wind and solar power in order to make coal more competitive. Trump's energy secretary, former Texas governor Rick Perry, sponsored a scheme to counter rapidly falling costs to generate electricity from solar and wind. Perry ordered a study of federal taxes and subsidies for solar and wind electricity. He wanted to show that they created an unfair economic burden on coal-fired power plants. He believed solar and wind added risks that the electricity grids would fail.

Perry put Travis Fisher in charge of this study. Fisher was a Trump political appointee who had worked for the Institute for Energy Research, an organization that opposes renewable energy. Fisher wrote the Institute's 2015 report that claimed renewable energy policies are "the single greatest emerging threat" to America's electric power grid, a greater threat than cyberattacks by the Russians, than terrorism, even than extreme weather.

Bloomberg News described the Institute and its advocacy arm, the American Energy Alliance, as the "influential force in shaping

Donald Trump's plans to dismantle Obama administration climate initiatives."

When Perry's Energy Department study came out it was almost a brochure for the oil and coal industries. Senator Chuck Grassley of Iowa, a conservative Republican and Trump supporter, denounced it as "anti-wind." (Coal mining brings a lot less money to Iowa than the wind farms that dot corn and soybean fields.)

Then in 2019 the mercurial Trump and his budget staff announced their intention to sell the Bonneville Power Administration in the Pacific Northwest, the Tennessee Valley Authority, the Southwestern Power Administration, and Western Area Power Administration. These four electric power grids created by FDR's New Deal would be unloaded at bargain prices.

The Trump budget declared, against an abundance of evidence, that "reducing or eliminating the Federal Government's role in electricity transmission infrastructure ownership, thereby increasing the private sector's role, and introducing more market-based incentives, including rates, for power sales from Federal dams would encourage a more efficient allocation of economic resources and mitigate risk to taxpayers." This was in many ways a solution in search of a problem since the four federally owned grids were well run, but it made perfect sense as a Trumpian rip-off of electricity customers to enrich Wall Street.

Corporate markets require a higher rate of return than does the U.S. government. And profits would be taxed at a rate that would be passed along to utility customers. This was a bad deal all the way around. Fortunately, Trump's scheme to rob taxpayers and give to the Wall Street rich failed.

Trump then tried another tack to benefit electric power plant owners. In the name of stopping what he said was overregulation, Trump took an axe to pollution control rules. He rejected Obama-era regulations to reduce the amount of toxic material coming out of electric power plant smokestacks. The disastrous effects were almost immediate.

The largest single source of sulfur dioxide in America is the Martin Lake Power Plant in east Texas. It spewed 56,198 tons of sulfur dioxide into the air in 2018, an increase of 54 percent from 2016, Obama's last year in office.

Sulfur dioxide was not the only deadly emission from coal-fired power plants which increased under Trump. Burning coal also produces tiny particles of toxic dust—aka acid rain—that can waft in the breeze for hundreds of miles until people breathe it in.

Trump's environmental rollbacks saved industry money, but on what I call the Universal Ledger, where all costs ultimately must be tallied, the price will be paid in the form of more asthma, cancer, heart attacks, and premature deaths. The damage from acid rain will be chronic and persistent.

Trump also helped the coal industry and owners of coal-fired power plants by relaxing rules to eliminate toxic coal ash ponds, many of them decades old, their dikes deteriorating. Many were positioned just above rivers on which millions of people relied for drinking water.

To get the most energy out of coal, electric utilities grind the black rocks finer than cosmetic face powder and blow the black mist into super-hot furnaces. Not everything combusts, however, leaving toxic ash laden with arsenic, cadmium, lead, and mercury, all toxic heavy metals. For more than a century electric power plant owners poured water onto their coal ash, creating a slurry that would flow downhill to a pond for storage. Instead of closing these deadly ponds, as Obama sought, which would slowly eliminate the risk that collapsing dikes would send the deadly mix into rivers, Team Trump went in the opposite direction.

Scott Pruitt, Trump's first Environmental Protection Agency administrator, set out to end tests of groundwater supplies near more than 400 coal-fired plants with slurry ponds. Testing would reveal the volume of heavy metals that had leaked into underground water supplies, many of which supply cities and towns with drinking water and farmers with irrigation water. For example, groundwater tests near Indiana sludge ponds found arsenic levels more than 45 times the maximum allowed under the U.S. Safe Drinking Water Act. In neighboring Illinois, orange and purple muck was leaching into the Vermillion River near coal-ash pits owned by the power-generating company Vistra Energy. High levels of radioactivity were found in groundwater near 11 Duke Energy power plants in North Carolina.

What all of these Trump pro-pollution policies have in common is that they would shift costs of mitigating the effects of toxic waste from energy producers to taxpayers.

On their way out the White House door in January 2021, Trump's minions issued a presidential permit for a $1 billion high-voltage transmission line that would transmit hydro power from Quebec to Massachusetts. But while the transmission line promoters and Team Trump described this plan as beneficial for the environment, it was obvious that the new power lines could also be used to move electricity from power plants burning coal and natural gas. "There is zero reliable evidence that the project would result in an actual, verifiable reduction in greenhouse gas emissions," observed Sue Ely, an attorney for the Natural Resources Council of Maine. "That's right. Zero." It was also economically wasteful in the view of Robert McCullough, a former top utility company economist. McCullough couldn't fathom how electricity customers would benefit because there was more capacity to transmit power between Quebec and New England than was being used or was likely to be needed.

Along the transmission corridor 25 towns voted against the project or rescinded their previous support. New Hampshire blocked an attempt to route the project through that state.

Team Trump's last-minute approval of the permit to build the transmission lines was issued in a way designed to obscure who would profit. The permit was issued in the name of a newly formed firm called NECEC Transmission, not exactly a memorable brand name that would resonate with the public. NECEC is owned, but not run, by Central Maine Power Company, which in turn is part of AVANGRID, Inc., which in turn is controlled by a company in Barcelona, Spain, called Iberdrola. Cheryl LaFleur, the sightless sheriff at FERC, was once the acting chief executive of a northeastern electricity monopoly that Iberdrola had acquired.

But none of these firms was the real beneficiary.

The major economic gains would go to Hydro-Québec, Canada's largest utility, enabling it to hoard water behind its dams in years of below-average rain and snow. Hydro-Québec would be obligated to provide power to Massachusetts utilities no matter what.

However, instead of releasing more water through its hydroelectric generators, it could buy cheap electricity made by burning coal in Canada's New Brunswick province and natural gas in New York. In terms of added greenhouse gases, that would be the equivalent of putting an extra 80,000 cars a year on the road, according to a detailed study by Energyzt Advisors LLC for environmental groups.

The project would benefit Hydro-Québec. Why did Trump abandon "America First" for a Canadian power utility?

The answer is that this deal would help Wall Street rake in more profits by reducing the costs of cleaning up environmental damage, shifting the burden onto people who did not vote for Trump.

15

The Shipping News

Elaine Chao's hearing for her nomination as Trump's transportation secretary was a cozy affair. Many of the senators on the Commerce Committee had worked with Chao in her previous government positions, as undersecretary of transportation during the George H. W. Bush presidency and as secretary of labor under George W. Bush. The tone of the hearing reflected that familiarity.

In her introductory remarks, Chao thanked Senator Rand Paul, from her home state of Kentucky, for his support of her nomination and quipped that she'd be "working to lock in the Majority Leader's support tonight over dinner." Chao is married to Senator Mitch McConnell, majority leader at the time, who, despite this obvious conflict of interest, declined to recuse himself from voting in support of his wife's nomination.

After she delivered that well-received joke, Chao introduced her family, who were seated behind her, devoting most of her words to her beloved father, James Chao, and sharing the family's classic immigrant story of coming to this country with very little and building a fortune.

James Chao and his wife, Ruth, were born in China in 1927 and 1930, respectively. They met in college in Shanghai during the last days of rule by Chiang Kai-shek and the corrupt Kuomintang Party. The year after Mao Zedong's communist army won the Chinese Civil War in 1949, the couple made their way to Formosa Island, now known as Taiwan, where martial law was imposed for almost four decades. While still in his 20s James, a merchant seaman, became a ship's captain, an early indication of his drive. He and Ruth married and had three of their six daughters there, including Elaine, who was born in 1953.

James came alone to America in 1958, earning a doctoral degree from St. John's University. Three years later Ruth and their three girls arrived, none of whom spoke any English. In 1964 James and Ruth founded their cargo ship company, the Foremost Group, in New York City. It specialized in shipping dry bulk cargo, such as iron ore, corn, soybeans, and wheat. Dr. Chao secured contracts to ship American rice to Vietnam during that war. They had three more daughters in the U.S. All six girls were as driven as their father; four of them have MBAs from Harvard. By the time Elaine was nominated as transportation secretary in January 2017, the Foremost Group's fleet had expanded to 22 ships, doing more than 70 percent of its business with China.

During his campaign, Trump frequently attacked China for taking American manufacturing jobs, stealing intellectual property, and making unfair trade deals. He spent a portion of virtually every campaign speech attacking the Chinese.

Why would Elaine Chao, whose family story ran counter to Trump's xenophobic rhetoric, sign up to be part of his administration? And why would she associate herself with him when her family's fortunes depended on Foremost having a strong relationship with China? One might also wonder why, as a potential heir to a shipping fortune, her nomination didn't generate controversy in her confirmation hearing. She would seem to have a blatant conflict of interest.

But the Senate confirmed her on a 93–7 vote, citing her insider experience in government, her understanding of the bureaucracy, and her political contacts that would help her get things done at the department.

Chao, it turned out, was Trump's kind of bureaucrat: able to remain silent around him no matter what he said about immigrants or China, and not the kind of person to oppose her boss publicly. She never spoke a word of criticism against Trump's frequent attacks on China for supposedly ripping off America. Even when he blamed China for Covid-19, trying to escape responsibility for his mishandling of the pandemic with explicitly racist attacks, Chao said nothing.

Chao had her own agenda, which was aiding the expansion of her family shipping empire as the secretary of transportation. The public record shows that she took many calculated actions that seemed to extend far beyond the bounds of federal law to advance her family's interests. Her conduct was so blatant and egregious that in 2019 she drew the attention of House Democrats whose duty was to exercise oversight on transportation.

While Chao was in office, the value of the Foremost Group grew on average by nearly a half-million dollars per day. The company more than doubled in size during Trump's four years in office, from $500 million worth of ships to almost $1.2 billion, according to data that VesselsValue, which monitors the oceangoing cargo ship industry, provided *DCReport*. Shortly after Chao resigned following the January 6, 2021, insurrection, the Department of Transportation inspector general recommended criminal charges be filed against her for misusing her office for personal gain.

Chao had always been a shrewd operator in Republican political circles, using her keen sense of the bureaucracy, her gift for silence, and her skills as a political infighter to thrive in administrative positions. Her greatest talent was creating an image of calm while doing little, a skill very much valued in Washington.

As labor secretary in the George W. Bush administration, image, not substance, was prominent. Chao infuriated labor leaders, some of whom considered her antiworker and condescending to working people. She oversaw burdensome new disclosure requirements for unions; corporations are not nearly so intensely regulated.

She also had a gift for making workers' complaints disappear. Approximately 70,000 complaints of wage theft—of employers paying less than minimum wage or refusing to issue final pay checks—were closed during her time at Labor after what the Government Accountability Office said was inadequate to nonexistent investigation. On Chao's watch investigators dropped cases when employers didn't answer an initial phone call or told investigators to call back. GAO investigators had a hard time finding case files with enough information even to know what happened to complainants. Most cases had been closed without even attempting recovery for the workers. One company admitted that it failed to pay a healthcare worker's wages for an entire year, yet her file was inexplicably closed by Chao's Labor Department.

The Labor Department also supervises the safety of coal mines, and Chao's tenure there was lethal for miners. One year, only 100 coal mines were inspected when seven times that many inspections were required by law. Many coal mine safety files were "missing, misdated, or mislabeled," according to the GAO. Some of the safety statistics that the Labor Department issued on her watch were simply made up, the GAO found.

One result of her hands-off approach to mine safety was a sharp rise in coal miner deaths, including from the 2006 Sago Mine disaster, when 12 miners died after the mine roof collapsed. Sago Mine's controlling owner was Wilbur Ross, who became Trump's commerce secretary.

These apparent lapses in leadership as the head of the Labor Department were not an obstacle to further employment when Chao left government service and moved into the private sector. In fact, they may have been an advantage when it came to her appointments to the boards of Wells Fargo and Rupert Murdoch's News Corp, two companies that were embroiled in scandals during her tenure with them.

Chao and McConnell were worth perhaps $3 million in 2007, around the time she left the Bush administration for the private sector. In the decade between then and the beginning of the Trump administration, their wealth grew substantially because Chao inherited part of her mother's $59 million fortune. Government ethics forms require only broad disclosures; in 2017 the couple officially listed Chao's inheritance at between $5 million and $25 million;

Forbes estimated it at $9 million. On her financial disclosure form she listed more than 80 investment accounts, eight of them valued at $1 million or more. In 2020 the Center for Responsive Politics, a nonprofit which has tracked the role of money in American elections and lobbying over four decades, put a more precise figure on the couple's total wealth: $34,137,534.

Between that chummy Senate confirmation hearing in January 2017 and Chao's indignant exit from the Trump administration after the Capitol riot of January 2021, Chao appears to have done all she could to make her father's shipping business more valuable.

What didn't happen was the promised major improvements to America's crumbling transportation systems. Candidate Trump had promised voters that right out of the box he would submit a massive $550 million plan to rebuild and improve public infrastructure. Soon after he became president, the plan doubled to more than $1 trillion, and later to $1.5 trillion.

In August 2017, Chao at his side, Trump declared, "This administration is working every day to deliver the world class infrastructure that our people deserve and frankly that our country deserves." The following February he called a White House meeting "to discuss America's depleted infrastructure," again using Chao as a willing prop. By April 2019 Kellyanne Conway, senior counselor to the president, was referring to her boss's promises as "infrastructure week." But what Americans got instead were a con man's phony promises repeated again and again until they became a running national joke, fodder for HBO's Bill Maher and John Oliver along with standup comics in clubs across the country.

No infrastructure plan ever appeared. Trump, who has never done a day of public service work, had no idea how Washington worked, or how to pull together the political forces to create a massive program. For her part, Chao mostly just stood at Trump's side; she left no record of campaigning for the nonexistent plan, except for making an anodyne comment now and then about the need for maintaining infrastructure.

Chao was busy growing her family fortune and increasing the prominence of her father's Washington access in the eyes of the Chinese. Mere weeks after she was sworn in, she started channeling Trump's behavior in using taxpayer money for personal and family benefit. Just as Trump steered federal dollars to his golf courses, Mar-a-Lago, and his Washington hotel, Chao steered attention to her family's cargo ship business. Official favoritism for Chao family interests quickly became apparent inside the Transportation Department, though unknown to the public.

Chao abused her position and wasted taxpayer money by planting stories in Chinese-language media emphasizing her father's deep connections in the Trump administration. In her first year in office, her official calendar showed, she held 21 interviews or meetings with Chinese-language media representatives. In most of them she talked up her father and his shipping company, and in some stories they appeared together. Her intended audience was Chinese state-owned or -influenced organizations that call themselves news organizations but serve as propaganda arms of the Chinese dictatorship.

Chao's father added to the impression that the family business was in deep with Trump. In more than a dozen interviews, with

Elaine at his side and often with the Transportation Department flag behind them, he touted her influence in setting U.S. government policy under Trump. He also bragged about his own access to Trump aboard Air Force One.

And it wasn't just publicity and the prospect of more business with the Chinese government that Chao expected from Transportation staff. The Department had a computer folder containing photographs the staff had collected of Chao's father. In January 2018, Chao directed the staff to revise her father's page, personal work that the assigned staffer confirmed to investigators when asked about it two years later.

Chao sent an email to two of her subordinates on September 24, 2017, identifying her father in the subject line. She indicated that he had purchased a product that had stopped working, had been sent back for repair, and after six weeks had not been returned to him or replaced. Chao directed her staff to contact the merchant to resolve her dad's problem. She never showed that kind of dedication when it came to low-wage workers cheated out of their pay or the safety of coal miners.

This unlawful mixing of personal and family interests became obvious during planning for the 50th anniversary celebration of Congress's creating the Department of Transportation. More than 500 people were invited to the March 2017 event in Washington. Internal government documents list more than 100 of these as "Dr. Chao's" guests, referring to her father. Government staff prepared detailed itineraries for Secretary Chao's family and negotiated for and booked a private Amtrak rail passenger car for her father and his guests to travel from New York to Washington and back. The cost was paid by the Foremost Group.

In arranging the celebration of a U.S. government agency's birth, Chao did something else highly unusual, the inspector general discovered: she directed her staff to send press releases and documents only to Chinese news organizations. The Transportation Department staff "reached out to Chinese press to offer interviews of the secretary and Dr. Chao," the government acting as the publicity agent for her family business.

Two months later Secretary Chao went to New York City, where the Chinese Consolidated Benevolent Association was holding a parade in honor of her and her father. Our government has ethics rules for the inevitable conflicts that arise from personal and official actions of presidential appointees. In most of Chao's joint appearances with her father and sometimes her sister Angela, however, no ethics advice was sought.

When a cabinet secretary attends a personal event, the rules say it is appropriate to be accompanied by her security detail and one or perhaps two staff to help move through crowds, check into hotels, and perform other chores most of us do ourselves. But along with security, Chao took at least eight of her staff—an entourage fit for a Hollywood diva—to one New York City event. She took four staff to other events.

Just 12 days after the benevolent association parade, Chao was back in Manhattan, this time for the 40th annual gala dinner of the Seamen's Church Institute. On the surface, that's a perfectly appropriate event for a Transportation Department secretary to attend.

This gala, however, honored the charitable foundation controlled by the Chao family for its gift to the State University of New York Maritime College in the Bronx, making this event personal, with little if any connection to Elaine Chao's official duties.

Chao, identified to the audience as the transportation secretary, and her sister, introduced as vice chair of the Chao family cargo ship business, accompanied their father to the stage. Again, no request was made of ethics officials about whether this was appropriate.

To strengthen her family's business connections with the communist leadership in Beijing, Chao "instructed" Transportation public affairs staff to distribute her seamen's speech "only to Chinese media outlets I specified. Call them NOW and tell them we are sending a story over. They will print what press release and speech says."

A little over a month later, Chao was at it again, giving the keynote address at the International Leadership Foundation, which "promotes the civic awareness, public-service and economic effectiveness of the Asian American Pacific Islander community." Her father also gave a speech.

Chao had actually solicited this opportunity to promote her father's business. She emailed the sponsoring foundation asking that she and her father be given speaking opportunities. The foundation obliged. At the dinner it even distributed 500 copies of *Fearless Against the Wind*, her father's autobiography, which is available only in Chinese. In connection with the event, Secretary Chao also gave a number of joint interviews with her father at the Transportation Department. The subject line of one email was "an interview with Dr. Chao and Secretary Chao," again reinforcing the impression that the U.S. Department of Transportation was endorsing her father's business.

At the same time, Chao assiduously minimized contact with American news organizations, never holding press conferences for domestic reporters on the transportation beat. In public appearances she would be introduced in glowing terms, step to the microphone to read a statement—often haltingly, as if she had not reviewed the material in advance—and then step away. The host would then announce that due to the secretary's busy schedule, she had to leave immediately.

There was more lurking unseen in the background of Chao's actions with implications for American diplomatic, trade, and national security interests.

Under Chao, records show, the agency budget made a series of cuts to programs that aid the struggling American maritime industry, and in particular proposed cuts to federal grants for small commercial shipyards as well as vital federal loan guarantees to American shipbuilding companies. Her agency's budget also proposed to slash spending for a grant program that helps keep five dozen American-flagged cargo ships ready for emergencies and wars. The budget sought to scale back plans to buy new ships that would train Americans as crew members. At the same time, her family financed scholarships in China and paid for a ship simulator to train Chinese seamen.

Congress, in bipartisan votes, rejected these cuts in Trump's first budget. Some were offered up again the next year. One opponent of the cuts was Representative Alan Lowenthal, a California

Democrat whose district includes one of the nation's largest cargo ports. "The Chinese government is massively engaged in maritime expansion as we have walked away from it," he said. "There is going to come a crisis, and we are going to call upon the U.S. maritime industry, and it is not going to be around."

While, like China, the Chao family was aggressively expanding its fleet and rapidly growing richer, Transportation's acting inspector general, Mitch Behm, was closing in on Chao. But in May 2020 Trump abruptly had Behm removed.

What, if anything, Chao and Trump, or more likely their proxies, said about Behm isn't known. Behm was the fifth inspector general whom Trump had his minions fire that April and May, each as they pursued investigations that threatened Trump or his allies. Then Trump installed Howard R. "Skip" Elliott, who was to hold dual jobs: one was looking for wrongdoing in the Department of Transportation as acting inspector general; the other was to continue in his existing job as the top official overseeing pipeline safety, a core function of the Transportation Department.

Representatives Gerry Connolly of Virginia, Peter DeFazio of Oregon, and Carolyn B. Maloney of New York, Democrats who led three committees with oversight of Transportation, found the whole matter infused with Trumpian arrogance. "Mr. Elliott doesn't seem to get it," they declared. "He wants to stay in a position at the Department and report directly to Secretary Chao, while at the same time supposedly taking on the 'independent' role of Inspector General—overseeing the Secretary. He can't do both. He has to choose, and so does Secretary Chao." The House Democrats told Elliott he must recuse himself from investigations involving that agency as well as Chao and her office.

Steven G. Bradbury, Transportation's general counsel, responded with the absurd claim that "there is no basis to suggest that [Elliott] cannot work on [inspector general] matters involving the Office of the Secretary" while also being Chao's subordinate at the pipeline safety office. Bradbury's letter was typical of the chutzpah demonstrated in the Trump era when issues of ethics and propriety were raised.

Adam Sullivan, the Transportation Department's assistant secretary for governmental affairs, told the House Democrats that their concerns about Chao's abuse of office for her family's benefit were baseless. "The allegation that the Secretary has used her official position to benefit her family's business is simply false," Sullivan wrote. "Of course, the Secretary is not involved with the management or operations of Foremost Group and has no financial stake in the company. Nor does the Department of Transportation regulate, promote, or benefit its business financially."

Sullivan was engaged in a narrow legalistic argument, not a practical one. For of course Secretary Chao did have a significant, albeit contingent, interest in the firm, just not an ownership stake. In using her government office to promote her father's fame and fortune she strengthened her own role within the family, increasing the likelihood that she would one day inherit a portion of her father's estate, which swelled during the Trump years.

Four weeks after Trump slunk off to Mar-a-Lago, unwilling to attend the inauguration of his successor, he suddenly evinced an awareness of the connections between McConnell, Chao, and

Beijing. This occurred after McConnell said Trump bore responsibility for the failed coup attempt on January 6.

"McConnell has no credibility on China because of his family's substantial Chinese business holdings," Trump declared in a February 16, 2021, email blast from his Trump Save America Political Action Committee. "He does nothing on this tremendous economic and military threat."

In December 2020, after it was clear Trump would be leaving soon, the inspector general's office found Chao's many abuses so egregious that referred her for criminal prosecution to two separate sections of the Justice Department. This could have waited, of course, for the next administration to address. But there was no prospect of Chao's being indicted. That's because she had her patron in the White House and her husband in the Senate—or, as Chao referred to them, "my two men."

After an extensive investigation, the inspector general confirmed that none of the staffers was paid for running personal errands and performing other favors. That simply means Chao stole from the taxpayers the value of the staffers' time, which can be a felony. The secretary's office of public affairs and other staff would later defend her conduct, normalizing her pursuing Chinese media and avoiding American journalists rather than recognizing her illegal abuse of government resources for personal and familial gain. Statements her closest aides made to inspector general investigators looking into Chao's conduct illustrate the need for strict ethics training and for equally strict enforcement of laws against misusing public office as Chao did.

16

Russian Money Man

Three weeks after Donald Trump's Electoral College victory in 2016, Wilbur Ross attended a party at the Gramercy Tavern, a tony restaurant in Manhattan's Flatiron District. He arrived early to meet privately with David J. Butters, the chief executive of Navigator Holdings and host of the night's festivities.

Ross is America's premier practitioner of *vulture capitalism*. He finds failing companies, sheds their existing loans, pensions, and other obligations in bankruptcy court, then borrows new money to pay himself and his partners fat fees and sends the companies on their way, zombie corporations lurching from one financial crisis to another. Ross claimed that his success picking over these emaciated enterprises had made his net worth $3.7 billion, though *Forbes* later estimated that was about six times his actual wealth.

Ross had met Donald Trump three decades earlier. Trump had sold junk bonds through the staid Merrill Lynch brokerage to acquire the unfinished white elephant of Atlantic City, the giant Taj Mahal casino hotel. The deal fell apart almost instantly, as I and a few others had predicted it would. Just six months after the Taj opened, Trump had to give up half his stake to bondholders, but that debacle made Trump and Ross commercial allies.

Back then, Ross told me that he was struck by how ordinary people responded to Trump; not as a scoundrel who failed to pay his bills but as a business hero. It made no apparent sense, but Ross was so impressed by Trump's hold on his fans that he advised his clients to keep Trump in control of the business. That ultimately allowed Trump to collect at least $82 million more from his casinos, even as they went through four bankruptcies before he was finally ousted.

Taj management also knowingly laundered money for customers, paying a $10 million fine, and later consented to a finding that it was "willfully violating" the Bank Secrecy Act.

The party Butters hosted on Navigator's dime in November 2016 celebrated Ross's becoming Trump's secretary of commerce. Navigator had reason to celebrate: through his investment firm, Ross owned between 30 and 60 percent of Navigator shares over a span of years—an investment that carried a dark secret. Navigator operates a fleet of 38 smallish ships, known as "handysize," that transport dangerous petrochemical gases, notably liquified natural gas, which, as explained in an earlier chapter, can be powerfully explosive.

What no one would know from the more than 50 pages detailing his financial investments that Ross would soon file with federal ethics officials was who hired Navigator's ships. That information emerged only months later, when someone leaked files from Appleby, a Bermuda law firm that specializes in setting up secret offshore accounts for people and companies dodging taxes, alimony, and debt collectors.

In a report called *The Paradise Papers* dated November 2017, the International Consortium of Investigative Journalists revealed that Navigator's primary customer was Silbur, a giant Russian energy firm. Two men who are infamously close to Vladimir Putin control Silbur.

One is Gennady Timchenko, an oligarch who was Putin's judo partner when they were younger and who remains his most valuable business ally. In 2014 President Obama put 17 Russian companies and banks on a sanctions list to punish Putin's invasion of Crimea. Timchenko played a significant role in all but three.

The other key man at Silbur was Kirill Shamalov, who became a billionaire after marrying the dancer Katerina Tikhonova, who just happens to be Putin's younger daughter. Such is the way of the Putin kleptocracy.

That Ross was the controlling shareholder of a company that depended for its profits on staying in the good graces of two men so intimately connected to Putin raised crucial national security questions. Chief among these was just how deeply the Kremlin had infiltrated Trump's circle. How much of Ross's wealth came from working with Kremlin agents in business—or possibly in crime? What hidden obligations might Ross have to the Kremlin? And did Putin have any compromising material on Ross? These and other national security issues would have prompted Republicans in Congress to reject any cabinet nominee with similar connections in any previous administration, but the GOP-controlled Senate confirmed Ross.

Silbur was just one of many deep and lucrative connections between Ross and the shadowy world of businesses and criminal enterprises operating under Putin's protective umbrella. And it was far from the most troubling in terms of business integrity or national security.

In 2014 Ross had become a significant shareholder in and vice chairman of the failing Bank of Cyprus. A large and exceptionally wealthy Russian expatriate population enjoys life on that Mediterranean isle. Bank of Cyprus has two vice chairs. Putin approved the other.

Ross bought into the bank after it became mired in losses and scandal growing out of its business with Russian customers. The bank was notorious for laundering Russian money. One hallmark of this relationship was that deposits were entirely out of proportion to the economy of Cyprus. In 2013 the Cypriot economy was about $23 billion, but Bank of Cyprus had $31 billion on deposit, according to Moody's, an American investment analytical firm. The leading German intelligence service estimated that Russians accounted for $26 billion of those deposits. No one who knows about banking, intelligence, or law enforcement had any doubt that the bank was a center of white-collar criminal enterprise.

Spokespeople for Ross said he saw an opportunity to profit by rescuing an undervalued and troubled bank. If that was his goal, the steps he took were odd. Ross brought in a new chief executive, Josef Ackermann, the disgraced former head of Deutsche Bank, the only bank that would extend loans to Trump because of his history of nonpayment.

Under Ackermann, Deutsche Bank had laundered an estimated $10 billion of Russian money. It paid more than $630 million in fines when it was caught, part of about $22 billion in penalties levied against it for misconduct during Ackermann's tenure. One former Deutsche Bank risk analyst told the *New Yorker*, "Deutsche Bank was structurally designed by management to allow corrupt individuals to commit fraud."

With a reputation like that, you might think Ross would have avoided Ackermann. That's because America has long had "Know your customer" rules that require banks to flag unusual and suspicious activity and to refuse deposits, loans, and wire transfers unless people can explain the sources of their funds and the business purpose of their money movements. Ross's vulture capitalism depended on arranging risky loans for failing companies, making it particularly dangerous for him to associate with known money launderers, and especially with Ackermann, whose name was well known on Wall Street. If bankers feared making loans in bankruptcy deals Ross was orchestrating, that would ruin his business.

But Ross's partners in the Bank of Cyprus deal seemed to have no such concerns. The biggest was the Renova Group, the aluminum, oil, and telecom giant owned by Russian oligarch Viktor Vekselberg, which bought more than 5 percent of the Cypriot bank's stock.

Another investor in the Bank of Cyprus was Dmitry Rybolovlev. He's the oligarch who paid Trump $95 million in 2008 for a gaudy Palm Beach mansion worth maybe a third that much, tore it down, and later sold off parts for a fraction of what he paid. That inflated purchase price allowed Trump to repay an overdue $40 million Deutsche Bank loan. It is conceivable that Putin or one of his top aides ordered Rybolovlev to pay Trump given that the real estate deal makes no business sense but makes plenty of sense as a payoff. Putin had twice sanctioned Rybolovlev for not doing what he was told, once with a year in jail on a trumped-up murder charge and once with about $250 million in fines for supposed pollution violations.

When Ross became vice chairman of the Bank of Cyprus, he succeeded Vladimir Strzhalkovsky, who had served as a KGB officer in St. Petersburg (then Leningrad) alongside Col. Vladimir Putin in the old Soviet Union. Strzhalkovsky at one time ran Intourist, the Kremlin's tourism agency. It provided cover for Russian spies and was suspected of hiding cameras in hotels to capture *kompromat*. That's what Russian intelligence calls damaging material that can turn people into conduits of information and even into traitors.

Bank of Cyprus had at least one notable American customer: Paul Manafort, who was Trump's unpaid campaign manager in 2016 when Kremlin agents got a private meeting at Trump Tower with Manafort, Donald Trump Jr., and Jared Kushner. Don Jr. denied and lied about that meeting for more than a year. Manafort had opened the accounts at Bank of Cyprus when he was secretly on the payroll of the Kremlin-backed regime in Ukraine, which was ousted by a popular uprising in 2014.

In picking Ackermann to run the Bank of Cyprus, Ross did not attempt to separate himself from the illicit cash flows that sustain numerous Russian criminal gangs, many of which are under the protection of the Kremlin. He chose to associate with oligarchs that U.S. intelligence regarded as state-backed criminals.

No cabinet member in American history had ever come as close to the kind of deep and financially rewarding connections to a hostile foreign power as Wilbur Ross. These connections were part of a pattern of Trump, his family, and his cronies being in business with people connected to Putin's gang. Trump insisted he had no business in Russia, yet again and again going back nearly four decades, Russians showed up around Trump. And Trump infamously praised Putin while saying that he didn't trust U.S. intelligence agencies.

In America, Ross has been in civil litigation since 2015, accused of stealing $120 million from his investment partners. Those allegations never surfaced during his Senate confirmation, becoming public only when *Forbes* broke the story in August 2018.

When asked about this by Dan Alexander of *Forbes*, Ross denied any wrongdoing and then lied, saying, "The SEC has never initiated any enforcement action against me." The Securities and Exchange Commission had fined Ross $2.3 million in 2016 for charging investors unauthorized fees. Ross paid, but as is standard, he did so without admitting or denying responsibility. Alexander reported that numerous people told consistent stories about Ross's dishonest conduct. "He'll push the edge of truthfulness and use whatever power he has to grab assets," New York financier Asher Edelman told *Forbes*.

Before being sworn in as commerce secretary, Ross agreed in writing to resign from various positions and dispose of his financial interests in an astonishing array of global investments that raised concerns with the Office of Ethics. Ross and his third wife, Hilary

Geary Ross, disclosed 483 asset, income, and retirement accounts worth at least $51 million and perhaps as much as $524 million.

Ross negotiated to divest only about 80 of these holdings; the others were deemed unlikely to pose ethical concerns. He pledged to put the proceeds from assets he sold in Treasury bonds to eliminate even the appearance of conflicts of interest. In addition to this, on the day he was sworn in, Ross reported 134 transactions selling his stocks and bonds valued at almost $214 million. In doing so, Ross was eligible for a particular benefit of presidential appointees: he did not have to declare any capital gains for income tax purposes. Instead, the gains transferred untaxed to the new investment. Taxes would come due only when he sold them, assuming the badly depleted Internal Revenue Service had enough staff to make sure he correctly reported the sales, perhaps years later.

Ross also made three stock purchases the day he took office, two of them in a small pharmaceutical company called Atara Biotherapeutics and the third in Wex Inc., a troubled payment-processing and financial company in Maine. Altogether, Ross bought less than a quarter-million dollars' worth of stock. But he dumped the Wex shares after ethics officials took note of them. One aspect of Wex's billion-dollar-plus annual business was providing management information services to U.S. government vehicle fleets. It was an audacious purchase for a commerce secretary, ripe with potential for profiteering from inherent conflict of interest.

Five of the investments he sold were in the Cayman Islands, in the island of Jersey off the coast of England, and in other tax havens. He also sold his most troubling investment, his Bank of Cyprus shares.

Ross earned at least $36.8 million in 2017 and probably much more. That's because the financial disclosure forms, as Trump said near the start of his campaign, were not designed for people of great wealth. Unfortunately, Congress has done nothing to update the forms, which have a top category of $50 million or more, without specifying any higher figure.

Ross, Education Secretary Betsy DeVos, Treasury Secretary Steven Mnuchin, and Linda McMahon, the Small Business Administration chief, all reported net worth in the hundreds of millions of dollars or more. Given that, these forms should add disclosure categories for individual investments at $100 million, $250 million, $500 million, and $1 billion.

Ross didn't make all of the stock sales he promised to complete before he was sworn in on the last day of February 2017, five weeks after Trump assumed office. This is not a minor matter.

"Your failure to divest created the potential for a serious criminal violation on your part and undermined public confidence," David J. Apol, the acting director of the White House Ethics Office, wrote Ross in July 2017. Ross claimed these were merely "inadvertent errors," a claim that is difficult to believe. Ross built his fortune by applying extraordinary diligence to ferreting out fine financial details of companies that were seeking refuge from creditors in bankruptcy court.

When lawyer and economist James S. Henry documented Ross's Bank of Cyprus dealings for *DCReport*, we were concerned that readers simply would not believe a U.S. cabinet member could be in so deep with so many disreputable people and so many high-level agents of a hostile foreign power. Because of that, we did something news organizations never do: we ran footnotes, more than a hundred of them. Henry later wrote to the U.S. Senate urging an investigation, suggesting Ross's sale of his Bank of Cyprus shares did not absolve his conduct. "Exiting a brothel in a hurry doesn't explain what you were doing there in the first place," Henry wrote.

In early 2019 when Emory A. Rounds III became head of the Office of Government Ethics, he took an unprecedented action involving a cabinet secretary's ethics filings. He revoked the 2018 certification of compliance with ethics regulators that his predecessor had granted Ross "because that report was not accurate and he [Ross] was not in compliance with his ethics agreement at the time of the report."

Further confirmation of Ross's ethical noncompliance came in December 2020 as the Trump administration was winding down. The Commerce Department's inspector general issued a report showing that Ross had repeatedly violated ethics rules. He had failed to list all of his assets in his ethics disclosure reports and had held on to some investments that he swore under oath had been sold. In one case, he shorted a stock rather than selling it. Ross was allowed to get away with it all because he claimed these were just inadvertent mistakes. But Trump's choice of the ethically challenged Ross for his cabinet was no inadvertent mistake.

17

Promises, Promises

On Donald Trump's way out the White House door he did something revealing how he lied and cheated his way into office and about where his allegiances genuinely are. On January 4, 2021, two days before the insurrection and 16 days before Trump's term ended, his administration proposed a new rule on drug prices, a major issue in both the 2016 and 2020 campaigns. The regulation would cause a major change in drug pricing, but it wasn't a rule that anyone who listened to his many promises would have expected.

Promising to lower drug prices was a brilliant campaign strategy. The issue had been building for years. In 2003 President George W. Bush proposed the first significant expansion of Medicare benefits since the program began in 1965 by adding Part D to provide some relief from rising drug prices.

But that law barred our government from negotiating for lower wholesale drug prices, which continued rising. Novo Nordisk, for example, raised the price of its widely used Novolog insulin

353 percent from its introduction in 2001 to 2016. Some other insulin makers raised prices even higher.

Six out of ten Americans were on at least one prescription drug by 2016 and one in ten Americans said they knew someone who died because they couldn't afford their drug regimen. Surveys show that a quarter to a third of Americans on a prescription medication skip getting a refill at least once a year because they don't have the money. The Kaiser Family Foundation, which studies health care, reported that about 12 percent of Americans often cut pills in half or skipped a dose. Skipping doses or taking less of a drug than prescribed kills an estimated 125,000 people each year, the Centers for Disease Control reported in 2016.

Trump campaigned on a claim that he was the only person who could lower drug prices. Unlike politicians who he said had no idea how to wrest lower prices from the drug companies, on Day One as president Trump promised that drug prices would drop dramatically. Such were the virtually magical superpowers he claimed to possess. A few days before the 2016 New Hampshire primary Trump told a rally, "We pay about $300 billion more than we are supposed to, than if we negotiated the price, so there's $300 billion on Day One we solve."

"If we negotiated the price of drugs," he told MSNBC's Joe Scarborough the next morning, "we'd save $300 billion a year."

It was a bizarre and fact-free claim, typical of Trumpian hyperbole. According to the federal Centers for Medicaid and Medicare Services, our federal government spent $298 billion on prescription drugs at that time. To believe Trump was to believe the big drug companies would hand over all the medications for free along with a check to Uncle Sam for a couple of billion dollars.

The spending reduction Trump promised meant prices would plummet by more than 70 percent, bringing them well below what was paid by the governments of Britain, Canada, France, Germany, Japan, and South Korea, all of which negotiated the wholesale prices they paid for drugs. No one but Trump and those who saw him as a demigod believed that.

When reporters asked Trump and his campaign staff about the fantastical $300 billion number they refused to respond. Besides, it was one of those big incomprehensible numbers. Trump wanted to own the image of price cutter extraordinaire. He didn't care about the number.

When Day One came and Trump was president, drug prices kept rising. All he did was talk about lowering them. Over the next four years, the most he did was suggest that, maybe, perhaps, he might invoke existing law to require pharmaceutical companies to sell our government drugs at the average price of other large countries. But it was all talk, no action.

Come the 2020 presidential campaign and the pandemic, Trump resumed touting his negotiating skills. Once he even claimed he had already achieved success slashing drug prices. "Drug prices are coming down—first time in 51 years—because of my administration, but we can get them down way lower working with the Democrats," Trump declared during some May 2019 comments in the Rose Garden. But prices had not come down. It was just another lie.

Trump even felt the need to push back against the power of the drug companies as he campaigned for a second term. "When you see the Drug Companies taking massive television ads against me, forget what they say (which is false), YOU KNOW THAT DRUG PRICES ARE COMING DOWN, BIG," he tweeted in August 2020.

That month he switched back to promising that drug prices would fall, provided he won a second term. "We think we're going to cut prescription drug prices 50, 60, even 70%," he told a New Hampshire rally.

Trump did, now and then, say that Democrats stymied drug price reductions by refusing to cooperate. That excuse made no sense because he had failed to take action in 2017 and 2018 when Republicans controlled the House and Senate.

Trump had plenty of legal authority to force drug prices down without Congressional cooperation. At least two federal laws gave Trump the power to declare that our government wouldn't pay exorbitant prices for drugs. He could have invoked a law known as Section 1498, which is most often used in military procurement. That law gives the president the power to override a patent if prices, including drug prices, are excessive or supply is inadequate.

During the 2001 anthrax scares, Bayer, the German owner of a powerful drug called Cipro, refused to lower its price. Cipro is a uniquely effective tool to stop the growth of the deadly anthrax bacteria in an infected person's lungs. President George W. Bush threatened to invoke Section 1498 unless Bayer cut its price. That threat prompted Bayer to halve the price of Cipro. Strange as it is to imagine, the second President Bush negotiated more effectively than Trump.

Trump even could have just declared that our government had better things to do than enforce rules against importing drugs from other countries such as Canada, where drug prices are much lower, noted Dean Baker, an economist who has proposed effective ways to lower drug prices.

Eventually, Trump took decisive action on drug prices. It was the first Monday of 2021, just 16 days before he would leave the White House. In the Federal Register, where rules changes are published and people can comment before any changes occur, he proposed a new policy in implementing the 40-year-old Bayh-Dole law. That law, like Section 1498, gives our government power to "march in" and seize control of a drug patent developed with taxpayer funding when the owner charges excessively high prices or holds back supply. Of course, the patent owner would be compensated, but any seizure would be immediate with payment after negotiations or litigation.

An early hint of Trump's last-minute action could be found in his administration's contracts with drug companies in 2020 to develop Covid-19 vaccines. Except for Pfizer, which used its own funds for research and development, the vaccines were all paid for with government money. That made them liable to the Bayh-Dole march-in rights over high prices or inadequate supply. March-in rights under Bayh-Dole have never been invoked, no doubt because the Pharmaceutical Research and Manufacturers of America, or PhRMA, has made clear that it would litigate. It's doubtful that any administration would waste political capital fighting by invoking march-in rights. Instead, the law's power is the negotiating leverage it gives a president to challenge greedy and recalcitrant drug companies during national emergencies by jawboning, as George W. Bush did.

Trump's proposed new rule would have removed that leverage. It would make marching-in on any patented drug under the Bayh-Dole law impossible. In political terms, the goal of the new proposed rule seemed clear—to make it harder for the incoming Biden administration to do what Trump failed to do, negotiate lower drug prices. In economic terms, the proposed new rule showed that Trump was siding with the drug companies against the voters who supported him because they believed he would bring drug prices down. While the proposed new rule was consistent with the Trump Administration's animus to government regulations, this gratuitous last-minute action was a slap in the face of those voters who believed Trump would bring down drug prices.

18

Family First

D onald Trump arrived in the White House so ignorant and unprepared for his new job that senior aides had to explain, among many other things, why the USS *Arizona* memorial for dead sailors exists at Pearl Harbor and that Finland is a country.

That ignorance created opportunity for his son-in-law Jared Kushner and Jared's wife, Ivanka, who walked into the White House with tumultuous pasts and very troubled finances. They walked out having made in four years at least $172 million from outside activities and possibly as much as $640 million, as their ethics filings revealed. During his last year on the Trump White House staff, Jared also set up a holding company in a Caribbean tax haven.

No Trump appointments better illustrate the potential for America's becoming a kleptocracy than the influence that Jared and Ivanka wielded in the Trump White House. They repeatedly used connections to foreign leaders to their own benefit. Ivanka got trademark rights from China by the dozens, covering everything from purses to voting machines. Japan and Russia granted or renewed her intellectual property licenses. All three nations extended this generosity close to the time when they attended meetings at which they sought White House favors.

Citizens for Responsibility and Ethics in Washington, an anti-corruption watchdog that frequently sued for access to government documents in the Trump era, kept track of this convenient calendar: "In 2017, Ivanka's business won preliminary approval for three Chinese trademarks on the same day that she dined with Chinese President Xi Jinping at Mar-a-Lago. In May 2018, Ivanka's business was awarded 'registration' approval from the Chinese government for five trademark applications, with an additional one getting 'first trial approval.' The same week, President Trump announced he would try to save jobs at ZTE, the Chinese telecommunications giant closely tied to the government. A month later, Ivanka's business got registration approval for three more Chinese trademarks, on the same day her father announced he'd lift sanctions against ZTE."

Ivanka had a hand in creating the tax-favored Opportunity Zones that were part of Trump's 2017 tax law. The zones were supposed to create jobs in high-unemployment neighborhoods that paid well, but several studies have found little job creation resulted. Most of the benefits flowed to real estate investors.

Among these beneficiaries was Jared Kushner, who held a significant stake in a company called Cadre, which set up Opportunity Zone deals. Jared at first failed to disclose this investment, as required by federal ethics law. When he did disclose it, he put its value at between $5 million and $25 million. He also promised to sell it when an ethics official said it posed a conflict of interest. He never did. By the time he left Washington, his Cadre stake had grown to a value between $25 million and $50 million. Of course, if Jared has a conflict of interest in an investment, so does Ivanka.

Ivanka also owned a slice of her father's Washington hotel. In the first three years of his presidency, the hotel made her $13 million, she disclosed in ethics reports. In 2020, when the pandemic hit travel and entertainment businesses hard, she still earned $1.5 million.

Filing those reports is mandatory, but Jared and Ivanka sought approval to file "voluntarily" rather than under penalty of perjury, as the law requires. Trump himself sought permission to file his statements without signing them under penalty of perjury. The Office of Government Ethics said no. That helps explain why, when Trump filed for the first time as president, nearly 90 percent of the wealth he had crowed about as a candidate disappeared from his report.

Ivanka's last disclosure report also contained a revealing change. She had valued her share of the hotel at between $5 million and $25 million. But in her 2020 report, she dropped the value to $100,000 to $250,000. It was an indication that with her father leaving the White House, the hotel's value plummeted because no one needed to stay there to pay tribute to Trump.

As for Jared, Trump showed again and again that he trusted Jared despite numerous early instances of atrocious judgment in finance and in working for the campaign. Jared took part in a June 2016 Trump Tower meeting that reeked of disloyalty. A British agent representing the Kremlin had emailed Donald Trump Jr. that Moscow wanted to help his father win the election. Don Jr.

wrote back, "Love it," and then took the meeting a few days later. Jared and Paul Manafort also attended.

All three men tried to keep that meeting secret for a year. When the email came out, all three men insisted the meeting was an inconsequential discussion of cross-border adoptions. What none of them did was what any loyal American should have done: refused the meeting or at least called the FBI afterward to speak with counterintelligence officials.

In December 2016, Jared again demonstrated his disloyalty. He approached Sergey Kislyak, the Russian ambassador to the U.S., and asked to use the Russian embassy's secure communications link to contact the Kremlin without the knowledge of American national security agencies. Ponder that for a moment. Ask yourself what would have happened if anyone close to Obama or any other previous president had done this. What would congressional Republicans have done with such information?

Kislyak, trained in both diplomacy and gathering intelligence, wisely declined Jared's request, but he recognized its value to Russia. So Kislyak informed his superiors in Moscow using an unsecured link, and soon the whole world knew about Jared's request. Kislyak had fired a shot across the bow of the incoming administration, a warning that the Kremlin could leak damaging secrets if Trump or his team ever crossed the modern czar. And for the next four years Trump praised Putin again and again.

Ivanka's past record was also troubling. In 2008 she had lied to potential buyers in the Trump SoHo high-rise, a scandal-ridden project which involved Russian gangsters and financiers from start to finish. Ivanka announced that 60 percent of the units had been sold, four times what she knew was the actual number. "We're in a very fortunate position where we have enough sales, and now we are strategically targeting certain buyers," she declared, her brothers, Don Jr. and Eric, at her side.

Donald Trump was entitled to 18 percent of any Trump SoHo profits, court papers later revealed. He signed a letter authorizing a financial restructuring of the project, whatever money it had secured suddenly vanished, reappearing in an Icelandic bank then under the thumb of a Russian oligarch. Litigation about that deal remains active. Trump's name, by the way, was removed from the building after his brand became toxic during his presidency.

The office of the Manhattan district attorney Cyrus Vance Jr. spent two years building a criminal case against Ivanka, Don Jr., and others over the Trump SoHo project. Investigators obtained emails in which the older Trump children coordinated their lies to prospective buyers, many of them Europeans. However, Vance killed that case after some unhappy buyers got refunds and a Trump lawyer made a $25,000 contribution to Vance's reelection campaign. The Trumps, their lawyer, and Vance all insist all their actions were proper and the donation irrelevant.

Jared's poor judgment had long been on display. In 2007 he made a deal to buy a Manhattan office building badly in need of renovation. He paid $1.8 billion, a record for a New York City property. The building had a subway stop in the basement and a devilish address: 666 Fifth Avenue. The 41-story building stands just down the street from Trump Tower.

The price paid per square foot doubled the previous record Manhattan sale. The deal was highly leveraged. Jared had to sell more than 17,000 New Jersey apartments his family owned to come up with a $50 million down payment. Mortgages covered the other 97 percent of the purchase price.

Even fully occupied, the rents were not nearly enough to cover the interest payments on the property, let alone taxes and operating expenses. Jared, then in his 20s, had made the deal soon after he took charge of the family real estate business because his father, Charles, was in federal prison for tax evasion.

Soon tenants started leaving 666 Fifth Avenue, and the Great Recession drove down rents that new tenants might pay. The building's value fell by more than half, putting the Kushners deep underwater even after selling off parts of the building. The Kushners were at risk of the kind of disaster Trump experienced in 1990 when he couldn't pay his bills, forcing him to give up an airplane, yacht, the Plaza Hotel, and other properties.

Jared had taken out loans with what are known as cross-collateralization clauses. If he failed to make payments on any one loan, all of his debts could be called in immediately. He and his father, by then released from prison, began a desperate search for an angel, talking to prospects in China, Qatar, the United Arab Emirates, and Saudi Arabia.

Tom Barrack, an Arabic-speaking real estate mogul in Florida who would later become president of the Trump inauguration committee, arranged the Middle East connections. Barrack would later leverage his White House connections to try to sell nuclear technology to Saudi Arabia.

Having a personal financial relationship with a foreign entity is usually an automatic disqualifier for Americans seeking a high-level security clearance with the U.S. government. It's a simple question of loyalty. So Jared's quest to find financing abroad should have eliminated him from consideration. On top of this, however, there were numerous errors and omissions in Jared's and Ivanka's SF86 filings. That's the primary document used to determine fitness for a security clearance. Jared, for instance, omitted from his SF86 that Trump Tower meeting with the Kremlin agents, his request to Kislyak to use secure Russian diplomatic communications, and a meeting he had had with the head of a Russian "bank" that the FBI regards as a front for Russian spying. The FBI had caught spies at the bank's Manhattan office posing as bankers. Any one of those omissions too would be reason to deny a security clearance.

Yet, after an Ethics Office investigation lasting more than a year, Jared and Ivanka got their clearances, including access to the President's Daily Brief.

Although Trump denied playing any role in this investigation, in early 2019 it was revealed that he had personally ordered the clearances for his daughter and son-in-law. The New York Times reported that both his White House chief of staff, Gen. John F. Kelly, and White House Counsel Don McGahn wrote memos to the file to shield themselves from any future fallout by arguing that they merely did as Trump ordered.

Jared and Ivanka were not alone in getting clearances that their conduct did not merit. Tricia Newbold, one of the White House employees who works on security clearances, told a House committee that at least 25 Trump staffers got clearances over objections from those whose job was to vet applicants.

Newbold told the committee that "two current senior White House officials" were among those given clearances despite "a wide range of serious disqualifying issues involving foreign influence, conflicts of interest, concerning personal conduct, financial problems, drug use, and criminal conduct." The background check of one person, publicly described only as "Senior White House Official 1," uncovered "significant disqualifying factors, including foreign influence, outside activities ('employment outside or business external to what your office at the [Executive Office of the President] entails'), and personal conduct."

Malcolm Nance, who has held clearances and written five books on national security in the Trump years, said he was shocked that Jared and Ivanka got clearances at any level, especially given Jared's failure to list the three meetings with Russians seeking to influence our government. "If you have to make a single correction on your SF86 you probably won't get a security clearance," Nance told me. "Make two and you are out for sure."

Sarah Kendzior, a journalist turned scholar of autocratic governments, says that nepotism is an early sign of an emerging regime dedicated not to democracy and freedom but to perpetuating itself. "Oligarchs and plutocrats often operate in a similar way to the mafia," Kendzior told me, "maximizing family structure for power and profit, only it's not recognized as such when cloaked in prestige and respectability. Children are viewed as secret-keepers, public relations tools, and, later in life, ideal vessels for money laundering. Loyalty is the most treasured virtue, far above honor or talent or love, and the greatest guarantee of loyalty can be found in kin ties."

That would explain not only the security clearances but why Trump gave his son-in-law such a broad portfolio of issues in which neither of them had a wisp of expertise. Trump had no training in diplomacy, but he had a nose for developing lucrative relationships and knew he could trust Jared to do what he wanted and to keep secrets within the family.

Soon after joining his father-in-law's team, Jared began freelancing foreign policy. American taxpayers have invested a fortune in developing diplomacy and policies with deeply informed experts on every country. Jared blithely ignored this expertise. He not only infuriated State Department diplomats, but risked drawing the United States into conflicts for no good reason. Jared conducted meetings and phone calls that Secretary of State Rex Tillerson knew nothing about. Most significant, Jared got himself in tight with Saudi Crown Prince Mohammed bin Salman, known as MBS, a connection which may pay off in the future as Jared again seeks investors for projects as a private citizen, as he did before his White House years. Jared's freelancing Middle East policy also played a role in inciting sedition against King Abdullah II of Jordan, which ended with arrests of three prominent Jordanians for inciting sedition.

After Jared made an unannounced visit to Saudi Arabia in late October 2017, the intelligence services of at least four countries intercepted communications in which MBS boasted that he had Kushner "in his pocket." It was MBS, we now know, who in 2018 ordered the death of *Washington Post* columnist Jamal Khashoggi, a critic of the Saudi government. Khashoggi was assassinated and dismembered in the Saudi consulate in Istanbul. Neither Trump nor Jared has ever criticized that murder.

Trump's first trip abroad as president was to Saudi Arabia in May 2017. He praised the Saudis for promoting peace and fighting terrorism even though the royal family funds 57 terrorist groups.

In contrast, Trump condemned Qatar for financing terrorists, which it does, but far less so than the Saudis. The Saudi royals detest the Qatari royal family because they own Al Jazeera, which uses satellite technology to beam accurate news reports into Saudi Arabia. The Saudi royal family regards accurate news as a threat to its hold on power, but they can't stop the broadcasts. [For 16 months I was a columnist on economic and regulatory issues for Al Jazeera America.]

Two weeks after Trump's visit, the Saudis and their allies imposed an economic blockade on Qatar. The U.S. State Department and Pentagon tried to remain neutral. Trump, of course, claimed credit. "During my recent trip to the Middle East I stated that there can no longer be funding of Radical Ideology. Leaders pointed to Qatar—look!" he tweeted. Following this, he tweeted that it was "good to see the Saudi Arabia visit with the King and 50 countries already paying off. They said they would take a hard line on funding extremism, and all reference [sic] was pointing to Qatar. Perhaps this will be the beginning of the end to the horror of terrorism!"

Trump's senseless attacks on Qatar and praise for the Saudis demonstrated his utter ignorance of the Middle East. But his animosity to Qatar also appears to be related to Jared's 666 Fifth Avenue debacle.

Qatar was one of the first places where the Kushner family had sought an angel to bail them out at 666 Fifth Avenue. But after studying the numbers, the Qataris said no. Then, in April 2017, a few weeks after Trump became president, Charles Kushner met with Ali Sharif Al-Emadi, the Qatari finance minister, at the St. Regis Hotel in New York. That meeting was held to secure financing for 666 Fifth Avenue, the *Intercept* reported almost a year later. A spokesperson for the Kushner Companies confirmed that but said it was Al-Emadi who sought the meeting, not the Kushners. The Kushners also claimed that "before the meeting, Kushner Companies had decided that it was not going to accept sovereign wealth fund investments." How curious, then, that just weeks after the St. Regis meeting, Donald Trump, who relied on Jared for Middle East information, denounced Qatar, home to America's most important Middle East military base, and claimed credit for the Saudi economic blockade.

* * *

How Jared and Ivanka made between $172 million and $640 million while holding unpaid White House jobs poses serious questions about the intersection of their financial interests and U.S. national security. Again and again Jared demonstrated appallingly poor judgment. Still, he retained the complete confidence of his father-in-law, which reinforces Trump's own gullibility and poor judgment.

While Jared was working in the White House, Freddie Mac, the federally sponsored mortgage loan corporation, approved almost $850 million of 10-year interest-only mortgages issued to the Kushner Companies. Not having to pay down the principal on the 18 mortgages increases the cash flow to the Kushner family, who could spend it as they chose or invest in other projects. It also poses the risk that a decade later, when the loans come due, the real estate market may have fallen and the Kushners may not be able to repay.

How well the properties are maintained could also be an issue. Jared is prominent in "Slumlord Millionaire," an episode in the Netflix series *Dirty Money*. In April 2021, a Maryland judge, in a 252-page decision, found that Jared and his brother Joshua had ripped off tenants for $322,000 in improper fees, failed to maintain the properties, and misled people about conditions in 17 apartment complexes. New renters often weren't allowed to inspect apartments until move-in day.

Jared and Ivanka rented a house in late 2016 on favorable terms from Andrónico Luksic, a Chilean billionaire seeking a big favor from the Trump administration. The 8,200-square-foot house was in Kalorama, a tony Washington neighborhood, located just around the corner from where Barack and Michelle Obama moved when his second term ended.

Luksic charged them $15,000 a month. That would not cover the interest on a rental property mortgage, nor would it cover property taxes and insurance. Even if Luksic paid cash for the $5.8 million house, the cost of his capital has a value that needs to be accounted for. The "Javanka" home got some attention, not because of the rent but because the couple denied Secret Service agents use of their bathrooms. The agents used a bathroom at the Obama residence instead, until the Obamas said no more. The Secret Service then rented part of another house for $300 a month just to have a toilet and sink. Luksic, by the way, never got the approvals he needed for a copper and nickel mine in Minnesota.

While working in the White House, Ivanka and Jared scored

a much bigger deal than their below-market rent on the Kalorama mansion.

The Kushner Companies sought massive loans in 2018 for the thousands of apartments they had acquired in the years before Trump became president. At that time, an Obama appointee ran what is formally called the Federal Home Loan Mortgage Corporation, better known as Freddie Mac. Two months later, the Kushners dropped their loan applications, suggesting that they expected the loans to be denied.

Then Trump appointed a new head of Freddie Mac in February 2019. Presto: Freddie Mac granted the Kushners mortgages totaling $786 million. The terms were generous, the underwriting questionable.

The Kushners needed only to pay interest, not principal. Not having to pay down the loan balance meant more cash flowing to the Kushner Companies, in which Jared had retained his 50 percent stake, though not direct control, after he joined the White House.

Interest-only mortgages impose greater risk on the lender. Unless the properties are well maintained and rise in value over the life of the loan, the lender may never recoup all the money that has been borrowed. The Kushner loans were for ten years with a balloon payment at the end, another risk for the lender.

Profit projections the Kushners submitted to justify the size of the loans proved wildly optimistic. Profits on the largest apartment complex loan came in 31 percent below what the Kushners projected, according to Freddie Mac records analyzed by ProPublica. Indeed, all 16 loans fell short of their projected profit, half of them by at least 10 percent.

A shortfall of just 5 percent strongly indicates a likelihood that a mortgage will eventually sour, according to research by John Griffin, a University of Texas finance professor.

That Freddie Mac made interest-only loans was even more surprising because the Kushners had an awful reputation as landlords. The Netflix series *Dirty Money* included an episode about Jared Kushner's property management style. The title: "Slumlord Millionaire."

Brian Frosh, the Maryland attorney general, sued 25 of the many Kushner Companies over abusive treatment of tenants in 2019. He said many apartments were so shoddily maintained that they posed health hazards to tenants. Lawyers for Jared Kushner, who owns half of the apartment company, and his relatives said the lawsuit was politically motivated.

Testimony from tenants took months. Tenants complained about refusals to eradicate vermin and make repairs, including when raw sewage flowed into a kitchen. Others said they agreed to rent a specific apartment that looked fine, only to be forced on moving day into a decrepit unit with filthy carpets, peeling paint, troublesome water faucets, and other problems.

Jacking up fees, the lawsuit revealed, was a core Kushner strategy to squeeze tenants for more money. The Kushners charged 15,289 would-be tenants a $50 application fee even though Maryland law limits the charge to half that. The Kushners charged more than 28,000 tenants a $12 "agent fee" when no agent existed. And a court-mandated fee in disputes between landlord and tenant was assessed at $80 even though the actual court fee was only $50.

Emily Daneker, the administrative law judge who heard the

testimony, noted that the Kushners charged this inflated fee 2,642 times over about two years. "These circumstances do not support a finding that this was the result of isolated or innocent mistakes," she wrote. Daneker's ruling required 252 pages to recount all the wrongs the Kushners perpetrated against financially vulnerable tenants. Despite this, the Kushners hailed her ruling against them as a victory because Frosh's staff failed to prove every accusation.

While in the White House, Jared held on to much of his stake in another real estate firm, Cadre, that he created with his brother, Joshua, and a friend, Ryan Williams, who came from Goldman Sachs. "Cadre is going to make us billionaires," Jared told colleagues when the commercial real estate brokerage launched in 2014.

Cadre is an offshore entity formed in the Cayman Islands, where laws guarantee secrecy. Among the known investors in Cadre are Jack Ma, the richest man in China when Trump assumed office, and Yuri Milner, who was on the Trump administration's report on oligarchs subject to American sanctions.

People and perhaps foreign governments whose identities are unknown invested $90 million in Cadre while Jared worked in the White House on a broad portfolio that included Middle East diplomacy. Cadre was seeking, and may have obtained, as much as $250 million with assistance from Goldman Sachs.

Cadre became a booming success once Trump assumed office. Its portfolio of American real estate grew fivefold between 2017 and 2019 to half a billion dollars.

Kushner didn't include Cadre on his first government ethics disclosure form in March 2017, even though he later valued his reduced stake at $25 million to $50 million. Because of this, among other problems and failures to disclose, national security professionals denied Kushner a security clearance, which would allow him to view sensitive government information, because they were concerned about "foreign influence" from Cadre investors. Kushner and the White House noted that he was not involved in Cadre management while working in the White House.

While foreign agents and governments invested in Cadre is secret, the *Guardian* and others reported that Saudi Arabia invested in the bailout of Jared Kushner's biggest asset purchase, 666 Fifth Avenue. That's the 41-story Manhattan office tower that Kushner bought with almost no money down in 2007 at a record-high price of $1.8 billion. Within little more than a year, the building's value plunged by more than half.

Kushner stuck it to taxpayers on his way out the White House door, too. After Trump lost the 2020 election, Kushner flew to Israel to tout the Trump administration's accomplishments. He met with Benjamin Netanyahu, the indicted prime minister, and other government officials. One week before Trump left office, Kushner charged his $24,335.20 hotel bill to the State Department.

While his trip may have been purely official business, it lined up well with two other significant matters of interest to the Kushner family. As Kushner was traveling to promote the Trump legacy with Israel, Trump pardoned Charles Kushner, Jared's father, who had served time for federal tax evasion and witness tampering. And that same month, the Kushner Companies applied for approval to sell $100 million worth of corporate bonds on the Tel Aviv Stock Exchange.

19

After Trump

That someone as unqualified and ill-suited to hold even a
lowly public office as Donald Trump made it to the White
House should prompt us to examine ways to protect our republic
and ensure that the liberties of the American people endure. The
damage Trump inflicted on our body politic did not end with his
presidency but spreads through conspiracy theorists and cowardly
Republicans who let fear of Trump overwhelm their oaths of office.

The promise was of an active, competent administration unshack-
led from Washington's standard operating procedure and with a
focus on only the Forgotten Men and Forgotten Women that would
create a booming economy, lower taxes and force American companies to bring factories and jobs back home. Taking aim at "elites"
and especially Wall Street, Trump vowed to "drain the swamp." He
told every rally he loved the people there, that he was sacrificing his
own financial wealth for the good of the country and many times
promising: "I will be your champion and I won't be playing golf."

He promised to Make America Great Again. But Trump is the

only president since Herbert Hoover in 1933 to leave office with an economy that was smaller per American than when he moved into the White House.

Instead of the promised greatness, Trump stocked the swamp with voracious Wall Street predators while abandoning or not enforcing rules to contain their worst behaviors.

From Trump we got an administration awash in profiteering, self-dealing, and conflicts of interest, run by unqualified and incompetent cabinet secretaries and agency managers. This was an era of eyes-wide-open blind trusts, infrastructure improvements that never materialized, denunciations of intelligence and law enforcement communities matched with lavish praise for the imaginary integrity of Vladimir Putin and his cronies. And all this before the pandemic, which Trump so completely mismanaged that hundreds of thousands of Americans died needlessly as he lied and denied about the virus.

We can repair that damage. Self-governance is all about taking responsibility and working to solve our problems and advance our society. Leaving the duties of citizenship to others in the mistaken belief that government won't respond to the people or, in the long wake of Watergate, that politics is dirty and unworthy of our involvement only helps those who grow ever richer by influencing government rules. Instead of acting like renters or, worse, squatters, we need to behave as what we are: the owners of our government. None of us will ever get all of what we want, but we can reach accommodations that benefit most and perhaps all of us through compromise. In democratic self-governance, bipartisanship, and the compromise agreements it enables, is a virtue.

Only we can assure the health of our democracy. And if we do not, we will pay a much higher price for the Trump era than we have already paid.

In his four years as president of the United States, Donald Trump bullied, cheated, denied, and lied because that's who he is. He is a con artist always looking for another mark, a man who has let billions of dollars slip through his fingers because prudence and judgment are concepts alien to his nature.

Paying debts is also alien to Trump's nature. During the 2016 campaign, he continually proclaimed his love and support for police, but he stiffed cities that incurred police overtime and other costs for providing security at his campaign rallies. Trump's refusal to pay for police protection contrasts with his many public statements claiming limitless love and support for police. "For you guys, anything I can do, I'll do," he told the International Association of Chiefs of Police in 2018.

Trump rallies needed heavy security because Trump frequently encouraged violence by his supporters, sometimes pointing out individuals who the crowd then kicked and beat. Trump urged his fans at one 2016 campaign rally to "knock the crap out of them. Okay, just knock the hell . . . I promise you I will pay for the legal fees." There were Trump fans who incurred legal fees but no record Trump paid any of them.

In cities Trump visited, researchers found that violent assaults reported to local law enforcement rose on average by 2.3 incidents per rally. There was no increased violence associated with Clinton rallies.

Clinton paid nearly every security bill sent by municipal

governments. So did Senator Ted Cruz of Texas, who ran in the 2016 Republican primaries. Senator Bernie Sanders of Vermont refused to pay for police protection at his 2016 Democratic Party primary rallies, but after drawing criticism, his campaign paid. Trump paid only in the few cases where the venue required a signed contract for security—and then not always in full and rarely on time. Those security costs stretched already tight municipal budgets for police, emergency medical technicians, and ambulances, as well as having firefighting crews on standby in some locales.

The city of El Paso has yet to see any of the $470,417 Trump owes for a 2016 rally. Taxpayers have given up hope Trump will pay the bill, City Councilman Peter Svarzbein told me in 2021. Nine other cities, from Burlington, Vermont, to Spokane, Washington, and Tucson, Arizona, to Eau Claire, Wisconsin, say the Trump campaign owes them more than $371,000. Five years later, their invoices all remain unpaid.

The young man who poked his finger into the chest of New York City's mayor is the same man who in his dotage riled up an angry mob near the White House, directing them to lay siege to our Capitol where they attacked the police, shouting "Hang Mike Pence." Trump's failed coup testifies to his incompetence. It also serves as a warning of how vulnerable our republic is to a future usurper who will be able to effectively organize the overthrow of our government from within.

Competence matters. Incompetence costs lives. In 2017, in my second Trump book, *It's Even Worse Than You Think*, I predicted that Trump wouldn't know what to do if a pernicious virus hopscotched around the world on jetliners causing a pandemic.

Based on three decades of studying the man, I know that he doesn't understand the principles of science, doesn't listen to advice he doesn't like, and refuses to accept facts that contradict his views.

There is one good thing Trump did for us. Just one. But to appreciate that we must first understand the evil he and his enablers fomented.

Trump cheated Americans during the 2016 election by working hand in glove with people who took money from the Kremlin and its allies, most notably his campaign manager Paul Manafort and Michael Flynn, a retired general. He cheated us even more by restricting the investigation of Special Counsel Robert Mueller, covering up the depth of Kremlin interference. Attorney General William Barr, who acted as if he were Trump's personal lawyer by lying about what Mueller's team found, helped that foul cause.

Trump cheated his supporters, desperate for relief after more than four decades adrift in the economic doldrums, by promising them tax cuts while ending the excessive influence Wall Street and big business wield in Washington. Instead, he slashed taxes for the rich and the corporations they own, enhancing the power of economic elites in our government while throwing crumbs to his less-wealthy supporters. In his tax law, Trump added an extra dollop of contempt for the "poorly educated" he claimed to love, showering himself and the rest of the Trump-Kushner family with more benefits as real estate investors. And he did it with borrowed money, which implies future tax increases to service the debt used to create the appearance of tax cuts.

That the vast majority of Americans hungered for what Trump insisted he alone could provide, a brighter economic future, is the fault of both parties for decades of malign neglect of people not rich enough to be part of the political donor class. That 90 percent of the population made relatively less income during Trump's four years in office than they did in the 1970s is due to our failure to make intelligent choices in who we elected and who they listened to once they reached Washington. Leaders of the Democratic Party, especially, need to ask themselves where they lost their way and how to redeem themselves so that working people will support them, not a financial and political swindler like Donald Trump.

Trump cheated workers with promises of rapid wage growth, more jobs, and economic growth of 4 to 6 percent per year. Instead, in his first three years, job growth ran about 3 percent below Obama's last six years, wages grew only modestly, and economic growth was subpar for the postwar era and not even close to his hot-air promises. In 2019 average income fell sharply, by $1,145 per household, my analysis of IRS data released in June 2021 showed. And among the 96 percent of taxpayers with incomes of less than $250,000 the news was even worse. That group had more income in 2016, Obama's last year, than in 2019 under Trump.

Remember those 1,100 Indiana factory jobs at a Carrier oven factory that Trump and Vice President Mike Pence claimed in December 2016 to have saved from moving to Mexico? More than 300 of them went south of the border, as the company had planned all along. And in 2020 alone Indiana companies exported more jobs to Mexico, China, India, and other countries than the 800 that were saved at Carrier.

Despite this and other examples of policy by publicity stunt about manufacturing jobs, here is the awful truth: our nation had

154,000 fewer factory jobs when Trump left office than when he became president. That's the opposite of his promise of abundantly more factory jobs.

This was just one of many distractions from reality, part of a political game of three-card monte presented by a master con artist.

Trump cheated us out of justice in pardoning Paul Manafort, General Michael Flynn, Roger Stone, Steve Bannon, and others.

Trump shamed us with his servile behavior, rushing to Asia to meet the hereditary dictator of North Korea, a meeting that produced nothing. He tore up the notes of his translator during his Helsinki meeting with Putin and later met with Putin alone, putting himself and our country in a compromising position, with no one to counter Russia's version of events. He abandoned our nation's history of standing up against human rights abuses as, again and again, he praised murderous autocrats, a stain on our nation's honor that will not fade for a long, long time, if ever.

Most damaging of all to the soul of America, Trump peeled back decades of progress toward reaching the promise of our Declaration of Independence, that we are all created equal. His racism, articulated at his campaign launch in June 2015, unleashed the worst instincts of bigots who no longer felt the need to keep quiet outside their homes and the company of friends who shared their small-minded views. Trump freed them from any constraints on speaking openly about their hatred of fellow Americans based on their skin color or religious faith. He even called at least some of these bigots "very fine people." Some Trumpers took his words as authority to attack and even kill in his name, as shown by defenses they tried to make in criminal proceedings.

Trump cheated us out of a valuable legacy: the unbroken history of peaceful transition of power from one administration to the next.

Long before Trump took his oath of office, I and others predicted that he would never peacefully leave the White House. One of those who said this was Tony Schwartz, who wrote *The Art of the Deal* for Trump.

Trump also cheated us out of integrity in high office as he tried to establish a kleptocracy, collecting tribute from favor seekers and pocketing many millions of taxpayer dollars as he partied at Mar-a-Lago and played golf every week. Just the four trips he made to Mar-a-Lago over five weeks in February and March 2017 cost taxpayers $13.6 million, the Government Accounting Office determined. He neglected his campaign promise always to work from the White House and never hit the links again. He even ordered Air Force flight crews, as well as Vice President Pence, to divert to his British Isles golf courses so he could rent them rooms and sell them dinners at taxpayer expense for his own profit.

Trips by his sons Don Jr. and Eric to the Dominican Republic, Uruguay, and the United Arab Emirates for Trump Organization business deals cost $396,000 just in temporary duty costs, such as hotel rooms for Secret Service agents.

When we finally get a full accounting, we will learn how much he benefited from forcing taxpayers to spend for his hotel rooms, golf cart rentals, meals, and other expenses at his properties. The bill, excluding necessary security costs, will run into many millions of dollars.

Even after his election loss Trump got from the Republican Party what he could not get from Mayor Abe Beame and FBI

Director James Comey: unquestioning personal loyalty, the law be damned. The Grand Old Party became a cult worshiping Trump.

It will take years, perhaps decades, to get back what Donald Trump cheated us out of, including a shared belief that voters should decide who will be granted the power to act in our name.

What we must do—now—is act in defense of our republic. Otherwise, over time we will lose our liberties; we will live under the boot of someone who possesses all of Trump's self-aggrandizing instincts but also knows how to manage power. A zealous competent manager with the work ethic Trump lacks could end our democracy even if some members of Congress and the courts continue to function as relics of a time when we were a free people.

In unleashing the forces of racial hatred, conspiracy theorizing, and do-nothing-ism, Trump cleared a path for would-be usurpers in the future. And do not doubt that others seek power, not in the limited fashion envisioned by the Framers of our Constitution, with its checks and balances, but on the dictatorial terms that were the norm until our republic first emerged almost 250 years ago.

*   *   *

Even the most ardent Trump supporters should realize by now that he sold us a bill of goods. There was no plan for infrastructure. There was no plan to denuclearize the Korean Peninsula, no plan to lower drug prices. There was never a replacement or improvement for Obamacare.

"America First" was nothing more than a slogan to distract from trade policies that destroyed Midwest soybeans sales to China, enriching Brazilian soybean farmers whose crops China then bought, while necessitating taxpayer welfare for Iowa farmers. The hypocrisy was even personal. Trump imported his Make America Great Again caps from Bangladesh; Ivanka Trump's failed clothing line featured dresses made in China.

Recovering from Trump—whether or not he is indicted, convicted, and sentenced to prison or home confinement—requires fixing structural flaws in our government. Let's start with tax returns. Ever since the unindicted tax cheat Richard Nixon, whose tax lawyer went to prison, it has been a tradition for presidential candidates and, when elected, presidents and their running mates to release their tax returns. Vice President Dick Cheney was the only person to deviate significantly from this, releasing only his summary pages for some years rather than his complete tax return. Trump has now shown that tradition is insufficient.

We cannot require a candidate to disclose tax returns as a condition of running for president. However, there is a lawful way to achieve the same result. Congress need only pass a law requiring the release of tax returns by the Internal Revenue Service when presidential and vice-presidential candidates reach some plateau that excludes fringe candidates who get a handful of votes. Raising a certain sum or filing to be on the ballot of a certain number of states could be used as thresholds for tax return disclosure.

The threshold needs to be low enough so that the American people learn early on about the candidates' tax-filing practices, income, and obligations. Disclosure just before the first week of primaries would be optimal. The IRS should release, minus personal details such as Social Security numbers, federal tax returns for the previous six years.

Why not just one year or two? The 2012 candidacy of Mitt Romney provides the answer. Romney talked about and planned to run long before he announced. That gave him time to arrange his finances and shape what we saw on the two years of partial tax returns that his campaign released.

Only because Mitt and Ann Romney acted with integrity to a question I asked them in 2011 do we know that they managed to create trusts worth roughly $100 million for their five sons without incurring any gift tax. At that time, the lifetime limit on untaxed gifts was not much more than $1 million. (The Romneys achieved this, I believe, by giving the sons stock in a newly formed company with no revenue, but which later became a profitable enterprise. That is perfectly legal, though Congress should examine whether it should be.)

Tax returns are secret only because Congress makes them so. Each year many tax returns are entered into the public record, material I have mined for decades, so there is no reason to let anyone who would lead our nation keep their tax filings secret. I favor similar disclosure for House and Senate candidates and federal judges.

Second, we need a law requiring that all financial assets of a president or vice president, other than personal residences and personal property like furniture and jewelry, go into a blind trust. No sitting president should be allowed to direct taxpayer money to enterprises they own, as Trump did for four years, nor shift property to close relatives, as Jared Kushner did.

Without getting into technicalities there are financial reforms that would protect the public from abuses of the sort Trump enacted and shield the incoming president and vice president from temptations that can affect our national security. For those who want to understand this issue better, I recommend Zephyr Teachout's 2016 book, *Corruption in America: From Benjamin Franklin's Snuff Box to Citizens United.*

A third necessary reform would be to write into law that certain specific acts by a sitting president, vice president, senator, representative, federal judge, or other civil officer are inherently impeachable. Codifying specific misconduct as impeachable would not diminish the broad constitutional description of high crimes and misdemeanors.

Criminal tax fraud, bribery, commercial bribery, extortion, or a judicial finding of perjury should all be codified as impeachable. So should commission of a felony like Trump's claim that he could shoot someone on Fifth Avenue without losing a vote and be exempt from a police investigation.

Impeachment is neither a civil nor a criminal process. It is a political one. The House has the sole power to impeach, the Senate the sole power to try with conviction requiring affirmative votes by two-thirds of senators "sitting." That doesn't mean 67 senators in our current 100-member Senate, but two-thirds of those who show up for the vote.

Congress should also prohibit the appointment of relatives in the first and second degrees from positions other than on honorary boards and commissions with minor duties. When John F. Kennedy made his brother Robert attorney general in 1961 he may have made a wise choice, but that decision should not excuse nepotism in a nation with no shortage of talent for high government positions.

As Sarah Kendzior and others have shown, nepotism is an early indicator of likely criminality and dictatorial tendencies.

Two other reforms would encourage integrity. One would be to strengthen our whistleblower laws. Various journalists, me included, got information from whistleblowers during the Trump years. But not until he was out of office did we learn about the use of secret subpoenas to seize telephone, email and other records of members of Congress who were critical of the president and some journalists under surveillance, which is anathema to a free society. That kind of action is outrageous, but it also shows the reason we need to strengthen whistleblower protections. Over several decades of writing about whistleblowers, I have seen how the laws have morphed from a shield for those who reveal misdeeds into a sword for attacking whistleblowers. Whistleblowers should be allowed a defense of public benefit and necessity, including in national security cases.

Another reform would end the practice of allowing candidates and officeholders to convert campaign and other donations to their personal use after leaving office. As his time in the White House drew to a close, Trump's enablers found an imaginative, cheap, and lucrative way to bring in more money via his political action committee. "Stop the Steal" became his new slogan, a clear shift from the MAGA concept of a better America to the narrow desires of lawlessly keeping Trump in office. In just eight weeks after Election Day 2020, Trump hauled in $255 million in donations. That was on top of about $240 million raised in less than three weeks before Election Day. The best part, for Trump anyway, was hidden in the fine print. His pitch for money focused on his need to hire lawyers to challenge the 2020 vote results, lawyers who he promised would prove he really won. The donors were the con man's latest marks. That became clear once Federal Elections Commission filings became public. Trump spent less than $9 million on lawyers and legal costs, about 4 percent of his haul. Only those who read the fine print knew that Trump could divert most of their contributions to maintain his lavish lifestyle, making him a wealthy beggar. That's not the image he sold of a self-made business genius with a Midas touch. Existing Super PAC rules—non-rules really—will let Trump use most of those hundreds of millions of donated dollars for his personal benefit. However, the costs of fighting possible criminal charges in New York and perhaps Georgia and Washington, D.C., may consume lots of that cash.

Worse still, Trump's exit fundraising was deceptive. Many donors didn't realize that they needed to uncheck a box or else their donation authorized Trump to keep tapping their checking or credit card accounts as often as he wanted. Usually, people have to opt in to monthly or weekly contributions, not opt out to avoid unlimited extra charges.

It was a mix of Ponzi scheme with elements of embezzlement. Trump tricked people into donating much more than they intended to give, which kept his campaign from going broke before Election Day. Then, after Election Day, he raised new money with baseless claims that Biden stole the election. Some of this new money was used to pay back those tricked into multiple unintended extra donations. Because of weak white-collar crime laws, this scheme may well go unpunished.

Stacy Blatt of Kansas City provides an excellent example of Trump's ripping off his supporters with the uncheck-the-box swindle. While in hospice care, Blatt heard Rush Limbaugh tell his radio audience that the Trump 2020 campaign needed money urgently. Blatt gave $500, half his monthly income, via WinRed, a commercial enterprise Trump used to process gifts. Over the next month, Trump's campaign tapped Blatt's bank account six more times, taking the dying man's last $3,000.

Victor Amelino gave $990 in September. He later discovered that the Trump people tapped his bank account weekly, draining nearly $8,000. "I'm retired. I can't afford to pay all that damn money," the 78-year-old California resident said. Amelino described Team Trump in one fitting word: "bandits." Federal Election Commission records revealed that Trump refunded $121 million to such donors, most of it after the election. But the scheme kept him from running out of cash just before Election Day.

Two reforms can stop abuses of Super PACs. First, former officeholders should be given a reasonable period, say, a year or two, to settle their campaign bills. Any remaining money must be donated to the federal government or, perhaps, public charities in which the politician and her family and staff play no role.

Second, the law should prohibit candidates and officeholders from passing on donations to other candidates. This is one of the most harmful ways that money corrupts our Congress, concentrating power in the hands of congressional leaders with large war chests from which they can hand out money to other politicians who do as party leaders tell them.

A better system would have taxpayers finance all elections

because, among other virtues, it would show us how each candidate would use a limited budget. Candidates who win and come in under budget would become national heroes, while those who can't discipline their campaign spending would run out of money or use it ineffectively. Had such a law been in place in 2016, the profligate Trump almost certainly would have gone broke before Election Day. Ditto in 2020, when his campaign staff drained his billion-dollar war chest early that year.

We should also recognize that Trump performed one important public service for America. He showed us just how vulnerable our democracy is to a would-be dictator interested in his own welfare above ours. For that, but nothing else, America owes Trump a thank-you.

Epilogue

Since I finished writing *The Big Cheat* in July 2021, revelation after revelation has shown that I understated how thoroughly Trump used the presidency to fleece America and enrich himself and his family. Those revelations should prompt us to question how vulnerable our democracy is to a master con man like Trump, and to Trump wannabes with the education and management skills to succeed in destroying our liberties should they make it to the White House.

Back in 2015, I warned that should Donald Trump became president he would never leave office peacefully. Critics called that statement outrageous. But that's exactly what we saw after Trump decisively lost both the popular vote and the Electoral College in 2020. Trump and his cronies plotted a coup, ultimately laying deadly siege to the United States Capitol on January 6, 2021, a date that will live in infamy. To this day he plots a return to power, raking in more than $250 million from supporters who want him to rule America.

EPILOGUE

Even as he desperately searched for ways to overturn the will of the people and rule as a dictator, Trump and his family relentlessly pursued ways to monetize his presidency. In the chapter "Family First," I document how Trump's son-in-law Jared Kushner pursued financing Kushner family projects in ways that harmed American national security interests in the Middle East.

Within weeks of Trump flying off in Air Force One rather than attend Joe Biden's inauguration, Kushner and Steve Mnuchin, Trump's treasury secretary, each launched investment firms to manage Persian Gulf money. In the ten years before Donald Trump became president, U.S. treasury secretaries made eight trips to the Middle East. Mnuchin made 18 trips in just four years. Mnuchin, a ruthless Wall Street banker of the kind Trump vowed to drive from "the swamp" in Washington, raked in $1 billion from the Middle East for his Liberty Strategic Capital fund.

Kushner spent long hours on the phone with the de facto Saudi ruler, the murderous Mohammed bin Salman, also known as MBS, who reportedly told an Emirati royal and others that he had Kushner "in his pocket." After Kushner left office, his Affinity Partners fund pocketed $2 billion in sovereign wealth from Saudi Arabia, even though a host of financial advisers warned MBS that Kushner's firm was woefully inexperienced, charged outrageous fees, and was "unsatisfactory in all aspects," the *New York Times* reported in April 2022.

That MBS sent Kushner the money anyway only reinforced the observation of law professor Richard Painter, the ethics chief for President George W. Bush, that Kushner, Ivanka Trump, and her two grown brothers "appear to people all over the world to be [Trump's] bagmen."

The Trumpian level of corruption would astound the Framers of our Constitution, who were in a snit after King Louis XVI gave Benjamin Franklin, our ambassador to the French court at Versailles, a bejeweled snuff box. We have become so accustomed to individual venality that it's hard to grasp when the venality is institutionalized, especially in the White House.

Since leaving office, Trump has benefited mightily from cowardice and perfidy among Democrats holding the power to prosecute crimes. A Manhattan grand jury, guided by two veteran prosecutors with deep knowledge of racketeering and fraud laws, built what they said was a solid case against Trump, only to be shut down by Alvin Bragg, the new district attorney in 2022. New York governor Kathy Hochul possesses unfettered authority to transfer that criminal case to state attorney general Letitia James, but she has refused. James, who ran for office promising to pursue Trump, has made no request to take charge of that criminal case even as she has sought publicity for her civil case against him.

The mystery of what happened to the $107 million raised for Trump's cheapskate 2017 inaugural was the focus of a lengthy investigation by Karl Racine, the District of Columbia attorney general. The fourth chapter in this book tells about the corrupt proposal to Stephanie Wolkoff to take donations off the books, which she refused, and how the Trumps then plotted to make her appear corrupt. Racine settled the case and Trump paid a fine, but the mystery of where the money went remains unsolved.

EPILOGUE

Trump may yet be brought to justice, but the spineless behavior of Bragg, Hochul, James, and Racine should never be forgotten.

Pardon my boasting, but my batting average on predictions about how Trump would behave in office holds steady at 1.000. I erred only in not realizing how cravenly Republican leaders like Mitch McConnell and Kevin McCarthy would bow to Trump, how cowardly federal judges would be when presented with evidence of corruption, and how feckless those four Democrats with prosecutorial power would be.

I do want to thank readers who found one error in this book, a typo. A payment to Wolkoff, most of it a pass-through she was ordered to send on to Trump cronies, was rendered as $21 million. Wolkoff said it was $25 million, adding that she didn't control or approve the pass-through.

Soon after the first of my many long interviews with Trump in 1988 I concluded that he would become a prominent force in American life. *Temples of Chance*, my 1992 casino exposé, documented his dishonesty and cited the prospect of his becoming president.

My hope is that Trump's legacy is not more corruption and hatred, but a realization by the American people of how much Trumpism threatens our precious liberties. Democratic self-governance requires the citizenry to be engaged so they elect only those whose conduct displays competence, dedication, respect for the law, and—most of all—integrity.

—David Cay Johnston
Rochester, New York
July 2022

Acknowledgments

More people than are mentioned below were instrumental in writing this book, which completes my Trump trilogy.

First, thanks to David Crook, my best friend and creator of *Wall Street Journal Sunday* before we cofounded DCReport.org in December 2016 along with my friend of four decades, Adam Leipzig, a longtime former Disney Studios executive and now publisher of *Cultural Daily*.

This book relied on the work of DCReport contributors Jillian S. Ambroz, Joe Maniscalco, Jordan Barab, Cheryl Collins, Alison Greene, Phil Mattera, Alicia Mundy, Sarah Okeson, Terry H. Schwadron, Erik Sherman, Grant Stern, Laura Vecsey, Dana Kennedy in France, Katya Gorchinskaya in Ukraine, and in Texas Kurt Eichenwald, my former colleague at the *New York Times*. Journalist Oleg Khomenok informed my understanding of Ukrainian and Russian affairs. I'm also grateful to John Byrne and Roxanne Cooper at *Raw Story*. Also Mary Trump and Carly Morgan.

ACKNOWLEDGMENTS

James S. Henry, who has waged a lonely fight across nearly five decades to expose corruption and illicit cash flows, helped explain the role Russian oligarchs played in Trump's activities. Mikhail Gershteyn, a Siberian-raised filmmaker and Rochester friend, translated documents.

Jeff Gottlieb, whose reporting won the *Los Angeles Times* a gold medal Pulitzer Prize for public service journalism; David McKay Wilson, who writes smart articles on local tax issues for Gannett's New York newspapers; and Alicia Mundy, an underappreciated veteran Washington investigative reporter, all provided memos that helped add context to anecdotes in these pages.

Writer Danelle Morton gave cheerful advice, and economist Dean Baker refreshed my memory on subtle economics issues.

My literary agent, Alice Fried Martell, a lawyer who has looked after me for three decades; my skilled editor on this and my previous book, Bob Bender; associate editor Johanna Li; copyeditor Judith Hoover; and Ben Wiseman, who designed the jacket; as well as Simon & Schuster's president Jonathan Karp and publisher Dana Canedy are all owed thanks.

Last but not least, my family, especially my youngest three daughters.

As with my previous seven books, I relied heavily on my daughter Amy Boyle Johnston, an artist with a master of fine arts degree. Amy possesses an amazing ability to ferret out significant but arcane details in obtuse materials. She also spotted connections I missed and kept my files in order, a daunting task.

Molly Leonard, a lawyer whom judges appoint to represent children in Canadian family court, and Kate Leonard, a lyricist whose

ACKNOWLEDGMENTS

first musicals are in production in New York City and Australia, copyedited parts of my fat-thumbs manuscript. My middle son, Andrew Drace, an Albuquerque truck driver, read and critiqued drafts of some chapters.

Most of all I appreciate the loving tolerance of my wonderful wife of nearly 40 years, Jennifer Leonard, the longtime chief executive of the Rochester Area Community Foundation. Jennifer not only raised our two daughters and helped raise my six older children, but she has been at my side during the 33 years I have covered Trump. For the past six years she endured my incessant observations about Trump and somehow still loves me.

—David Cay Johnston
Rochester, New York
July 2021

Notes

Introduction

2 *He had even cheated novice roulette players*: David [Cay] Johnston, "The Official Guide to Losing Roulette: A Casino Told It Wrong, and Regulators Allowed It," *Philadelphia Inquirer*, September 11, 1989, Page A1; David [Cay] Johnston, *Temples of Chance*, page 165 etc., Doubleday, 1992.

2 *Mayor Ed Koch . . . 15 days in jail*: Kirk Johnson, "Bulgari Pleads Guilty in a Sales-Tax Scheme," *New York Times*, December 6, 1986, https://www.nytimes.com/1986/12/06/world/bulgari-pleads-guilty-in-a-sales-tax-scheme.html.

2 *He'd even gotten away with forgery*: In The Matter of Donald Trump, New York City Tax Appeals Tribunal Determination TAT(H) 93-216(UB), October 11, 1996; David Cay Johnston, "New Evidence Donald Trump Didn't Pay Taxes," *Daily Beast*, June 15, 2016, https://www.thedailybeast.com/new-evidence-donald-trump-didnt-pay-taxes.

2 *fined $200,000*: Henry Stern, "Casino Fined $200,000 for Moving Black and Female Dealers for High Roller," Associated Press, June 5, 1991, https://apnews.com/article/e95c1d808471da3fe5e34ea201757da4.

3 *Ninety percent of American households*: Thomas Piketty and Emmanuel Saez, "Income Inequality in the United States 1913–2003," *Quarterly Journal of Economics* 118.1 (2003): 553–609, https://eml.berkeley.edu/~saez/pikettyqje.pdf; https://eml.berkeley.edu/~saez/ (scroll to phrase Tables and Figures Updated to 2018).

4 *payday lenders who charged*: Marquette National Bank v. First of Omaha

NOTES

Corp., U.S. Supreme Court, No. 77-1265, December 18, 1978, https://www .law.cornell.edu/supremecourt/text/439/299.

4 *Only three in ten jobs*: Wage Statistics for 2015, Social Security Administration, https://www.ssa.gov/cgi-bin/netcomp.cgi?year=2015.

4 *the acronym ALICE*: United for ALICE, United Way of Northern New Jersey, https://www.unitedforalice.org; David Cay Johnston, "Elites Fight Back against Mismeasures of Inequality," *Aljazeera America*, January 13, 2015, http://america.aljazeera.com/opinions/2015/1/child-poverty-alice unitedway.html.

5 *violent crime in the U.S. was on the wane*: Crime in the U.S. 2015, FBI, https://ucr.fbi.gov/crime-in-the-u.s/2015/crime-in-the-u.s.-2015/offenses -known-to-law-enforcement/violent-crime.

8 *Returned an extraordinary indictment*: "The People of the State of New York against The Trump Corporation, d/b/a the Trump Organization, Trump Payroll Corp., d/b/a The Trump Organization, Allen Weisselberg," Supreme Court of the State of New York, https://s3.documentcloud .org/documents/20982368/new-york-v-trump-org-allen-weisselberg.pdf.

9 *Eric Trump testified*: Steve "Aaron, et al, Plaintiffs, against The Trump Organization, Inc., a New York Corporation, and Donald J. Trump, an individual," videotaped deposition, February 9, 2011, US District Court for the Middle District of Florida, Tampa Division, Case No. 8:09-CV-2493, https://www.washingtonpost.com/wp-stat/graphics/politics/trump-ar chive/docs/depo-transcript-eric-trump-2-9-11.pdf.

10 *The eventual outcome*: Brian Ross Investigates, Law & Crime, August 25, 2020, https://www.youtube.com/watch?v=JLmQFvKLnlU.

10 *Trump issued a statement*: Karen Freifeld, Jonathan Stempel, and Jan Wolfe, "Trump Organization, CFO Are Charged in 'Sweeping' 15-year Tax Fraud," Reuters, July 1, 2021, https://www.reuters.com/article/us-usa -trump-new-york-idTRNIKCN2E73HH.

11 *belittled but did not challenge*: Caroline Vakil, "Trump Lawyer Claims Indictment Was Politically Motivated," The Hill, July 1, 2021, https://the hill.com/blogs/blog-briefing-room/news/561207-trump-lawyer-claims-in dictment-was-politically-motivated.

12 *In 2018, the* New York Times: David Barstow, Susanne, Craig, and Russ Buettner, "Trump Engaged in Suspect Tax Schemes as He Reaped Riches From His Father," *New York Times*, October 2, 2018, https:// www.nytimes.com/interactive/2018/10/02/us/politics/donald-trump-tax -schemes-fred-trump.html.

13 *immunity applied even if he committed murder*: David Cay Johnston, "Can Trump Really Get Away with Murder?," DCReport, December 17, 2019, https://www.dcreport.org/2019/12/17/supreme-court-to-decide-can -trump-really-get-away-with-murder/.

13 *Roberts wrote*: "Donald J. Trump, Petitioner v. Cyrus R. Vance, Jr., in His Official Capacity as District Attorney of the County of New York, et al.," Supreme Court of the United States, No. 19–635, July 9, 2020, https:// www.supremecourt.gov/opinions/19pdf/19-635_07jq.pdf.

1. Original Lie

16 *"I see a woman"*: Donald Trump Presidential Campaign Announcement Full Speech (C-SPAN), YouTube, June 16, 2015, https://www.youtube .com/watch?v=apjNfkysjbM; transcript, "Here's Donald Trump's Presidential Announcement Speech," *Time*, June 16, 2015, https://time .com/3923128/donald-trump-announcement-speech/.

17 *"he vowed to build a 'great wall'"*: Alexander Burns, "Donald Trump, Pushing Someone Rich, Offers Himself," *New York Times*, June 16, 2015, https://www.nytimes.com/2015/06/17/us/politics/donald-trump-runs-for -president-this-time-for-real-he-says.html.

18 *"We are looking to cast people"*: Aaron Couch and Emmet McDermott, "Donald Trump Campaign Offered Actors $50 to Cheer for Him at Presidential Announcement," *Hollywood Reporter*, June 17, 2015, https://www .hollywoodreporter.com/news/politics-news/donald-trump-campaign-of fered-actors-803161/.

18 *Corey Lewandowski*: Morgan Chalfant, "Email Suggests Trump Campaign Paid Actors $50 to Support the Donald at NYC Announcement," *Washington Examiner*, June 18, 2015, https://www.washingtonexaminer .com/red-alert-politics/email-suggests-trump-campaign-paid-actors-50 -support-donald-nyc-announcement.

18 *the American Democracy Legal Fund*: *American Legal Democracy Fund v. Donald J. Trump*, Federal Election Commission, Complaint MUR 6961, filed August 28, 2015, https://eqs.fec.gov/eqsdocsMUR/17044405282.pdf.

18 *Seven months after the announcement*: First General Counsel's Report, Federal; Election Commission, https://eqs.fec.gov/eqsdocsMUR/17044405316 .pdf.

19 *falsely told vendors*: Janet Babin, "Is Donald Trump Savings NYC Millions or Making Millions Off Taxpayers?," WNYC, https://www.wnyc.org

/story/donald-trump-saving-nyc-millions-or-making-millions-taxpayers/;
Libby Handros, "Trump, What's The Deal?," https://www.youtube.com
/watch?v=wYU2FJxsSeE.

20 *Trump put a number on it*: $8,737,540,000: Erin Carlyle, "Trump Exaggerating His Net Worth (by 100%) in Presidential Bid," *Forbes*, June 16, 2015, https://www.forbes.com/sites/erincarlyle/2015/06/16/trump-exaggerating -his-net-worth-by-100-in-presidential-bid.

20 *greater than $10 billion*: Katie Little, "Donald Trump: I'm Worth More Than $10 Billion," CNBC, July 17, 2015, https://www.cnbc.com/2015/07/15 /donald-trump-im-worth-more-than-10-billion.html.

21 *throwing little rocks at a baby*: Paul Schwartzman and Michael E, Miller, "Confident. Incorrigible. Bully: Little Donny Was a Lot Like Candidate Donald Trump," *Washington Post*, June 22, 2016, https://www.washington post.com/lifestyle/style/young-donald-trump-military-school/2016/06/22 /f0b3b164-317c-11e6-8758-d58e76e11b12_story.html.

23 *Trump was similarly threatening*: Andrea Bernstein, "Trump Pushed for a Sweetheart Tax Deal on His First Hotel. It's Cost New York City $410,068,399 and Counting," *Trump Inc.* podcast of ProPublica and WNYC, January 22, 2020, https://www.propublica.org/article/trump -pushed-for-a-sweetheart-tax-deal-on-his-first-hotel-its-cost-new-york -city-410-068-399-and-counting#175609.

2. Jobs Mirage

25 *Trump spoke at the New York Economic Club*: Tessa Berenson, "Read Donald Trump's Speech on Jobs and the Economy," *Time*, September 15, 2017, https://time.com/4495507/donald-trump-economy-speech-transcript/.

26 *net worth of the typical middle-income family*: Federal Reserve Survey of Consumer Finances, "Changes in U.S. Family Finances from 2016 to 2019," Table 2, https://www.federalreserve.gov/publications/files/scf20. pdf; Federal Reserve Survey of Consumer Finances, "Changes in Family Finances 1983 and 1989," Table 2, https://www.federalreserve.gov/econres /files/bull0192.pdf. Inflation adjustments by author from https://data.bls .gov/cgi-bin/cpicalc.pl.

26 *Trump promised economic growth*: Heather Haddon, "Donald Trump Says Tax Plan Could Lift GDP Growth to 6%," *Wall Street Journal*, September 28, 2015, https://www.wsj.com/articles/BL-WB-58216; Scott Horsley, "Trump Confident He Can Speed Economic Growth

to Rate Not Seen in Years," NPR, September 15, 2016, https://www.npr
.org/2016/09/15/494112503/trump-sets-audacious-goal-of-4-percent-eco
nomic-growth.

27 *Ladies and gentlemen, this is Masa of SoftBank*": Jordan Weismann, "A
Japanese Billionaire Just Showed How Corporations Are Going to Manipulate Trump," *Slate*, December 7, 2016, https://slate.com/business/2016/12
/softbanks-ceo-shows-how-corporations-can-manipulate-trump.html.

27 *Son's most lucrative investment*: Una Galani, "Valuing SoftBank in Alibaba's Aftermath," *New York Times*, September 22, 2014, https://dealbook
.nytimes.com/2014/09/22/valuing-softbank-in-alibabas-aftermath/.

28 *"Masa said he never would have done this"*: Donald Trump Twitter archive,
https://www.thetrumparchive.com/?searchbox=%22Masa+said%22.

28 *"Saudi Arabia, I get along with all of them"*: "Presidential Candidate Donald
Trump Rally in Mobile, Alabama," C-SPAN, August 21, 2015, https://
www.c-span.org/video/?327751-1/donald-trump-campaign-rally-mo
bile-alabama&start=856.

29 *Just as Trump claimed credit*: Glenn Kessler, "Did Ivanka Trump Create
'millions' of Jobs?," *Washington Post*, February 17, 2019, https://www.wash
ingtonpost.com/politics/2019/02/27/did-ivanka-trump-create-millions-jobs/.

29 *Trump soon elaborated*: Jason LeMiere, "Donald Trump Claims Ivanka
Has 'Created Millions of Jobs,' but Doesn't Explain How," *Newsweek*,
February 25, 2019, https://www.newsweek.com/ivanka-trump-donald
-jobs-daughter-1343101.

29 *declaring that Ivanka had "created 14 million jobs"*: Luke O'Neil, "Trump
Claims Ivanka Created 14m Jobs: The Entire Economy Only Added
6m," *Guardian*, November 13, 2019, https://www.theguardian.com
/us-news/2019/nov/13/trump-claims-ivanka-created-14m-jobs-the-entire
-economy-only-added-6m; Aaron Rupar, "Trump Just Claimed Ivanka
Created 14 Million Jobs: The Entire Economy Added 6 Million," *Vox*,
December 12, 2019, https://www.vox.com/2019/11/12/20961764/trump
-ivanka-created-14-million-jobs-whopper; Ian Millhiser, "Trump Claims
That His Daughter Created 10 Percent of All the Jobs in the United
States," *Vox*, April 8, 2020, https://www.vox.com/2020/4/8/21212802
/trump-ivanka-10-percent-jobs-walmart-15-million.

30 *ProPublica put the number at 797*: Daniela Porat, Lena Groeger, and Isaac
Arnsdorf, "What Happened to All the Jobs Trump Promised?," Pro-
Publica, updated May 7, 2019, https://projects.propublica.org/graphics
/trump-job-promises.

30 *Softbank really did follow through*: Biz Carson and Angel Au-Yeung, "SoftBank's Masayoshi Son Promised Trump He'd Invest $50 Billion and Create 50,000 U.S. Jobs: Did He Deliver?," *Forbes*, December 10, 2018, https://www.forbes.com/sites/bizcarson/2019/12/10/softbank-masay oshi-son-job-promise-president-donald-trump-progres/?sh=3d0a7 80028fc.

31 *but the Obama administration's antitrust experts had prevented*: Michael J. de la Merced, "Sprint and SoftBank End Their Pursuit of a T-Mobile Merger," *New York Times*, August 5, 2014, https://dealbook.nytimes .com/2014/08/05/sprint-and-softbank-said-to-abandon-bid-for-t-mo bile-us/.

31 *Son got approval to sell Sprint*: "Justice Department Settles with T-Mobile and Sprint in Their Proposed Merger by Requiring a Package of Divestitures to Dish," U.S. Department of Justice, July 26, 2019, https://www .justice.gov/opa/pr/justice-department-settles-t-mobile-and-sprint-their -proposed-merger-requiring-package.

3. Charity Doghouse

33 *"Donald was not a dog fan"*: Ivana Trump, *Raising Trump* (New York: Gallery Books, 2017), https://www.amazon.com/Raising-Trump-Ivana /dp/1501177281.

35 *"Mr. Trump had a cow"*: Dan Alexander, "How Donald Trump Shifted Kids-Cancer Charity Money Into His Business," *Forbes*, June 28, 2017, https://www.forbes.com/sites/danalexander/2017/06/06/how -donald-trump-shifted-kids-cancer-charity-money-into-his-business /?sh=3b2ac83e6b4a.

37 *"While people can disagree on political issues"*: Meghan Keneally, "Eric Trump's Charity Isn't the First in the Family to Come under Scrutiny," ABC News, June 7, 2017, https://abcnews.go.com/US/eric-trumps-charity -family-scrutiny/story?id=47887162.

38 *Michael Cohen testified*: Sam Wolfson, "Trump Used His Charity's Money to Pay for Portrait of Himself, Cohen Says," *Guardian*, February 27, 2019, https://www.theguardian.com/us-news/2019/feb/27/michael-cohen-testi mony-trump-painting-foundation-money; Kevin Stack and Steve Eder, "New Records Shed Light on Donald Trump's $25,000 Gift to Florida Official," *New York Times*, September 14, 2016, https://www.nytimes .com/2016/09/15/us/politics/pam-bondi-donald-trump-foundation.html.

NOTES

39 *alleging that Trump University was a scam*: Statement by A.G. Schneiderman On $25 Million Settlement Agreement Reached in Trump University Case, https://ag.ny.gov/press-release/2016/statement-ag-schneiderman-25 -million-settlement-agreement-reached-trump.

40 *Billy Graham received $100,000*: Jane C. Timm, "Trump's Foundation Wrote Many Checks On Path to Nomination," NBC News, October 5, 2016, https://www.nbcnews.com/politics/2016-election/trump-s-founda tion-wrote-many-checks-path-nomination-n659811.

40 *foundation paid $264,631*: David A. Fahrenthold, "Trump Boasts About His Philanthropy. But His Giving Falls Short of His Words," *Washington Post*, October 29, 2016, https://www.washingtonpost.com/politics /trump-boasts-of-his-philanthropy-but-his-giving-falls-short-of-his -words/2016/10/29/b3c03106-9ac7-11e6-aoed-abo774c1eaa5_story.html.

41 *"bizarre, this laundry list"*: David A. Fahrenthold, "Trump Directed $2.3 Million Owed to Him to His Tax-Exempt Foundation Instead," *Washington Post*, September 26, 2016, https://www.washingtonpost .com/politics/trump-directed-23-million-owed-to-him-to-his-charity -instead/2016/09/26/7a9e9fac-8352-11e6-ac72-a29979381495_story.html.

41 *"notice of violation"*: New York Attorney General's Office Issues Notice of Violation Directing Trump Foundation to Cease and Desist New York Solicitations, October 3, 2016, https://ag.ny.gov/press-release/2016 /new-york-attorney-generals-office-issues-notice-violation-directing -trump.

41 *The check mark was an admission of self-dealing*: Donald J. Trump Foundation Return of Private Foundation Calendar Year 2015, https://s3.document cloud.org/documents/3224099/Trump-Foundation-2015-tax-filing.pdf.

42 *Underwood got the president*: Shane Goldmacher, "Trump Foundation Will Dissolve, Accused of 'Shocking Pattern of Illegality,'" *New York Times*, December 18, 2018, https://www.nytimes.com/2018/12/18/nyregion /ny-ag-underwood-trump-foundation.html; A.G. Underwood Announces Stipulation Dissolving Trump Foundation under Judicial Supervision, With AG Review of Recipient Charities, Office of the [New York State] Attorney General, https://ag.ny.gov/press-release/2018/ag-underwood-an nounces-stipulation-dissolving-trump-foundation-under-judicial.

42 *"Trump breached his fiduciary duty"*: *People ex rel. James v. Trump*, Supreme Court, New York County, New York, 66 Misc. 3d 200 (N.Y. Sup. Ct. 2019) 112 N.Y.S.3d 467, https://casetext.com/case/people-ex-rel-james-v-trump.

43 *A party permit*: S. V. Date, "Dog Rescue Charity Linked to Lara Trump

245

NOTES

Funneling Money into Donald Trump's Pocket," *Huffington Post*, December 3, 2021, https://www.huffingtonpost.co.uk/entry/lara-trump-mar-a-lago-dog-rescue-charity_n_604becaac5b636ed337a6886?ri18n=true.

4. Off the Books

This chapter draws on extensive author interviews with Stephanie Winston Wolkoff.

46 *Gates had once worked*: Eric Tucker, "Ex-Trump Campaign Official Rick Gates Gets 45 Days in Jail," Associated Press, Dec. 17, 2019, https://apnews.com/article/politics-russia-trump-investigations-amy-berman-jackson-robert-mueller-f12c47c41699f46e5412f4a50224cba3.
46 *Gates would plead guilty*: *United States v. Richard W. Gates III*, Rick Gates Plea Documents, U.S. District Court for the District of Columbia, Crim. No. 17-201-2, https://www.documentcloud.org/documents/4386658-Rick-Gates-Plea-Documents.html.
47 *Among the guests at the Candlelight Dinner . . . Maria Butina*: "Trump's Inauguration: The Money behind the Most Expensive U.S. Presidential Debut," Episode 5, "Inauguration, Inc.," *New York Times*, June 26, 2019, video, at 9:21, https://www.nytimes.com/2019/06/26/the-weekly/trump-inauguration-expensive.html. Also on Butina attending the inaugural, see Craig Timberg, Rosalind S. Helderman, Andrew Roth, and Carol D. Leonnig, "In the Crowd at Trump's Inauguration, Members of Russia's Elite Anticipated a Thaw between Moscow and Washington," *Washington Post*, January 20, 2017, https://www.washingtonpost.com/politics/amid-trumps-inaugural-festivities-members-of-russias-elite-anticipated-a-thaw-between-moscow-and-washington/2018/01/20/0d767f46-fb9f-11e7-ad8c-ecbb62019393_story.html.
47 *Butina later confessed*: *United States of America v. Mariia Butina*, also known as Maria Butina, U.S. District Court for the District of Columbia, Criminal Case 18-218, guilty plea filed December 13, 2018, https://assets.documentcloud.org/documents/5626661/Maria-Butina-pleaded-guilty-to-conspiring-to-act.pdf.
47 *Viktor Vekselberg heads the Renova Group*: Shuki Sadeh and Refaella Goichman, "How Putin's Blacklisted Oligarch Friend Is Linked to Key Israeli Political Players," *Haaretz*, January 3, 2019, https://www.haaretz.com/israel-news/.premium-how-putin-s-blacklisted-oligarch-friend-is-linked

246

NOTES

-to-key-israeli-political-players-1.6803271; "Trump's Inauguration: The Money behind the Most Expensive U.S. Presidential Debut," Episode 5, "Inauguration, Inc.," at 8:58.

47 *the government has long suspected that Columbus Nova is a front*: US VC PARTNERS GP LLC et al. v. United States Department of the Treasury, Office of Foreign Assets Control et al., U.S. District Court for the Southern District of New York, 19 Civ. 6139, https://www.courthousenews.com /wp-content/uploads/2019/07/IntraterTreasury-COMPLAINT.pdf.

47 *Also attending was Alexander Mashkevitch*: Memorandum from Tom Adams and Dennis Aftergut to Representative Jackie Speier.

48 *the Kremlin has sought to develop Trump as an asset*: Luke Harding, "The Hidden History of Trump's First Trip to Moscow," (excerpted from his book *Collusion: Secret Meetings, Dirty Money, and How Russia Helped Donald Trump Win*), *Politico*, November 19, 2017, https://www.politico.com/maga zine/story/2017/11/19/trump-first-moscow-trip-215842/; Craig Unger, "When a Young Trump Went to Russia," *New Republic*, August 15, 2018, https:// newrepublic.com/article/150646/young-trump-went-russia, which includes a 1987 photograph of Trump and Ivana in St. Petersburg (Leningrad).

48 *The presence of these and other Russians*: Matthew Mosk and John Santucci, "Special Counsel Eyeing Russians Granted Unusual Access to Trump Inauguration Parties," ABC News, June 28, 2018, https://abcnews.go.com /Politics/special-counsel-eyeing-russians-granted-unusual-access-trump /story?id=56232847.

For a good summary of some of the many Russian connections, see Memorandum from Tom Adams and Dennis Aftergut to Representative Jackie Speier, September 19, 2018, https://speier.house.gov /_cache/files/d/c/dcf255c2-9171-4f10-958e-bcba1d41cfd1/0794257E962ED3AB 15F47FEECFC3F99C.2019-01-08-russian-glossary-updated.pdf.

48 *Trump held an unannounced meeting in the Oval Office*: Julie Vitkovskaya and Amanda Erickson, "The Strange Oval Office Meeting between Trump, Lavrov and Kislyak," *Washington Post*, May 10, 2017, https://www.wash ingtonpost.com/news/worldviews/wp/2017/05/10/the-strange-oval-office -meeting-between-trump-lavrov-and-kislyak/.

49 *Whether Russian money made its way to the inaugural committee*: Andrew Prokop, "Why Trump's Inauguration Money Is a Major Part of Mueller's Russia Investigation," *Vox*, updated August 14, 2018, https://www.vox .com/2018/7/5/17505728/trump-inauguration-mueller-russians-rick-gates; Mathew S. Schwartz, "Trump Inaugural Committee Hit with Subpoena,"

247

NPR, February 5, 2019, https://www.npr.org/2019/02/05/691522377 /trump-inaugural-committee-hit-with-subpoena.

49 *Many Russians of dubious character also bought Trump apartments*: Nathan Layne, Ned Parker, Svetlana Reiter, Stephen Grey, and Ryan McNeill, "Russian Elite Invested Nearly $100 Million in Trump Buildings, Reuters, March 17, 2017, https://www.reuters.com/investigates/special-report /usa-trump-property/; Craig Unger, "Trump's Russian Laundromat," *New Republic*, July 13, 2017, https://newrepublic.com/article/143586/trumps-rus sian-laundromat-trump-tower-luxury-high-rises-dirty-money-interna tional-crime-syndicate; Charles P. Pierce, "Trump Tower Was an Entire Ecosystem of Criminal Sketchballs in the '80s and '90s," *Esquire*, November 2, 2020, https://www.esquire.com/news-politics/politics/a34552314 /trump-tower-mobsters-criminals-80s/ (citing reporting by the late Wayne Barrett).

49 *Dmitry Rybolovlev, yet another Russian oligarch, rescued Trump*: Alexandra Clough, "Trump in Palm Beach: Did Russian Mansion Buyer Make Money?," *Palm Beach Daily News*, February 17, 2019, https://www.palm beachdailynews.com/news/20190217/trump-in-palm-beach-did-russian -mansion-buyer-make-money (detailing Rybolovlev's losses).

49 *Trump's inaugural committee, which reported raising a record $106,751,308*: 58th Presidential Inaugural Committee 2016 Form 990 tax return, https://apps .irs.gov/pub/epostcard/cor/814463688_201710_990O_2018041215256354.pdf.

49 *more than double the $53 million raised for Obama's first inauguration*: Presidential Inaugural Committee 2009 Form 990 tax return, https://cam paignlegal.org/sites/default/files/Obama%20Inaugural%20Committee _2008%20990.pdf.

51 *Somebody seems to have falsified some ticket purchase records*: Lee Fang, "Trump Inaugural Committee Falsely Lists Big Donation from 'Hidden Figures' Hero," *Intercept*, April 20, 2017, https://theintercept.com/2017/04/20/don ald-trumps-inauguration/.

52 *Wolkoff was paid $26 million*: Maggie Haberman and Kenneth P. Vogel, "Trump's Inaugural Committee Paid $26 Million to Firm of First Lady's Adviser," *New York Times*, February 15, 2018, https://www.nytimes .com/2018/02/15/us/politics/trumps-inaugural-committee-paid-26-mil lion-to-first-ladys-friend.html.

52 *$25 million of the $26 million*: Wolkoff, interview by author.

53 *The inaugural committee didn't pay to archive*: The Trump inaugural committee link redirects to https://24cashtoday.com.

NOTES

53 *Barrack issued a statement*: Jonathan O'Connell, "D.C. Attorney General Sues Trump Inaugural Committee over $1 Million Booking at President's Hotel," *Washington Post*, January 22, 2020, https://www.washingtonpost.com/business/economy/dc-attorney-general-sues-trump-inaugural-committee-over-1-million-booking-at-presidents-hotel/2020/01/22/aa4ffab6-3c90-11ea-b9od-5652806c3b3a_story.html.

54 *Jacquelin M. Kasulis*: "Former Advisor to Presidential Candidate Among Three Defendants Charged with Acting as Agents of a Foreign Government." Justice Department, July 20, 2021, https://www.justice.gov/opa/pr/former-advisor-presidential-candidate-among-three-defendants-charged-acting-agents-foreign.

5. Collecting Tribute

Zach Everson remarks are from author interviews and his 1100 Pennsylvania Avenue newsletter.

56 *What struck Everson . . . was where The Beast stopped*: PBS, "President Donald Trump Walks Parade Route on Inauguration Day 2017," YouTube, January 20, 2017, https://www.youtube.com/watch?v=gmQew6CSrU8.

56 *Senator Leland Stanford of California, a robber baron*: "Leland Stanford: American Politician and Industrialist," *Encyclopedia Britannica*, updated April 20, 2021, https://www.britannica.com/biography/Leland-Stanford.

56 *Under a contract with the federal government*: Courtney Bublé, "Trump's D.C. Hotel under Renewed Scrutiny," *Government Executive*, January 14, 2021, https://www.govexec.com/oversight/2021/01/trumps-dc-hotel-under-renewed-scrutiny/171418/.

58 *The Al Sabah family*: Alex Altman, "Donald Trump's Suite of Power," *Time*, undated, https://time.com/donald-trumps-suite-of-power/.

59 *money was pouring into*: Jonthan O'Connell, "Trump D.C. Hotel Turns $2 Million Profit in Four Months," August 10, 2017, *Washington Post*, https://www.washingtonpost.com/politics/trump-dc-hotel-turns-2-million-profit-in-four-months/2017/08/10/23bd97f0-7e02-11e7-9d08-b79f191668ed_story.html.

60 *Everson also observed John Legere*: David Shepardson, "T-Mobile Spent $195,000 at Trump Hotel in D.C. Since Merger Announcement," Reuters, March 5, 2019, https://www.reuters.com/article/us-sprint

-corp-m-a-trump/t-mobile-spent-195000-at-trump-hotel-in-d-c-since -merger-announcement-idUSKCN1QM1ZY.

61 *Adams felt paying tribute*: Zach Everson, "President's D.C. Hotel Has Received More Than 10 Percent of the Spending from the GOP Candidate for Kentucky Secretary of State's Campaign," 1100 Pennsylvania, November 4, 2019, https://www.1100pennsylvania.com/p/pence-and-mc connell-headlined-trump.

6. Don't Ask, Don't Know

64 *looking at space to rent*: Helene Cooper, "Why the Defense Dept. Is Looking to Lease Space in Trump Tower," *New York Times*, February 8, 2017, https://www.nytimes.com/2017/02/08/us/politics/trump-tower-de fense-department.html.

64 *found an owner*: Mark Hosenball and Phil Stewart, "Pentagon to Lease Privately Owned Trump Tower Apartment for Nuclear 'Football': Letter," Reuters, May 5, 2017, https://www.reuters.com/article /us-usa-pentagon-trumptower/pentagon-to-lease-privately-owned-trump -tower-apartment-for-nuclear-football-letter-idUSKBN1812B5.

64 *The apartment cost was $130,000*: Paul Sonne, "U.S. Military's Space in Trump Tower Costs $130,000 a Month," *Wall Street Journal*, July 19, 2017, https:// www.wsj.com/articles/u-s-militarys-space-in-trump-tower-costs-130 -000-a-month-1500428508.

65 *The 1808 law states that "no member"*: Statutes at Large, https://www.loc .gov/law/help/statutes-at-large/10th-congress/session-1/c10s1ch48.pdf.

66 *Trump's Old Post Office lease*: Evaluation of GSA's Management and Administration of the Old Post Office Building Lease," General Services Administration, Office of Inspector General, January 16, 2019, https:// www.oversight.gov/report/gsa/evaluation-gsas-management-and-ad ministration-old-post-office-building-lease; Electronic Reading Room, Freedom of Infoormation Act, General Services Administration (scroll down to "Old Post Office—Ground Lease" where it is in several parts), https://www.gsa.gov/reference/freedom-of-information-act-foia/elec tronic-reading-room.

67 *the notorious Roy Cohn*: Marie Brenner, "How Donald Trump and Roy Cohn's Ruthless Symbiosis Changed America," *Vanity Fair*, June 28, 2017, https://www.vanityfair.com/news/2017/06/donald-trump-roy-cohn-rela tionship.

NOTES

68 *Alexander Hamilton wrote in* Federalist 73: *President Reagan's Ability to Receive Retirement Benefits from the State of California,* 5 U.S. Op. O.L.C. 187, 188, 1981 WL 30896 (June 23, 1981) (quoting The Federalist No. 73).

68 *The leasing agency . . . let Trump keep his D.C. hotel:* Kevin Terry, Letter to Trump Old Post Office LLC from General Services Administration Public Buildings Service, March 23, 2017, https://www.gsa.gov/portal /getMediaData?mediaId=157798.

68 *a richly detailed report completed in 2019:* "Evaluation of GSA's Management and Administration of the Old Post Office Building Lease," General Services Administration, Office of Inspector General, January 16, 2019, https://www.oversight.gov/report/gsa/evaluation-gsas-manage ment-and-administration-old-post-office-building-lease.

7. Conflicts of Interest

73 *before Jimmy Carter assumed office:* "Texts of Carter Statement on Conflicts of Interest and Ethics; Appointees' Guidelines," *New York Times,* January 5, 1977, https://www.nytimes.com/1977/01/05/archives/texts-of -carter-statement-on-conflicts-of-interest-and-ethics.html.

73 *discovered that he and Rosalynn were more than $1 million in debt:* Kevin Sullivan and Mary Jordan, "The Un-celebrity President," *Washington Post,* August 17, 2018, https://www.washingtonpost.com/news /national/wp/2018/08/17/feature/the-un-celebrity-president-jimmy-carter -shuns-riches-lives-modestly-in-his-georgia-hometown/?utm_term =.9b4d1a640fbc.

73 *telling Fox News, "You know, under the law":* Ken Thomas, "Trump Says Executives Will Run Business Empire with His Children," *PBS News Hour,* December 11, 2016, https://www.pbs.org/newshour/politics/trump -says-executives-will-run-business-empire-children; Amanda Sakuma, *"New York Times* Live Tweets Closed-Door Meeting with Donald Trump," NBC News, November 22, 2016, https://www.nbcnews.com /politics/2016-election/new-york-times-live-tweets-closed-door-meet ing-donald-trump-n687316; Andy Sullivan, Emily Stephenson, and Steve Holland, "Trump Says Won't Divest from His Business While President," Reuters, January 11, 2017, https://www.reuters.com/article /us-usa-trump-finance/trump-says-wont-divest-from-his-business-while -president-idUSKBN14V21I.

75 *"You people with this phony Emoluments Clause":* Annie Karni, "Trump

NOTES

Dismisses 'Phony Emoluments Clause,' Defending Doral," *New York Times*, October 21, 2019, https://www.nytimes.com/2019/10/21/us/politics /trump-doral-emoluments-clause.html.

76 *Cap Cana was a massive resort project*: Jeff Horwitz, "Dominican Deal Tests Trump Pledge of No New Foreign Projects," Associated Press, February 9, 2017, https://apnews.com/article/90c95dfef76244e49dcce68296obcdob.

77 *court records show he had been paid $12 million*: Manuela Andreoni, "A Failed Project Where Everyone Lost, Except Trump," Univision, February 26, 2018, https://www.univision.com/univision-news/latin-america/trump -at-cap-cana-a-failed-project-where-everyone-lost-except-trump.

77 *The Hazourys issued a press release*: Jeff Horowitz, "Dominican Resort Deal Tests Trump's Pledge of No New Foreign Projects," Associated Press, February 10, 2017, https://www.vnews.com/Dominican-deal-tests-Trump -pledge-of-no-new-foreign-projects-8013636.

78 *Global Witness, a nonprofit*: "A Foreign Affair: Trump's Dominican Republic Deal," Global Witness, December 2018, https://www.global-witness.org/en/campaigns/corruption-and-money-laundering/a-foreign -affair-trumps-dominican-republic-deal/.

79 *Five Trump-branded projects*: Anjali Kamat, "Political Corruption and the Art of the Deal," *New Republic*, March 21, 2018, https://newrepublic .com/article/147351/political-corruption-art-deal.

79 *Trump-branded projects in . . . Panama*: Aggelos Petropoulos and Richard Engel, "A Panama Tower Carries Trump's Name and Ties to Organized Crime," NBC News, November 17, 2017, https://www.nbcnews.com /news/investigations/panama-tower-carries-trump-s-name-ties-organized -crime-n821706.

79 *which Trump often denounced*: Jeanna Smialek, "Trump Tried to Kill Anti-Bribery Rule He Deemed 'Unfair,' New Book Alleges," *New York Times*, January 15, 2020, https://www.nytimes.com/2020/01/15/business /economy/trump-bribery-law.html.

80 *Modi personally invited Ivanka Trump*: "Ivanka Trump to Attend India-US Entrepreneur Summit, PM Modi Tweets," *Times of India*, August 11, 2017, https://timesofindia.indiatimes.com/india/ivanka-trump-to-attend-india -us-entrepreneur-summit-pm-modi-tweets/articleshow/60010143.cms.

80 *he would give a policy speech on Indo-Pacific relations*: Vindu Goel and Maria Abi-Habib, "Donald Trump Jr. Retreats from Foreign Policy on India Trip," *New York Times*, February 23, 2018, https://www.nytimes .com/2018/02/23/world/asia/donald-trump-jr-india-modi.html.

NOTES

81 *he was paying a property specialist lawyer*: Jack Flemming, "Donald Trump's Beverly Hills home quietly sells for $13.5 million," *Los Angeles Times*, June 12, 2019, https://www.latimes.com/business/realestate/hot-property /la-fi-hotprop-trump-organization-beverly-hills-20190612-story.html.

81 *Trump sold the property for $13.5 million*: Jonathan O'Connell, Alice Crites, and David A. Fahrenthold, "Trump's Company Sells California Mansion to Firm Linked to Indonesian Billionaire, a Business Partner," *Washington Post*, June 13, 2019, https://www.washingtonpost.com /politics/trumps-company-sells-california-mansion-to-firm-linked-to -indonesian-billionaire-a-business-partner/2019/06/13/5d73206a-8de5 -11e9-adf3-f70f78c156e8_story.html.

81 *the real estate website Property Shark*: Robert Demeter, "How Much Did Home Prices Increase in LA County since the Downturn?" Property Shark, June 11, 2018, https://www.propertyshark.com/Real-Estate-Re ports/2018/06/11/how-much-did-prices-increase-in-la-county-since-the -downturn.

83 *Don Jr. flew to Jakarta*: Patsy Widakuswara, "Conflict of Interest Allegations Dog Trump Jr. on Indonesia Trip," VOA News, August 13, 2019, https:// www.voanews.com/usa/conflict-interest-allegations-dog-trump-jr-indo nesia-trip.

84 *Trump met with the Indonesian coordinating minister*: Jason Hoffman, "Trump Held Unannounced Meeting with Indonesian Minister in Oval Office," CNN, November 19, 2020, https://www.cnn.com/2020/11/19 /politics/trump-indonesia-luhut-binsar-pandjaitan-intl-hnk/index.html.

84 *What made the meeting noteworthy*: Patsy Widakuswara, "White House Mum on Trump Meeting with Indonesian Minister," Voice of America, November 18, 2020, https://www.voanews.com/east-asia-pacific /white-house-mum-trump-meeting-indonesian-minister.

8. Tax Scam

86 *Adam Smith, the philosopher and economist*: Adam Smith, *The Theory of Moral Sentiments*, chapter 3, http://knarf.english.upenn.edu/Smith /tms133.html.

86 *Trump said, "We are going to be discussing something so important"*: C-SPAN, September 28, 2015, https://www.c-span.org/video/?328396-1/donald -trump-news-conference-tax-policy.

87 *90 million of the 150 million—and related figures*: U.S. Internal Revenue

Service, Statistics of Income—2014 Individual Income Tax Returns Complete Report (Publication 1304).

87 *about 15 million people*: U.S. Bureau of Labor Statistics, "Labor Force Statistics from the Current Population Survey," https://data.bls.gov/timeseries /LNS11000000; U.S. Bureau of Labor Statistics, "Unemployment rate 5.0 percent in March 2016, U-6 at 9.8 percent," *TED: The Economics Daily*, April 5, 2016, https://www.bls.gov/opub/ted/2016/unemployment-rate-5-0 -percent-in-march-2016-u-6-at-9-8-percent.htm?view_full; U-6 measures unemployed, underemployed and workers discouraged from seeking jobs.

88 *"I have joined the political arena"*: "Trump: I Alone Can Fix the System," CNBC, July 21, 2016, https://www.cnbc.com/video/2016/07/21/trump-i -alone-can-fix-the-system.html.

89 *Lily Batchelder*: Lily L. Batchelder, "Opportunities and Risks in Individual Tax Reform," testimony before Senate Finance Committee, September 13, 2017, https://www.finance.senate.gov/imo/media/doc/Batchelder%20Tes timony.pdf.

90 *The Tax Policy Center's Howard Gleckman*: Howard Gleckman, "TaxVox: Campaigns, Proposals, and Reforms," Tax Policy Center, November 15, 2016, https://www.taxpolicycenter.org/taxvox/dont-confuse-trumps-tax -cuts-tax-reform.

90 *George Stephanopoulos pressed him*: *This Week*, ABC News, October 4, 2015, https://abcnews.go.com/Politics/week-transcript-donald-trump /story?id=34187405.

90 *do for $2,000 projects*: Road to the White House 2016: Presidential Candidate Donald Trump News Conference on Tax Policy, C-SPAN, September 28, 2015, (video starting at 15:48), https://www.c-span.org /video/?328396-1/donald-trump-news-conference-tax-policy.

91 *He told a rally in Scranton*: Rachel Martin, "Who Benefits from Donald Trump's Tax Plan?" NPR, November 13, 2016, https://www.npr.org/tran scripts/501739277.

91 *Trump went before the Economic Club of New York*: Donald Trump, Economic Club of New York, September 15, 2016, https://www.econclubny .org/documents/10184/109144/2016TrumpTranscript.pdf.

94 *Americans who made $40,000 to $50,000*: "T20-0010: Baseline Distribution of Income and Federal Taxes, All Tax Units, by Expanded Cash Income Level, 2017," Tax Policy Center, December 24, 2019, https://www.taxpolicy center.org/model-estimates/baseline-distribution-income-and-federal -taxes-feburary-2020/t20-0010-baseline.

NOTES

94 *In 2018 the Trump tax law*: Tax Policy Center, https://www.taxpolicycenter
.org/model-estimates/baseline-distribution-income-and-federal-taxes
-feburary-2020/t20-0012-baseline.

95 *"The richest 1 percent received a $278,540 lifetime tax cut"*: Laurence Kot-
likoff, "Did the Rich Get All of Trump's Tax Cuts?," *Forbes*, July 23, 2019,
https://www.forbes.com/sites/kotlikoff/2019/07/23/did-the-rich-get-all
-of-trumps-tax-cuts/?sh=7c080784f209.

96 *But in 2019 the pretense ended*: Tim O'Donnell, *The Week*, July 23, 2019,
https://theweek.com/speedreads/854487/trump-have-article-2-where
-have-right-whatever-want-president.

97 *"I don't benefit. I don't benefit"*: Christina Wilkie, "Trump Walks Back His
Pledge That Reform Won't Make Him Richer," CNBC, October 11, 2017,
https://www.cnbc.com/2017/10/11/trump-walks-back-his-pledge-that-tax
-reform-wont-make-him-richer.html.

97 *Trump, however, stood to benefit to the tune of $146,000*: David Cay John-
ston, *"DCReport* Exclusive: Trump Earned $153 Million in 2005; He Paid
$36.6 Million in Taxes," *DCReport*, March 14, 2017, https://www.dcreport
.org/2017/03/14/taxes/.

98 *Disclosure forms showed their income*: Rebecca Beitsch, "Kushner, Ivanka
Trump reported up to $640 million in outside income during White
House years," *The Hill*, February 8, 2021, https://thehill.com/homenews
/administration/537851-kushner-ivanka-trump-reported-up-to-640m-in
-outside-income-during.

98 *Trump paid zero income taxes in 15 years*: Russ Buettner, Susanne Craig, and
Mike McIntire, "Long-Concealed Records Show Trump's Chronic Losses
and Years of Tax Avoidance," *New York Times*, September 27, 2020, https://
www.nytimes.com/interactive/2020/09/27/us/donald-trump-taxes.html.

99 *under a 1992 law he personally lobbied for*: "Credit Availability and Economic Recovery," C-SPAN, November 21, 1991, https://www.c-span.org
/video/?22846-1/credit-availability-economic-recovery.

99 *according to confidential tax documents obtained by the* New York Times:
Russ Buettner, Susanne Craig, and Mike McIntire, "The President's
Taxes," *New York Times*, February 20, 2020, https://www.nytimes.com
/interactive/2020/09/27/us/donald-trump-taxes.html.

100 *documents obtained by Jesse Drucker and Emily Flitter*: Jesse Drucker and
Emily Flitter, "Jared Kushner Paid No Federal Income Tax for Years,
Documents Suggest," *New York Times*, October 13, 2018, https://www
.nytimes.com/2018/10/13/business/jared-kushner-taxes.html.

NOTES

9. Polishing Apple

101 *Trump's tax cut law took away many benefits*: Amir El-Sibaie, "2018 Tax Brackets," Tax Foundation, January 2, 2018, https://taxfoundation.org/2018-tax-brackets/.

103 *The income tax it owed . . . was $88 billion*: James S. Henry, "Apple's Sweetheart Tax Deal," *DCReport*, January 26, 2018, https://www.dcreport.org/2018/01/26/apples-sweetheart-tax-deal/.

104 *what British Journalist Nick Shaxson calls "Treasure Islands"*: Nicholas Shaxson, "Treasure Islands: Uncovering the Damage of Offshore Banking and Tax Havens," (New York: St. Martin's Griffin, 2012).

105 *His law forgave 77 percent of the taxes they owed*: 35 percent rate reduced to 8 percent is 77.1 percent less for offshore money invested in factories and equipment. For cash and near cash, the tax rate on repatriating was 15.5 percent, a reduction of 55.7 percent.

106 *the same level of investment Exxon had been making*: Mathew Gardner, "How Exxon's Empty $50 Billion Promise Made Its Way into Trump's SOTU," Institute on Taxation and Economic Policy, January 31, 2018, https://itep.org/how-exxons-empty-50-billion-promise-made-its-way -into-trumps-sotu/.

108 *$42 billion per year*. Phoebe Wall Howard, "Ford F-series Trucks Second only to iPhone in Sales. Here's Why That's Important," *Detroit Free Press*, June 24, 2020, https://www.freep.com/story/money/cars/ford/2020/06/24 /ford-f-150-super-duty-pickups-economic-impact/3246206001/.

109 *More than two-thirds of the poorest households*: Steven M. Rosenthal and Theo Burke, "Who Owns US Stock? Foreigners and Rich Americans," Tax Policy Center, October 20, 2020, https://www.taxpolicycenter.org /taxvox/who-owns-us-stock-foreigners-and-rich-americans.

10. The Koch Papers

This chapter draws on the roughly 1,000 pages of internal Oxbow documents in my possession and the five-part series I wrote in 2019 for *DCReport*. This link will generate the series, though in reverse order: https://www.dcreport.org/?s=Koch+Papers&search_button=Search.

113 *India banned it*: Sudarshan Varadhan and Abinaya Vijayaraghavan, "India Allows Conditional Import of Petcoke; Cement Shares Rise," Reuters,

August 17, 2018, https://www.reuters.com/article/us-india-petcoke
/india-allows-conditional-import-of-petcoke-cement-shares-rise-id
USKBN1L20X6.

114 *Bill did so well on his own*: Jef Feeley, "Bill Koch Ordered to Sell Oxbow
Carbon in Investor Dispute," *Bloomberg*, August 1, 2018, https://www
.bloomberg.com/news/articles/2018-08-01/bill-koch-ordered-to-sell-ox
bow-carbon-in-dispute-with-investor.

11. Wall Scam

127 *Chants of*: "BUILD THAT WALL!" Donald Trump Chants After Major
Endorsement, NewsNow from Fox (Phoenix), May 25, 2016, https://www
.youtube.com/watch?v=ZGSAhNZnisk.

127 *mightier than the Great Wall of China*: "Trump Compares Border Wall to
Great Wall of China," *PBS NewsHour*, May 1, 2016, https://www.youtube
.com/watch?v=bApzgA8J2lU.

127 *"We will build a great wall"*: "Trump: We Will Build a Great Wall Along
the Southern Border," Fox Business, August 31, 2016, https://www.you
tube.com/watch?v=2J9y6s_ukBQ.

128 *would cost $21.6 billion*: Julia Edwards Ainsley, "Trump Border 'Wall' to
Cost $21.6 Billion, Take 3.5 Years to Build: Internal Report," Reuters,
February 10, 2017, https://www.reuters.com/article/us-usa-trump-immi
gration-wall-exclusive/exclusive-trump-border-wall-to-cost-21-6-billion
-take-3-5-years-to-build-internal-report-idUSKBN15O2ZN.

128 *let contracts for 135 miles of fence*: Perla Trevizo and Jeremy Schwartz,
"Records Show Trump's Border Wall Is Costing Taxpayers Billions More
Than Initial Contracts," *Texas Tribune* and ProPublica, Oct. 27, 2020,
https://www.texastribune.org/2020/10/27/border-wall-texas-cost-rising
-trump/.

129 *President Trump gave his "blessing"*: Stephanie Saul, "Kris Kobach Wants
to Build the Wall His Way, and Says He Has the President's Blessing,"
New York Times, January 25, 2019, https://www.nytimes.com/2019/01/25
/us/politics/kris-kobach-wall-funding.html.

130 *I'm credible and a real person*: Ben Collins and Brandy Zadrozny, "Founder
of Viral Fundraiser for Trump's Border Wall Has Questionable News
Past," NBC News, December 20, 2018, https://www.nbcnews.com
/tech/tech-news/founder-viral-fundraiser-trump-s-border-wall-has-fake
-news-n950636.

130 *Kolfage had boasted*: Salvador Hernandez, "The GoFundMe Border Wall Is Finished. It's Not Stopping Migrants from Coming In," BuzzFeed, June 2, 2019, https://www.buzzfeednews.com/article/salvadorhernandez /border-wall-gofundme-sunland-park-residents-migrants.

131 *sliced through the steel barrier*: Nick Miroff, "Smugglers Are Sawing Through New Sections of Trump's Border Wall," *Washington Post*, November 2, 2019, https://www.washingtonpost.com/national/smugglers-are-sawing -through-new-sections-of-trumps-border-wall/2019/11/01/25bf8ce0-fa72 -11e9-ac8c-8eced29ca6ef_story.html.

131 *Topol acted on complaints*: Grant Stern, "Florida Officials Open Fraud Investigation of Border Wall Fundraising Effort," *DCReport*, June 4, 2019, https://www.dcreport.org/2019/06/04/florida-officials-open-fraud-inves tigation-of-border-wall-fundraising-effort/.

131 *a federal grand jury in Manhattan*: Leaders of 'We Build the Wall' Online Fundraising Campaign Charged with Defrauding Hundreds of Thousands of Donors," U.S. Attorney's Office for the Southern District of New York, August 20, 2020, https://www.justice.gov/usao-sdny/pr/leaders-we-build -wall-online-fundraising-campaign-charged-defrauding-hundreds-thou sands.

132 *only 69 miles of fencing*: "Schedule Considerations Drove Army Corps of Engineers' Approaches to Awarding Construction Contracts through 2020, Government Accountability Office," June 17, 2021, https://www .gao.gov/assets/gao-21-372.pdf.

12. Opportunity Knocks

133 *America had only 15 cases*: Kathryn Watson, "A Timeline of What Trump Has Said on Coronavirus," CBS News, April 3, 2020, https://www .cbsnews.com/news/timeline-president-donald-trump-changing-state ments-on-coronavirus/.

134 *"This was unexpected"*: Deirdre Shesgreen, David Jackson, and John Fritze, "From 'Great' to 'Blindsided': How Trump Changed His Coronavirus Message Amid Fear, Confusion in the White House," *USA Today*, March 10, 2020, https://www.usatoday.com/story/news/politics /2020/03/10/coronavirus-trump-shifts-message-crisis-grows-stocks-plum met/4966450002/.

134 *"This came up—"*: "Remarks by President Trump, Vice President Pence, and Members of the Coronavirus Task Force in Press Briefing," Trump

White House, March 16, 2020, https://trumpwhitehouse.archives.gov
/briefings-statements/remarks-president-trump-vice-president-pence
-members-coronavirus-task-force-press-briefing-3/.

134 *"Nobody ever expected"*: "Remarks by President Trump, Vice President
Pence, and Members of the Coronavirus Task Force in a Fox News
Virtual Town Hall," Trump White House, March 24, 2020, https://
trumpwhitehouse.archives.gov/briefings-statements/remarks-president
-trump-vice-president-pence-members-coronavirus-task-force-fox-news
-virtual-town-hall/.

134 *a pandemic that could kill*: Lawrence K. Altman, MD, "Is This a Pandemic?
Define 'Pandemic,'" *New York Times*, June 8, 2009, https://www.nytimes.
com/2009/06/09/health/09docs.html; Robin Marantz Henig, "Experts
Warned of a Pandemic Decades Ago. Why Weren't We Ready?," *National
Geographic*, April 8, 2020, https://www.nationalgeographic.com/science
/article/experts-warned-pandemic-decades-ago-why-not-ready-for-corona
virus.

134 *President George W. Bush recognized*: Gardiner Harris, "Bush Announces
Plan to Prepare for Flu Epidemic," *New York Times*, November 5, 2005,
https://www.nytimes.com/2005/11/02/politics/bush-announces-plan-to
-prepare-for-flu-epidemic.html.

134 *President Obama initiated*: Victoria Knight, "Obama Team Left Pandemic Playbook for Trump Administration, Officials Confirm," Kaiser
Health News via *PBS NewsHour*, May 15, 2020, https://www.pbs.org
/newshour/nation/obama-team-left-pandemic-playbook-for-trump-ad
ministration-officials-confirm.

134 *In 2017 the Pentagon warned*: Ken Klippenstein, "Exclusive: The Military
Knew Years Ago That a Coronavirus Was Coming," *Nation*, April 1,
2020, https://www.thenation.com/article/politics/covid-military-short
age-pandemic/.

134 *ran a tabletop exercise*: David E. Sanger, Eric Lipton, Eileen Sullivan,
and Michael Crowley, "Before Virus Outbreak, a Cascade of Warnings
Went Unheeded," *New York Times*, March 19, 2020, https://www.nytimes
.com/2020/03/19/us/politics/trump-coronavirus-outbreak.html.

135 *consider a $3.7 million PPP loan*: "Tracking PPP Loans: Irongate Azrep
Bw LLP," ProPublica, June 1, 2021, https://projects.propublica.org/corona
virus/bailouts/loans/irongate-azrep-bw-llc-2021437406.

135 *Our government made more than 7 million such PPP loans*: "PPP Data,"
U.S. Small Business Administration, various dates, https://www.sba

.gov/funding-programs/loans/coronavirus-relief-options/paycheck-pro
tection-program/ppp-data.

136 *"Vote for me, Hawaii!!" he tweeted*: Sopan Deb, "On Donald Trump's
Claim That He 'Employs Many People' at Honolulu Hotel," CBS News,
March 8, 2016, https://www.cbsnews.com/news/donald-trump-claims-he
-employs-many-people-at-honolulu-hotel/.

137 *Minority-owned businesses had an especially tough time*: "Minority-Owned
Businesses Were Last In Line to Receive Loans, Latest PPP Data Show,"
Associated Press via CBS News, January 4, 2021, https://www.cbsnews
.com/news/minority-owned-businesses-were-last-to-receive-ppp-loans
-adding-to-their-despair/.

137 *Terence Dickson owns*: Stacy M. Brown, "Terra Café Owner: Government
Ignores Black-Owned Small Businesses," *Baltimore Times*, May 1, 2020,
http://baltimoretimes-online.com/news/2020/may/01/terra-cafe-owner
-government-ignores-black-owned-sm/.

138 *But qualifying for forgiveness is a difficult hurdle*: "COVID-19 Federal Efforts
Could Be Strengthened by Timely and Concerted Actions," Government
Accountability Office, September 2020, https://www.gao.gov/assets/gao
-20-701.pdf.

138 *Treasury Secretary Steven Mnuchin told Congress*: Mark Niquette and Zach-
ary R. Mider, "Names of Small-Business Borrowers from Paycheck Protection Program Won't Be Released, Mnuchin Says," *Time*, June 13, 2020,
https://time.com/5852828/mnuchin-ppp-borrowers-names-secret.

138 *Eleven news organizations sued for the PPP and Economic Disaster loan
data*: Jonathan O'Connell, Andrew Van Dam, Aaron Gregg, and Alyssa
Fowers, "More Than Half of Emergency Small-Business Funds Went to
Larger Businesses, New Data Shows," *Washington Post*, December 2, 2020,
https://www.washingtonpost.com/business/2020/12/01/ppp-sba-data/.

138 *More than two dozen loans totaling more than $3.6 million*: Ben Popken and
Andrew W. Lehren, "Release of PPP Loan Recipients' Data Reveals Trou-
bling Patterns: Tenants Paying Rent at Trump Organization and Kushner
Companies Properties Are Beneficiaries of PPP Loans," NBC News,
December 2, 2020. https://www.nbcnews.com/business/business-news
/release-ppp-loan-recipients-data-reveals-troubling-patterns-n1249629.

141 *Erik Sherman, a DCReport financial reporter, explains*: Erik Sherman,
"How Big Banks Have Undercut the PPP COVID-19 Loan Program,"
DCReport, May 15, 2020, https://www.dcreport.org/2020/05/15/how-big
-banks-have-undercut-the-ppp-covid-19-loan-program/.

NOTES

143 *a reporter asked Trump, "Will you commit publicly"*: "Remarks by President Trump, Vice President Pence, and Members of the Coronavirus Task Force in Press Briefing," Trump White House Archives, March 22, 2020, https://trumpwhitehouse.archives.gov/briefings-statements/remarks -president-trump-vice-president-pence-members-coronavirus-task-force-press-briefing-8/.

143 *A day earlier a reporter had asked Trump about "reports that the coronavirus"*: "Remarks by President Trump, Vice President Pence, and Members of the Coronavirus Task Force in Press Briefing," Trump White House Archives, March 21, 2020, https://trumpwhitehouse.archives.gov/brief ings-statements/remarks-president-trump-vice-president-pence-mem bers-coronavirus-task-force-press-briefing-7/.

145 *The top 5 percent received more than half*: O'Connell et al., "More Than Half of Emergency Small-Business Funds Went to Larger Businesses, New Data Shows."

145 *"poorly designed and irresponsibly run"*: Rey Mashayekhi, "'Poorly Designed and Irresponsibly Run': PPP Scrutiny Mounts After SBA Data Dump," *Fortune*, December 11, 2020, https://fortune.com/2020/12/11 /ppp-scrutiny-sba-trump-administration-big-companies-small-busi nesses-covid-relief/.

146 *These fake borrowers bought* Lamborghinis: "Second Man Allegedly Buys Lamborghini with Coronavirus Loans," *Guardian*, August 5, 2020, https://www.theguardian.com/us-news/2020/aug/05/lamborghini-corona virus-fraud-second-case.

146 *Hannibal Ware issued an eight-page report*: "White Paper: Risk Awareness and Lessons Learned from Prior Audits of Economic Stimulus Loans," Small Business Administration, Office of Inspector General, April 3, 2020, https://www.sba.gov/sites/default/files/2020-04/SBA_OIG_White Paper_20-11_508.pdf.

146 *his staff had discovered "potentially rampant fraud"*: "SBA Inspector General Inspection Report: Inspection of Small Business Administration's Initial Disaster Assistance Response to the Coronavirus Pandemic," Report No. 21-02, Small Business Administration, Office of Inspector General, October 28, 2020, https://www.sba.gov/sites/default/files/2020-11 /SBA%20OIG%20Report%2021-02.508.1.pdf.

13. Dangerous Favors

149 *In 2017 SoftBank purchased Fortress*: "SoftBank Group Completes Acquisition of Fortress Investment Group," Fortress Press Release, December 27, 2017, https://www.fortress.com/shareholders/news/2017-12-27-softbank -group-completes-acquisition-of-fortress-investment-group.

150 *David Swensen, the very successful manager*: William D. Cohan, "Cash for Fortress, a Bath For Investors," CNN Money, June 10, 2009, https:// money.cnn.com/2009/06/10/news/companies/fortress.fortune.

150 *the prospectus was missing a disclosure section titled "Greed"*: Michelle Celarier, "The Fall of Fortress," Institutional Investor, April 5, 2017, https://www .institutionalinvestor.com/article/b1505p66vqo6cy/the-fall-of-fortress.

150 *Fortress generously forgave all but $48 million of the debt*: David Enrich, Russ Buettner, Mike McIntire, and Susanne Craig, "How Trump Maneuvered His Way Out of Trouble in Chicago," *New York Times*, October 27, 2020, https://www.nytimes.com/2020/10/27/business/trump-chicago-taxes .html; the Fortress mortgage is at Cook County Clerk's Office, https:// www.ccrecorder.org/recordings/recording/show/340081751/.

151 *she launched a broad investigation*: Russ Choma, "New York's AG Is Investigating One of the Biggest Mysteries on Trump's Balance Sheet," *Mother Jones*, August 25, 2020, https://www.motherjones.com/politics/2020/08 /new-yorks-ag-is-investigating-one-of-the-biggest-mysteries-on-trumps -balance-sheet.

151 *SoftBank's Fortress division extended a $57 million loan*: "SoftBank subsidiary issues loan to Kushner for Jersey City project," *The Real Deal*, January 23, 2019, https://therealdeal.com/2018/01/23/softbank-subsidiary -issued-57m-loan-to-kushner-companies/.

151 *One Journal Square*: Devin Gannon, "Kushner's Controversial One Journal Square Project Receives Approval to Bring 1,700 Units to Jersey City," 6SQFT, January 6, 2021, https://www.6sqft.com/one-journal-square-jer sey-city-kushner-companies-approval-and-new-renderings-january-2021.

152 *the city government refused the family's request for a package of subsidies*: Bernard Condon, "Kushner Plans to Build Twin-Towers in New Jersey Unraveling," Associated Press, April 23, 2018, https://apnews.com/article /364077cb70de446cb4f48f4bcddao23e.

152 *Jared's sister Nicole Kushner Meyer hosted an investment seminar*: Emily Rauhala and William Wan, "In a Beijing Ballroom, Kushner Family Pushes $500,000 'Investor Visa' to Wealthy Chinese," *Washington*

NOTES

Post, May 6, 2017, https://www.washingtonpost.com/world/in-a-beijing
-ballroom-kushner-family-flogs-500000-investor-visa-to-wealthy-chi
nese/2017/05/06/cf711e53-eb49-4f9a-8dea-3cd836fcf287_story.html.

153 *the Kushners told business publications*: Shawn Boburg, "Kushner Tapped
Program Meant for Job-Starved Areas to Build a Luxury Skyscraper,"
Los Angeles Times, June 1, 2017, https://www.latimes.com/business/la-fi
-kushner-eb5-20170601-story.html.

153 *not the first Fortress loan to the Kushner family*: Ben Walsh, "Fortress Makes
Loan to Kushner Cos.' Jersey City Project," *Barron's*, January 23, 2018,
https://www.barrons.com/articles/fortress-makes-loan-to-kushner-cos
-jersey-city-project-1516726648.

153 *a business called New Fortress Energy*: "Our Vision and Mission," New
Fortress Energy, undated, https://www.newfortressenergy.com/about.

155 *Karl Alexy, chief safety officer*: Rebecca Leber, "Oil-Train Spills Are Worse
Than Ever, and Obama's New Safety Rules Aren't Enough," *New Republic*,
July 23, 2014, https://newrepublic.com/article/118824/obama-administra
tions-oil-train-safety-rules-arent-enough.

14. Expensive Juice

159 *Each year America generates about 4 trillion kilowatt hours of electricity*: "What
Is U.S. Electricity Generation by Energy Source?," U.S. Energy Information Administration, March 5, 2021, https://www.eia.gov/tools/faqs
/faq.php?id=427&t=3.

160 *Just five weeks later they announced that they would shut down*: Alex Kuffner,
"New Owners to Shutter Outmoded Brayton Point Power Station in 2017,"
Providence (RI) Journal, October 8, 2013, https://www.providencejournal
.com/article/20131008/News/310089995.

160 *Powelson declared, "The jihad has begun"*: David Cay Johnston, "How Donald
Trump Is Raising Your Electric Bill," *Daily Beast*, May 31, 2017, https://
www.thedailybeast.com/how-donald-trump-is-raising-your-electric-bill.

163 *The Detroit Democrat said that mixing these electricity financing and trading
interests*: Author interviews with retired Senator Carl Levin.

166 *Scott Pruitt . . . set out to end tests of groundwater supplies*: Margaret Talbot,
"Scott Pruitt's Dirty Politics," *New Yorker*, March 26, 2018, https://www
.newyorker.com/magazine/2018/04/02/scott-pruitts-dirty-politics.

167 *"There is zero reliable evidence"*: "Explainer: Why the CMP Corridor Is
a Bad Deal for Maine and the Climate," Natural Resources Council of

263

NOTES

Maine, July 9, 2020, https://www.nrcm.org/blog/why-cmp-corridor-is
-bad-deal-maine-climate/.

15. The Shipping News

172 *Approximately 70,000 complaints of wage theft*: Gregory D. Kutz, "Case Studies from Ongoing Work Show Examples in Which Wage and Hour Division Did Not Adequately Pursue Labor Violations," Department of Labor, testimony before the Committee on Education and Labor, House of Representatives, July 15, 2008, https://www.gao.gov/assets/gao-08-973t.pdf.

174 *In 2020 the Center for Responsive Politics*: Glenn Kessler, "Mitch McConnell Got 'Rich' the Old Fashioned Way," *Washington Post*, June 2, 2020, https://www.washingtonpost.com/politics/2020/06/02/mitch-mcconnell-got-rich-old-fashioned-way/.

174 *In August 2017, Chao at his side*: Politico Staff, "Full Text: Trump's Comments on White Supremacists, 'Alt-left' in Charlottesville," *Politico*, August 15, 2017, https://www.politico.com/story/2017/08/15/full-text-trump-comments-white-supremacists-alt-left-transcript-241662.

176 *Chao directed her staff to contact the merchant*: "Watchdog Faulted Elaine Chao for Misuse of Office as Transportation Secretary," NBC News, March 3, 2021, https://www.nbcnews.com/politics/politics-news/watchdog-faulted-elaine-chao-misuse-office-transportation-secretary-n1259547.

180 *"The Chinese government is massively engaged"*: Michael Forsythe, Eric Lipton, Keith Bradsher, and Sui-Lee Wee, "A 'Bridge' to China, and Her Family's Business, in the Trump Cabinet," *New York Times*, June 2, 2019, https://www.nytimes.com/2019/06/02/us/politics/elaine-chao-china.html.

16. Russian Money Man

183 *Wilbur Ross attended a party*: Max Abelson, "Wilbur Ross and the Era of Billionaire Rule," *Bloomberg Businessweek*, January 26, 2017, https://www.bloomberg.com/news/features/2017-01-26/wilbur-ross-and-the-cabinet-of-billionaires.

183 *that was about six times his actual wealth*: Dan Alexander, "Why Forbes Is Dropping Wilbur Ross' Net Worth—Again," *Forbes*, July 23, 2019, https://www.forbes.com/sites/danalexander/2019/07/23/why-forbes-is-dropping-wilbur-ross-net-worthagain.

NOTES

184 *allowed Trump to collect at least $82 million more*: Shawn Tully, "How Donald Trump Made Millions Off His Biggest Business Failure," *Fortune*, March 10, 2016, https://fortune.com/2016/03/10/trump-hotel-casinos-pay-failure/.

184 *Taj management also knowingly laundered money*: United States of America Department of the Treasury Financial Crimes Enforcement Network, In the Matter of: *Trump Taj Mahal Associates*, Number 2015-02, Assessment of Civil Penalty, https://www.fincen.gov/sites/default/files/enforcement_action/20150302%20Assessment%20of%20Civil%20Money%20Penalty%20Trump%20Taj%20Mahal%20(post-approval%20by%20bankruptcy%20court).pdf.

184 *What no one would know from the more than 50 pages*: Executive Branch Personnel, Public Financial Disclosure Report (OGE Form 278e), Ross, Wilbur L., filed December 19, 2016, https://extapps2.oge.gov/201/Presiden.nsf/PAS+Index/A28CA739CF331E63852583A600727D04/$FILE/Wilbur-L-Ross-2018-278.pdf.

185 *In a report called* The Paradise Papers: *Paradise Papers: Secrets of the Global Elite*, International Consortium of Investigative Journalists, November 2017, https://www.icij.org/investigations/paradise-papers/.

185 *One is Gennady Timchenko*: "#101 Gennady Timchenko," Bloomberg Billionaires Index, *Bloomberg*, May 31, 2021, https://www.bloomberg.com/billionaires/profiles/gennady-timchenko/?sref=C7iJPlqU.

185 *The other key man at Silbur was Kirill Shamalov*: Jack Stubbs, Andrey Kuzmin, Stephen Grey, and Roman Anin, "The Man Who Married Putin's Daughter and Then Made a Fortune," Reuters, December 17, 2015, https://www.reuters.com/investigates/special-report/russia-capitalism-shamalov/.

186 *In 2014 Ross had become a significant shareholder*: James S. Henry, "Another Cabinet Pick with Secret Ties to Putin and Oligarchs," *DCReport*, February 25, 2017, https://www.dcreport.org/2017/02/25/another-cabinet-pick-with-secret-ties-to-putin-and-oligarchs/.

186 *the Cypriot economy was about $23 billion*: Matthew Boesler, "Shreveport, Louisiana Has a Bigger Economy Than Cyprus," *Business Insider*, March 17, 2013, https://www.businessinsider.com/size-of-cyprus-economy-in-context-2013-3.

186 *Bank of Cyprus had $31 billion on deposit*: "Seeing Red: Russian Cash Caches Critical for Cyprus," *National Herald*, May 24, 2020, https://www.thenationalherald.com/cyprus_economy/arthro/seeing_red_russian_cash_caches_critical_for_cyprus-335541.

186 *Russians accounted for $26 billion of those deposits*: Markus Dettmer and

Christian Reiermann, "Aid to Cyprus Could Benefit Russian Oligarchs," *Spiegel International*, May 11, 2012, https://www.spiegel.de/international /europe/german-spy-agency-says-cyprus-bailout-would-help-russian -oligarchs-a-865291.html.

187 *Under Ackermann, Deutsche Bank laundered*: Ben Protess, Jessica Silver-Greenberg, and Jesse Drucker, "Big German Bank, Key to Trump's Finances, Faces New Scrutiny," *New York Times*, July 19. 2017, https:// www.nytimes.com/2017/07/19/business/big-german-bank-key-to-trumps -finances-faces-new-scrutiny.html.

187 *"Deutsche Bank was structurally designed"*: Ed Caesar, "Deutsche Bank's $10-Billion Scandal," *New Yorker*, August 22, 2016, https://www.new yorker.com/magazine/2016/08/29/deutsche-banks-10-billion-scandal.

187 *The biggest was the Renova Group*: "Renova Group Became a Shareholder of Bank of Cyprus," Cyprus Property Info, September 20, 2014, http:// cyprusproperty.info/news/122.

187 *Another investor in the Bank of Cyprus was Dmitry Rybolovlev*: Linette Lopez, "The Bank of Cyprus' Biggest Shareholder Is a Russian Oligarch with an Insane Real Estate Portfolio," *Business Insider*, March 18, 2013, https://www.businessinsider.com/dmitry-rybolovlev-bank-of-cyprus -2013-3.

188 *It is conceivable that Putin*: Michael Cohen, author interview; Frank Cerabino, "A New Twist in the Old Saga of That Palm Beach Mansion Trump Made a Killing Off Of," *Palm Beach Post*, September, 11, 2020, https:// www.palmbeachpost.com/story/news/columns/2020/09/11/michael-co hens-take-trumps-sale-palm-beach-estate-russian/3468953001/.

188 *Putin had twice sanctioned Rybolovlev*: Julie Zeveloff, "The Wild Life of the Billionaire Oligarch Who Just Bought an $88 Million Apartment for His Daughter," *Business Insider*, December 20, 2011, https://www .businessinsider.com/dmitry-rybolovlev-buys-most-expensive-pent house-new-york-2011-12.

188 *Vladimir Strzhalkovsky, who had served as a KGB officer*: "Russians, Including Putin Ally, Join Bailed-in Bank of Cyprus Board," Reuters, September 10, 2013, https://www.reuters.com/article/bankofcyprus/rus sians-including-putin-ally-join-bailed-in-bank-of-cyprus-board-idUSL 5NoH63FF20130910.

188 *Bank of Cyprus had at least one notable American customer: Paul Manafort*: Aggelos Petropoulos and Richard Engel, "Manafort-Linked Accounts on Cyprus Raised Red Flag," NBC News, March 29, 2017, https://www

.nbcnews.com/news/world/manafort-linked-accounts-cyprus-raised-red
-flag-n739156.

189 *Ross . . . accused of stealing $120 million from his investment partners*: Dan
Alexander, "New Details about Wilbur Ross' Business Point to Pattern of Grifting," *Forbes*, August 7, 2018, https://www.forbes.com/sites
/danalexander/2018/08/06/new-details-about-wilbur-rosss-businesses
-point-to-pattern-of-grifting/.

190 *Ross also made three stock purchases*: Steven Mufson, "Commerce Secretary
Wilbur Ross Made at Least $30 Million Last Year, Ethics Filing Shows,"
Los Angeles Times, September 13, 2018, https://www.latimes.com/business
/la-fi-wilbur-ross-20180913-story.html.

191 *"Your failure to divest created the potential"*: Steven Mufson, "Government
Ethics Office Scolds Wilbur Ross over Stock Sales," *Washington Post*,
July 12, 2018, https://www.washingtonpost.com/business/economy/gov
ernment-ethics-office-scolds-wilbur-ross-over-stock-sales/2018/07/12/4d
fa24c2-863d-11e8-8553-a3ce89036c78_story.html.

191 *lawyer and economist James S. Henry documented*: David Cay Johnston,
"Another Cabinet Pick with Secret Ties to Putin and Oligarchs,"
DCReport, February 25, 2017, https://www.dcreport.org/2017/02/25/another
-cabinet-pick-with-secret-ties-to-putin-and-oligarchs/.

192 *He revoked the 2018 certification of compliance*: Executive Branch Personnel,
Public Financial Disclosure Report (OGE Form 287e), Ross, Wilbur L.,
U.S. Office of Government Ethics Certification, Certification Declined
on 2/15/19 by Rounds, Emory, https://extapps2.oge.gov/201/Presiden.nsf
/PAS+Index/A28CA739CF331E63852583A600727D04/$FILE/Wilbur-L
-Ross-2018-278.pdf.

192 *The Commerce Department's inspector general issued a report*: "Investigation
into Multiple Allegations That Secretary of Commerce Wilbur L. Ross,
Jr., Failed to Comply with His Ethics Agreement and Violated Conflict
of Interest," U.S. Department of Commerce, Office of Inspector General,
December 3, 2020, https://www.oig.doc.gov/Pages/Investigation-into
-Multiple-Allegations-That-Secretary-of-Commerce-Wilbur-L-Ross-Jr
-Failed-to-Comply-with-His-Ethics-Ag.aspx.

17. Promises, Promises

193 *proposed a new rule*: "Rights to Federally Funded Inventions and Licensing of Government Owned Inventions," *Federal Register*, January 4,

NOTES

2021, https://www.federalregister.gov/documents/2021/01/04/2020-27581
/rights-to-federally-funded-inventions-and-licensing-of-government
-owned-inventions.

193 *barred our government*: Dana Milbank and Claudia Deane, "President
Signs Medicare Drug Bill," *Washington Post*, December 9, 2003, www
.washingtonpost.com/archive/politics/2003/12/09/president-signs-medi
care-drug-bill/989689c0-dec3-4e78-8879-8f5e5b840f21/.

193 *Novolog insulin 353 percent*: William T. Cefalu, et al., "Insulin Access and
Affordability Working Group: Conclusions and Recommendations," *Diabetes Care*, June 2018, https://care.diabetesjournals.org/content/41/6/1299.

194 *Skipping doses*: Megan Leonhardt, "Americans Are Skipping Medically
Necessary Prescriptions Because of the Cost," CNBC, February 27, 2020,
https://www.cnbc.com/2020/02/26/people-skipping-medically-necessary
-drugs-because-they-cost-too-much.html.

194 *spent $298 billion*: NHE Fact Sheet, National Health Expenditure
Data, Centers for Medicare and Medicaid Services, December 16,
2020, https://www.cms.gov/research-statistics-data-and-systems/statis
tics-trends-and-reports/nationalhealthexpenddata/nhe-fact-sheet.

195 *"Drug prices are coming down"*: Aaron Blake, "Trump's Gripe-Filled News
Conference, Annotated," *Washington Post*, May 22, 2019, https://www
.washingtonpost.com/politics/2019/05/22/trumps-gripe-filled-press-con
ference-annotated/.

195 *"When you see"* and *"we're going to cut prescription drug prices"*: "Prescription
Drugs," *Martinsville Bulletin*, Sept. 9, 2020, https://martinsvillebulle
tin.com/news/national/govt-and-politics/prescription-drugs/article
_ca02d5c9-4c41-5dc2-a37b-457f154a5b67.html.

196 *That law gives*: 28 U.S. Code § 1498—Patent and copyright cases, https://
www.law.cornell.edu/uscode/text/28/1498.

196 *Bush threatened*: Keith Bradsher with Edmund L. Andrews, "A Nation
Challenged: CIPRO; U.S. Says Bayer Will Cut Cost of Its Anthrax Drug,"
New York Times, October 24, 2001, https://www.nytimes.com/2001/10/24
/business/a-nation-challenged-cipro-us-says-bayer-will-cut-cost-of-its
-anthrax-drug.html.

197 *That made them liable*: 35 U.S. Code § 203—March-in rights, https://www
.law.cornell.edu/uscode/text/35/203.

18. Family First

199 *having made in four years at least $172 million*: Bess Levin, "Jared and Ivanka Made Up to $640 Million While Working in Washington, or 457,142 Stimulus Checks," *Vanity Fair*, February 8, 2021, https://www.vanityfair.com/news/2021/02/jared-kushner-ivanka-trump-white-house-income.

199 *Ivanka got trademark rights from China*: "China Grants More Trademark Approvals for Ivanka Trump Firm—Including Voting Machines," Reuters, November 6, 2018, https://www.reuters.com/article/us-china-usa-ivanka/china-grants-more-trademark-approvals-for-ivanka-trump-firm-including-voting-machines-idUSKCN1NB0TL.

200 *Japan . . . granted or renewed*: Tommy Beer, "Ivanka's Trademark Requests Were Fast-Tracked in China After Trump Was Elected," *Forbes*, September 22, 2020, https://www.forbes.com/sites/tommybeer/2020/09/22/ivankas-trademark-requests-were-fast-tracked-in-china-after-trump-was-elected/?sh=78ec399d1d60.

200 *Russia . . . granted or renewed*: Caroline Zhang, "Russia Renewed Ivanka Trump's Trademarks Shortly before the 2016 Election," Citizens for Ethics, January 24, 2019, https://www.citizensforethics.org/reports-investigations/crew-investigations/russia-ivanka-trump-trademarks-2016-election.

200 *Citizens for Responsibility and Ethics in Washington*: About CREW, https://www.citizensforethics.org/about.

200 *Ivanka had a hand in creating the tax-favored Opportunity Zones*: Emily Stewart, "Ivanka Trump Reportedly Advocated for a Tax Break She and Jared Kushner Could Profit From," *Vox*, December 12, 2018, https://www.vox.com/policy-and-politics/2018/12/12/18137834/jared-kushner-ivanka-trump-opportunity-zone.

201 *Jared and Ivanka sought approval*: Sheelah Kolhatkar, "Ivanka Trump Tries to Quiet the Ethics Critics," *New Yorker*, March 31, 2017, https://www.newyorker.com/news/news-desk/ivanka-trump-tries-to-quiet-the-ethics-critics.

201 *Trump himself sought permission*: Charles S. Clark, "Trump Plan to Submit Unsigned Financial Disclosure Draws Mixed Reviews," Government Executive, May 22, 2017, https://www.govexec.com/management/2017/05/trump-plan-submit-unsigned-financial-disclosure-draws-mixed-reviews/138061.

201 *when Trump filed for the first time as president*: "Trump's 2017 Financial

Disclosure," OpenSecrets.org, June 16, 2017, https://www.opensecrets
.org/trump/trump-2017-financial-disclosure.

201 *A British agent representing the Kremlin*: Jo Becker, Adam Goldman and
Matt Apuzzo, "Russian Dirt on Clinton? 'I Love It,' Donald Trump Jr.
Said," *New York Times*, July 11, 2017, https://www.nytimes.com/2017/07/11
/us/politics/trump-russia-email-clinton.html.

202 *Jared again demonstrated his disloyalty*: Meghean Keneally, "A Closer Look
at the Meetings with Russians the Trump Team Failed to Disclose," ABC
News, October 12, 2017, https://abcnews.go.com/Politics/closer-meetings
-russians-trump-team-failed-disclose/story?id=50397154.

202 *In 2008 she lied to potential buyers*: David Smith, "Trump Jr and Ivanka
Trump 'Knew They Were Lying' over Ploy to Sell Condos, Book Claims,"
Guardian, January 9, 2020, https://www.theguardian.com/us-news/2020
/jan/09/trump-jr-ivanka-trump-condos-scheme-book.

203 *Donald Trump was entitled to 18 percent of any Trump SoHo profits*: Jim
Zarroli and Alina Selyukh, "Trump SoHo: A Shiny Hotel Wrapped in
Glass, But Hiding Mysteries," NPR, November 7, 2017, https://www.npr
.org/2017/11/07/560849787/trump-soho-a-shiny-hotel-wrapped-in-glass
-but-hiding-mysteries.

204 *Jared . . . made the deal*: Julia Horowitz and Cristina Alesci, "Kushner
Companies Offloads Troubled 666 Fifth Avenue Flagship," CNN Money,
August 3, 2018, https://money.cnn.com/2018/08/03/news/companies/kush
ner-666-fifth-avenue-brookfield/index.html.

205 *he had personally ordered the clearances for his daughter and son-in-law*: Mag-
gie Haberman, Michael S. Schmidt, Adam Goldman, and Annie Karni,
"Trump Ordered Officials to Give Jared Kushner a Security Clearance,"
New York Times, February 28, 2019, https://www.nytimes.com/2019/02/28
/us/politics/jared-kushner-security-clearance.html.

205 *Tricia Newbold, one of the White House employees*: Rebecca Kaplan,
"Whistleblower Says 25 People Given White House Clearance
Despite Rejections," CBS News, updated April 1. 2019, https://www
.cbsnews.com/news/house-panel-interviews-whistleblower-tricia-new
bold-about-white-house-security-clearances/.

207 *Jared's freelancing*: David Ignatius, "Inside the palace intrigue in Jordan and a
thwarted 'deal of the century,'" *Washington Post*, June 12, 2021, https://www.wash
ingtonpost.com/opinions/2021/06/11/jordan-saudi-trump-netanyahu-deal/.

207 *the intelligence services of at least four countries intercepted communications*:
Dan Merica, "Intercept: Saudi Crown Prince Bragged about Kushner

Relationship," CNN, March 22, 2018, https://www.cnn.com/2018/03/22
/politics/jared-kushner-mohammed-bin-salman/index.html.

207 *ordered the death of* Washington Post *columnist Jamal Khashoggi*: Shane Harris, Greg Miller, and Josh Dawsey, "CIA Concludes Saudi Crown Prince
Ordered Jamal Khashoggi's Assassination," *Washington Post*, November 16, 2018, https://www.washingtonpost.com/world/national-security
/cia-concludes-saudi-crown-prince-ordered-jamal-khashoggis-assassina
tion/2018/11/16/98c89fe6-e9b2-11e8-a939-9469f1166f9d_story.html.

208 *the Saudis and their allies imposed an economic blockade on Qatar*: "Qatar
Row: Trump Claims Credit for Isolation," BBC News, June 6, 2017,
https://www.bbc.com/news/world-middle-east-40175935; Wayback
Machine, Trump Twitter archive, June 6, 2017, https://web.archive
.org/web/20170606120637/https:/twitter.com/realDonaldTrump/sta
tus/872062159789985792, https://web.archive.org/web/20170606133708
/https:/twitter.com/realDonaldTrump/status/872084870620520448, and
https://web.archive.org/web/20170606134456/https:/twitter.com/real
DonaldTrump/status/872086906804240384.

209 *meeting was held to secure financing for 666 Fifth Avenue*: Clayton Swisher and
Ryan Grim, "Jared Kushner's Real-Estate Firm Sought Money Directly
from Qatar Government Weeks Before Blockade," *Intercept*, March 2,
2018, https://theintercept.com/2018/03/02/jared-kushner-real-estate
-qatar-blockade.

209 *The Kushners also claimed*: "Greg Price, Kushner Qatar Meeting Confirmed, but Dad Insists He Didn't Take Money," *Newsweek*, March 19,
2018, https://www.newsweek.com/kushner-dad-qatar-money-851230.

209 *Freddie Mac . . . approved almost $850 million*: David Kocieniewski and
Caleb Melby, "Kushner Cos. Gets $800 Million Federally Backed Apart-
ment Loan," *Bloomberg*, May 23, 2019, https://www.bloomberg.com/news
/articles/2019-05-23/kushner-cos-gets-800-million-federally-backed
-apartment-loan; Heather Vogel, "Trump, Inc.: The Kushners' Freddie
Mac Loan Wasn't Just Massive: It Came with Unusually Good Terms,
Too," ProPublica, October 1, 2020, https://www.propublica.org/article
/the-kushners-freddie-mac-loan-wasnt-just-massive-it-came-with-un
usually-good-terms-too.

210 *the couple denied Secret Service agents use of their bathroom*: Peter Jami-
son, Carol D. Leonnig, and Paul Schwartzman, "The $3,000-a-Month
Toilet for the Ivanka Trump/Jared Kushner Secret Service Detail,"
Washington Post, January 14, 2021, https://www.washingtonpost.com

/dc-md-va/2021/01/14/secret-service-bathroom-ivanka-trump-jared -kushner.

211 *The Kushner Companies sought massive loans*: Heather Vogell, "The Kushners' Freddie Mac Loan Wasn't Just Massive. It Came With Unusually Good Terms, Too," ProPublica, October 1, 2020, https://www.propublica .org/article/the-kushners-freddie-mac-loan-wasnt-just-massive-it-came -with-unusually-good-terms-too.

212 *A shortfall*: John M. Griffin and Alex Priest, "Is COVID Revealing a CMBS Virus?," SSRN, Aug. 10, 2020, https://ssrn.com/abstract=3671162.

212 *Emily Daneker*: Alison Knezevich, "Jared Kushner's Apartment Company Violated Consumer Laws in Maryland, Judge Rules," *Baltimore Sun*, April 21, 2021, https://www.baltimoresun.com/maryland/bs-md-west minster-case-decision-20210429-03rvxoj32najldswlsaytx6fbq-story.html.

213 *Daneker's ruling required*: "Consumer Protection Division, Office of the Attorney General, Proponent, v. Westminster Management, LLC, et al., Respondents," OAG-CPD-04-19-34292, https://s3.documentcloud.org /documents/20693965/westminstermgmtdec042921.pdf.

213 *Kushner charged his*: Department of State expense filing, https://www .usaspending.gov/award/CONT_AWD_19IS4021F0123_1900_191S70 18D0004_1900.

213 *"Cadre is going to make us billionaires"*: Vicky Ward, "Jared Kushner May Have an Ethics Problem—to the Tune of $90m," *Guardian*, June 16, 2019, https://www.theguardian.com/commentisfree/2019/jun/15/jared-kush ner-cadre-corruption-ethics-foreign-funding.

213 *Cadre became a booming success*: Jon Swaine, "Company Part-owned by Jared Kushner Got $90m from Unknown Offshore Investors Since 2017," *Guardian*, June 10, 2019, https://www.theguardian.com/us-news/2019 /jun/10/jared-kushner-real-estate-cadre-goldman-sachs.

213 *Kushner didn't include Cadre*: Meredith Lerner and Linnaea Honl-Stuenkel, "OGE Reverses Course on Jared Kushner's Cadre conflict," Citizens for Responsibility & Ethics in Washington, July 13, 2020, https://www .citizensforethics.org/reports-investigations/crew-investigations/oge-re verses-course-on-jared-kushners-cadre-conflict/.

214 *Trump pardoned*: "Statement from the Press Secretary Regarding Executive Grants of Clemency," Trump White House, December 23, 2020, https:// trumpwhitehouse.archives.gov/briefings-statements/statement-press-sec retary-regarding-executive-grants-clemency-122320/.

214 *Kushner Companies applied*: Peter Grant, "Kushner Cos. Plans to Raise

NOTES

$100 Million by Selling Bonds in Israel," *Wall Street Journal*, December 29, 2020, https://www.wsj.com/articles/kushner-cos-plans-to-raise-100-mil lion-by-selling-bonds-in-israel-11609275706.

19. After Trump

215 *many times promising*: "Donald Trump: I Will Be your Champion," ABC15Arizona, August 24, 2016, https://www.youtube.com/watch?v=ag z42UhlOew.

217 *"For you guys"*: "President's Remarks at International Association of Chiefs of Police Convention," C-SPAN video at 10:08, October 8, 2018, https:// www.c-span.org/video/?452576-1/president-trump-addresses-chiefs-po lice-convention.

217 *Trump frequently encouraged violence*: Ainara Tiefenthäler, "Trump's His tory of Encouraging Violence," *New York Times*, March 14, 2016, https:// www.nytimes.com/video/us/100000004269364/trump-and-violence.html.

217 *by 2.3 incidents per rally*: Niraj Chokshi, "Assaults Increased When Cities Hosted Trump Rallies, Study Finds," *New York Times*, March 16, 2018, https://www.nytimes.com/2018/03/16/us/trump-rally-violence.html.

217 *Clinton paid nearly . . . Cruz . . . Sanders*: Dave Levinthal, "Why the Trump Campaign Won't Pay Police Bills," Center for Public Integrity, June 1, 2019, https://publicintegrity.org/politics/donald-trump-police -cities-bills-maga-rallies/.

220 *90 percent of the population made relatively less income*: Carter C. Price and Kathryn A. Edwards, "Trends in Income from 1975 to 2018," RAND Edu cation and Labor, September 2020, https://www.rand.org/content/dam /rand/pubs/working_papers/WRA500/WRA516-1/RAND_WRA516-1 .pdf.

220 *job growth ran about 3 percent below Obama's last six years*: David Cay John ston, "Why Trump Gets a 'C' on the Economy," *DCReport*, April 29, 2019, https://www.dcreport.org/2019/04/29/why-trump-gets-a-c-on-the -economy/.

220 *That group had more income*: David Cay Johnston, "You Can Thank Donald Trump If You're Feeling Poorer Today," *DCReport*, June 4, 2021, https:// www.dcreport.org/2021/06/04/you-can-thank-donald-trump-if-youre -feeling-poorer-today/.

220 *those 1,100 Indiana factory jobs at Carrier*: Michael Sainato, "'He Pulled the Wool Over Our Eyes': Workers Blame Trump for Moving Jobs Overseas,"

Guardian, July 10, 2019, https://www.theguardian.com/us-news/2019/jul/10/trump-workers-jobs-overseas-factories.

220 *Indiana companies exported more jobs*: David J. Lynch, "Trump's Carrier Deal Fades as Economic Reality Intervenes," *Washington Post*, October 26, 2020. https://www.washingtonpost.com/business/2020/10/26/trump-carrier-manufacturing-jobs/.

221 *more factory jobs*: All employees, thousands, manufacturing, seasonally adjusted, Bureau of Labor Statistics Series CES3000000001, https://data.bls.gov/timeseries/CES3000000001?amp%253bdata_tool=XGtable&output_view=data&include_graphs=true.

221 *"very fine people"*: Rosie Gray, "Trump Defends White-Nationalist Protesters: 'Some Very Fine People on Both Sides,'" *Atlantic*, August 15, 2017, https://www.theatlantic.com/politics/archive/2017/08/trump-defends-white-nationalist-protesters-some-very-fine-people-on-both-sides/537012.

221 *authority to attack and even kill in his name*: Michael Kunzelman and Alanna Durkin Richer, "'Blame Trump' defense in Capitol riot looks like a long shot," ABC News, February 27, 2021, https://abcnews.go.com/Politics/wireStory/blame-trump-defense-capitol-riot-long-shot-76152193.

222 *played golf every week*: Sophie Germain, TrumpGolfCount.com, December 30, 2020, https://trumpgolfcount.com.

222 *Just the four trips he made to Mar-a-Lago over five weeks*: "Presidential Travel: Secret Service and DOD Need to Ensure That Expenditure Reports Are Prepared and Submitted to Congress," U.S. Government Accountability Office, January 2019, https://www.gao.gov/assets/gao-19-178.pdf.

222 *neglected his campaign promise*: Chris Cilizza, "Donald Trump's Huge Golf Hypocrisy," CNN, January 4, 2018, https://www.cnn.com/2018/01/03/politics/donald-trump-golf-analysis/index.html.

222 *ordered air force crews . . . diverted*: Ellen Ioanes, "Trump's Turnberry Resort Has Made Nearly $200,000 from US Military Visits Since He Took Office," *Business Insider*, September 18, 2019, https://www.businessinsider.com/259-air-force-crews-refueled-at-the-airport-trump-turnberry-2019-9.

222 *Trips by his sons . . . cost $396,000*: "Report to Congressional Requesters [on] Presidential Travel," GAO, January 2019, https://www.gao.gov/assets/gao-19-178.pdf.

225 *Romney acted with integrity*: David Cay Johnston, "Romney's Gift from Congress," Reuters, January 12, 2012, https://www.reuters.com/article/idIN36912619520120131.

Index

INDEX

INDEX

INDEX

INDEX

INDEX

greenhouse gas emissions, 167, 168
Griffin, John, 212
gross domestic product (GDP), 26
Guardian, 214
Guilfoyle, Kimberly, 128, 130
Gulf War, 59
Gurgaon Trump Towers, 80

Hamilton, Alexander, 68
Hawaii, 135–36, 140, 142
Hazardous Materials Transportation
    Act, 156
Hazoury, Ricardo and Fernando,
    77, 78
health care
    drug patents, 196–98
    drug prices, 193–98, 223
    Medicare, 94, 96, 109, 142, 193
    Obamacare, 223
Henry, James S., 191–92
Hillcrest Asia Limited, 82
Hiroshima, 155
Hollwich Kushner Architecture, 139
Hollywood Reporter, 18
Homeland Security, Department
    of, 128
Honolulu, 135
Hoover, Herbert, 216
House Oversight Committee, 38
Hoy, 78
Hydro-Québec, 167–68

Iberdrola, 167
immigration, 19
    see also Mexico, Mexicans
impeachment
    Impeachment Clause in the
        Constitution, 65

reforms of laws on, 226
    of Trump, 40
India, 79–80, 113, 220
Indian Point, 122
Indonesia, 82–84
infrastructure, 174–75, 223
inspector general (IG), 68–69, 71–72,
    180, 182
Institute for Energy Research,
    163–64
insulin, 193–94
Intercept, 209
International Association of Chiefs
    of Police, 217
International Consortium of
    Investigative Journalists, 185
International Leadership
    Foundation, 178
Intourist, 188
Intrater, Andrew, 47
Iraq, 58–59
Irongate Azrep Bw, 136
IRS (Internal Revenue Service), 41,
    90, 100, 220
    audits by, 99, 113, 114, 117–21,
        124–25
    Candidates' tax returns and, 224–25
    Koch and, 112–25
    presidential inauguration and, 50
    Ross and, 190
    Trump and, 39, 43, 99
    see also taxes
Israel, 214
It's Even Worse Than You Think
    (Johnston), 218

Jakarta, 83
James, Letitia, 151

INDEX

INDEX

INDEX

INDEX

INDEX

INDEX

INDEX

It's Even Worse Than You Think

NEW YORK TIMES BESTSELLER

It's Even Worse Than You Think
What the Trump Administration
Is Doing to America

Revised and Updated

DAVID CAY JOHNSTON

"David Cay Johnston is one of this country's most important journalists." —*The Washington Monthly*